NO, I DON'T GET DANGER MONEY

NO, I DON'T GET DANGER MONEY

CONFESSIONS OF AN ACCIDENTAL WAR CORRESPONDENT

LISETTE REYMER

First published in 2025

Allen & Unwin Aotearoa New Zealand
Level 2, 10 College Hill, Freemans Bay
Auckland 1011, New Zealand
+64 (9) 377 3800
auckland@allenandunwin.com
www.allenandunwin.co.nz

83 Alexander Street
Crows Nest NSW 2065, Australia
+61 (2) 8425 0100

EU Authorised Representative: Easy Access System Europe, Mustamäe tee 50, 10621 Tallinn, Estonia, gpsr.requests@easproject.com

A catalogue record for this book is available from the National Library of New Zealand.

ISBN 978 1 991142 26 9

Design by Megan van Staden
Set in Tiempos text
Printed and bound in Australia by the Opus Group

10 9 8 7 6 5 4 3

It'll be old news soon,
But for now, it's a hell of a yarn.

NORWAY
DENMARK
UNITED KINGDOM
Glasgow
IRELAND
Dublin
Birmingham
Cardiff
London
NETHERLANDS
The Hague
Brussels
BELGIUM
GERMANY
Paris
FRANCE
Lucerne
SWITZERLAND
Chur
ITALY
Barcelona
Madrid
PORTUGAL
SPAIN
Praia da Luz
Tunis

Helsinki
Stockholm
ESTONIA
RUSSIA
LATVIA
LITHUANIA
Moscow
BELARUS
POLAND
Warsaw
Bucha
Kyiv
Kraków
Przemyśl
Lviv
Kharkiv
CZECHIA
UKRAINE
Izyum
SLOVAKIA
Dunaivtsi
Dnipro
Donetsk
MOLDOVA
Siret
HUNGARY
Mykolaiv
Chișinău
Odessa
ROMANIA
Crimean
Peninsula
CROATIA
BOSNIA AND
HERZEGOVINA
SERBIA
Black Sea
MONTENEGRO
BULGARIA
NORTH
MACEDONIA
ALBANIA
Gallipoli
GREECE
TURKEY
Kahramanmaraş
Adana
İskenderun

CONTENTS

BEFORE WE START

I've been accused by some of my closest friends of talking a bit too much about how many stamps my passport has in it.

'Oh, you travel quite a bit do ya, Lisette?' they'll tease, trying to get me to stop before I get a roll on.

'Go on, tell us about the special one for Jordan . . .' they'll continue, poking fun at what they know full well is my favourite stamp anecdote.

I maintain that my record of adventures is a beautiful thing, and more often than not the border force officer will agree with me, commenting something along the lines of 'Wow, you've been busy!' while searching for a free spot to press some fresh ink. But I can also appreciate that those 'I remember when . . .' friends can grow a bit tiresome — and so I want to make it clear from the outset that this book isn't about me harping on like some veteran of the front line, because *that* I certainly am not. It's about sharing, for the first time, the truth behind each of those stamps. The ludicrous, the outrageous, the untold stories that would never make the cut for TV.

I hope you enjoy the journey as much as I did. And if you do ever want to see a pretty impressive passport . . . I'm more than willing to travel for a show and tell.

CAMBRIDGE, NEW ZEALAND

On 11 September 2001, George Bush sat in a classroom, the Twin Towers fell, television sets flickered with fresh tragedy, and the world changed forever.

It was also the day I got my first scoop.

My brother, and favourite sibling at the time (I run a healthy rotation system), came bounding down the stairs, yelling at my mum, who was slicing through a stack of ham sandwiches lined with butter so thick it looked like cheese.

'A plane just hit the Twin Towers!' he announced.

My mum, now dividing sandwiches into five separate lunchboxes for her five hungry children, replied, without missing a beat, 'When will you lot learn not to trust everything you hear from those radio disc jockeys?' But my brother switched on the television anyway and suddenly our rowdy household stood in a very unfamiliar quiet. We weren't allowed to watch TV on weekdays, let alone in the mornings, but Mum made an exception that day.

While around me the school routine eventually slowly hummed back to life, I sat glued to the news. My sister started to debate why she only got three sandwiches and my brother got five, but I didn't have time to add my seven-year-old complaints to the pile-on. I was busy. By the time I was sitting at my primary-school desk, pencil in hand and 1B5 at the ready, I had my angle decided. Our teacher had told us to write about how we heard the news that morning. 'This is history,' she explained.

But I knew everyone would tell the same story, and I was determined to stand out. I proceeded to write a two-page tale of how my dad knew someone who died in the towers that morning. 'Mum was bursting out with tears. Dad was shocked when he heard it at the cowshed,' I wrote.

My inspiration was something as mundane as one of the farm workers knowing someone who knew someone who lived in New York. To call it an embellishment of the truth would be incredibly generous — it was, absolutely, a shameless lie. But when we each took turns to read our stories to the class, mine was by far the most riveting. My classmates couldn't believe it and I think I even collected a hug or two with a bowed head. My patient teacher almost definitely knew it was an attention-grab but never said anything. God bless Mrs Kneebone. And, for some still unknown reason, my parents also never thought to challenge it when they read my story after school that day. Perhaps they were fostering my early love for storytelling? Or perhaps they had misinterpreted my dream to be a journalist as a dream to work for the tabloids.

I have, since then, worked hard to hone my craft. For example, I now stick to the facts. But when I look at the past three and a half years and the stories I have told, a tiny bit of me wishes that some of them had been made up, exaggerated for impact or sharpened with a dramatic edge. There have been more than a few occasions where the story has felt far too sad to be even twistedly thrilled about, as journalists often are. The reality is: the truth that follows in these pages is wilder than fiction, and not even seven-year-old Lisette would have had the creative licence to conjure it all up. I did let her loose on some of the names, though, as many of the characters we met along the way preferred to keep a low profile for reasons that will be very obvious to you all.

AUCKLAND, NEW ZEALAND
May 2021

'We'd like to offer you the job of Europe Correspondent.'

I was sitting across the table from two of the big bosses, who I knew well, and a lady from HR, who I had only met earlier that morning, in the final interview of what had been a gruelling selection process. I had been up all night working on my final presentation, and so when they told me the news I almost instantly started crying. It was exhaustion, relief and joy all tied up in one pretty embarrassing blubbery mess.

When I left the office, dabbing my eyes with a tissue, most in the newsroom assumed I had missed out, and nobody came anywhere near me. I went straight upstairs to the rooftop where a camera was already set up and just 20 minutes later I was on air doing a live cross into the 6 p.m. news bulletin, having whispered to my friend Simon, behind the lens, 'I got it' just moments beforehand.

Despite the family rules around television on weekdays when we were kids, an exception was made every night at 6 o'clock, or, more accurately, for the 6 o'clock news. The news mattered in our house and my parents very rarely missed it. My dad would always be late home from the cowshed after the evening's milking, and when we heard the washhouse door open and the tap turn on as he tried to rid himself of farm stench, we'd all jump into action. Mum would get his dinner out of the oven and someone would hit rewind on the VCR, while I'd say a silent prayer that the news hadn't been recorded on the tape I had just pulled apart to make a black witch wig out of. We'd push play and Mum would carry on with the dishes in the kitchen, unable to even see the TV but constantly tut-tutting over the state of the nation while Dad provided his own political commentary. If any of us kids started talking too loudly the tape would get paused and my dad would start to huff; and every day when it got to weather, Mum would walk around the breakfast bar from the kitchen to get a better look. She'd perch on the edge of the couch and make a comment on the presenter's outfit, while my dad would grumble that there wasn't enough rain, or there was far too much rain.

'Thanks for nothing, Jim,' he'd say to the TV.

My Opa was the only person I knew who was more loyal to the news than my dad. I have a distinct memory of him picking me up from an after-school art class and moving faster than I'd ever seen him move, rushing to the car and racing down the rural back roads of Ōhaupō because he didn't want to miss the start of the news. I wish so badly that he had lived long enough to see what career I chose. He would have been my toughest critic and my biggest fan, and his buddies at the golf course wouldn't have heard the end of it.

Despite the pre-established passion for current affairs arising from our family obsession with the news, becoming a journalist was entirely my own choice. My mum and dad are the antithesis of tiger parents. Both opinionated people, they raised opinionated children and we would have fierce debates about almost anything at the dinner table, during which the volume would escalate to a point where no one could really hear anything the other person was saying, least of all Mum's pointless pleas for 'inside voices!' But other than a clear directive to be a good person, work hard and vote National (I'm certain my dad now considers me a raging liberal), I never felt any pressure to do anything in particular.

I have always been driven and I've always been competitive; but above all, I've always been a little sister. For as long as I can remember, I have admired my siblings above anyone else and given that there's four of them, there has always been plenty of admiration fuelling my own ambitions. There's a five-year age gap between me and the next one, and as I grew up watching their many achievements stack up, I truly believe it warped my perspective of how realistic it was to do 'wow' things: secure a school prefect position, win a trip to Europe as a teenager with the Prime Minister, graduate with a Master's degree, build a radio station, buy your first home in your mid-twenties, run marathons or race an Ironman or row for New Zealand. And while I am yet to replicate any of these achievements, it was purely a copy-cat approach that from the outset saw me dare to dream big. A correspondent job was that for me: a pinnacle point of any journalist's career, and an opportunity to collect new adventures in new places and make my family as proud as they'd always made me. And while saying goodbye to them was by far the toughest part of the assignment, I was one step closer to being just like them when I grew up and I couldn't have been more excited.

TOKYO, JAPAN
July 2021

'We're only going for three weeks!' The ridicule began as soon as I arrived at Auckland Airport with three large suitcases and a carry-on bag, all bursting at the zips.

'No, Tokyo is just my halfway point, I'm moving to London!' I justified, and then repeated at least another twenty times, to anyone who looked at my overloaded trolley with even a hint of judgement. The world was still finding its way through Covid and the Olympic committee had chartered a special flight to take journalists and athletes to Tokyo. I was so excited at the prospect of covering the Olympic Games that I didn't dwell too much on the fact I wouldn't be coming back to New Zealand for what I thought would be two years. By the time we arrived in Japan, however, I had been well and truly reminded. Over the course of the flight, dozens and dozens of people — some I knew, some I didn't — appeared at my seat one at a time, dropping off a single puzzle piece and congratulating me on my new job. It took the entire flight for me to collect the full set of pieces and complete the picture: a photograph of me and my brother underlined by the message 'Travel safe, very proud of you. Lots of love, Bjorn.' He secured a return to favourite sibling with that, although (I should note) not for the first time since 2001.

Everything about Tokyo was surreal. An international event of that scale taking place amid a pandemic was always going to be strange, and without fans the stands were depressingly empty. The media would cheer for the athletes, trying to build some atmosphere, and when we met them afterwards for interviews we would pass on messages from family members who so desperately wanted to be there. The Olympics was operating as one giant bubble, with everyone getting regular Covid tests, wearing masks and conducting interviews from a distance. The masks didn't help with the heat. The air was thick with humidity and to make matters worse, we had been given long-sleeved black shirts to wear as a team uniform. It was so torturous that at the rowing venue several days in, one of the Kiwi medallists threw us some bargaining power, promising to give me an exclusive interview if our bosses agreed to let us wear a short-sleeved T-shirt for the rest of the games. It didn't work.

I've never coped well in the heat. I once took a holiday in

Rome with my sister during a heatwave and have never been forgiven for 'completely ruining it' for her with my complaints. So before I even landed in Japan I knew I was K-popping with the devil. I was sweating profusely the minute I got off the plane and within days started losing my voice, which was seemingly exacerbated by long stints talking on air. During my first live cross I was forced to swallow halfway through, trying to oil my struggling throat.

'Are you okay? It sounded like a fly flew in your mouth,' one of the producers messaged me afterwards.

Embarrassed, I retreated into my air-conditioned room and barely left for the rest of the night, but I think it backfired because when I went back out into the humidity the following day I felt worse than ever. The sun was already burning at 8:30 a.m., and as I stood talking to camera outside the rowing venue for the mid-morning bulletin in New Zealand I became increasingly breathless. There was a lot of panic and a lot of sweat and it all made the breathlessness much worse.

My phone pinged with a message from the big boss: 'Hi, I hope you are OK . . . don't worry about needing to take time off . . . chill and rest up.' My thoughts started spiralling almost immediately, imagining a newsroom all murmuring about the wrong person being chosen for the Europe job; a sentiment I was rapidly starting to agree with.

I managed to get through the next two days without any major issues, but the humidity kept soaring and in temperatures around 40 degrees I was rolling the dice every time I went on air. A live cross about the triathlon was the final straw. We had been filming all morning and not drinking enough water, and the minute the light was turned on my face I felt my legs go weak and I was struggling to breathe all over again. I am certain now that I was suffering from both a panic attack and heatstroke, and I was seconds from fainting. My voice was completely gone, my sentences became jumbled and I saw John, the camera operator, take a step out from behind his camera, getting ready to catch me.

'Fuck I'm so sorry, I don't know why this keeps happening,' I messaged the producer, Paul Mayow, who luckily also happens to be one of the kindest humans in news (probably even the world).

'No worries mate, I just hope you're OK. Just that bloody Tokyo heat.'

Not everybody saw it like that. With Covid always on the mind, we had emails come in to the newsroom expressing concern for my health and diagnosing me with the virus. Within hours, the phone call came: the decision had been made that I couldn't be on air while this was happening; it was a bad look.

It felt even worse. I was choking on my most important assignment to date and I didn't know how to fix it. I was on the phone frantically trying to convince the managers that I was okay and fine to be on air, but in private I had already convinced myself that I would never be able to do a live cross again.

After a day's rest, which I spent lying with ice pressed against my neck and forehead whenever possible, I was given permission to go back on air — but I knew I was being watched closely. For the next week it felt like there was a boa constrictor wrapped around my throat every time I did a live cross, but I would hold a fan in front of my face right up until the final second, say a prayer to the television gods and hope for the best. By week two, I must have been adjusting to the heat slightly and was through the worst of it. By week three, I had made a vow to never complain about working in the cold when I finally made it to Europe.

I turned 27 on the final day of the Olympics. Nine years earlier I had turned eighteen in Europe after watching my sister Anna row at the London Olympics, and my mind was already drifting to turning 30 in Paris. At the wrap party that night we toasted with cheap, high-percentage Japanese canned drinks and soaked up the sunset from our apartment balcony. It was perfect; not even the thought of the weeks ahead in quarantine, or the irritable bowel of one of our crew, could take away from that moment. After a horrendous start to my overseas adventure, I was relieved to have proven to myself that I could still do live crosses. And as I boarded the flight to London, I concluded that there was still *some* life left in my career.

LONDON, UNITED KINGDOM
August 2021

A decade earlier, when I was just starting out at Broadcasting School in Christchurch, I had managed to wrangle a day of work experience in the TV3 newsroom. I was typically nervous and trying to avoid getting in the way, but by mid-afternoon the producer of the day must have grown sick of entertaining me so rang up one of the new camera operators to come and collect me before leaving for a shoot. His name was Daniel Pannett, and we spent the afternoon filming something, somewhere; a story so unremarkable I have never been able to recall any of the details. The more I've thought about it in the years since, the more I'm convinced it was a made-up job, designed purely to keep me busy and out of the office.

What I do remember, though, is that we stopped at a service station on the way because Daniel wanted to stock his car with snacks — which was all I needed to see of the industry to know I was in the right place. It was surreal, then, ten years later, to touch down in London as the Europe Correspondent and meet the Europe cameraman I would be working with in my new role. Daniel Pannett. It was the first time I'd seen him since that extremely forgettable shoot. Methven's finest export, Daniel had already been in London for more than two years by that point, and was very patient with me as I gushed over the various famous landmarks, walking the streets with rose-tinted glasses that I'm not sure I've ever taken off. I felt like I had won the journalism lottery. We were filming in front of Buckingham Palace, outside Westminster Abbey, on a red double-decker bus going over Tower Bridge, and my arm was getting bruised from all the pinching. To be clear: I was pinching myself; it wasn't a weird case of Daniel pinching his new colleague.

The first place I lived in London was an outrageous apartment in Shoreditch, one of the trendiest parts of the city. It's full of cool shops and cool people and very cool graffiti-covered streets — the type of graffiti that tourists pay too many pounds for an art tour of, not the type you spend far too many pounds to paint over. I definitely wasn't a natural fit for the level of cool I was surrounded by, but I put my faith in osmosis.

'Isn't that Jack the Ripper territory?' our veteran foreign editor John Hale queried when I told him where I had settled, but it had been many years since John had lived in England and while it had absolutely been Jack the Ripper territory once upon a time, I assured him I was safe. Ironically, he expressed more concern over me living in Shoreditch than he ever did over us heading to Ukraine.

My apartment building included a concierge named Sam who became incredibly invested in our work and was possibly more relieved than my mum whenever we arrived back in one piece from a war zone. I had the place to myself and there was absolutely no way I could afford it, but I rented it off a family I knew from New Zealand who very generously redefined 'mates rates'. It very quickly felt like home, but it was also our office. Daniel and I would spend hours there, drinking red wine, listening to the Eagles and cooking up pitches for where we wanted to go next.

Every newsroom in the world has a list of people who might be soon going to die, and there is a stash of pre-written and pre-edited television packages, known as obits, ready to put straight to air for those particular VIPs. I shudder to think how many journalists over the past few decades have written and voiced an obit for Queen Elizabeth, only for it to be updated and redone by another journalist a couple of years later. I was sent to London with strict instructions to redo the Queen's obit as soon as I landed. I told Daniel I wasn't going to leave the UK until she had died, rightly predicting it was likely to happen in the next five years but incorrectly predicting it would be the biggest story we'd ever have the privilege of covering. Daniel didn't care as much for the royals, and made it clear from day one that his dream assignment would be to a place like Gaza. We agreed that this seemed a long shot, but I promised I'd at least try to find a story in a place like that.

As unlikely as a war zone seemed, the Europe Bureau staff had a history of being deployed to places slightly more high-risk than what you would regularly cover in New Zealand; whether that was tear-gas-fuelled riots or wildfires or scenes of terror. As a result, part of every correspondent's initiation process is the attending of a hostile environments training course and Daniel and I were both shipped off to a forest in Kent to get our certificates. The course is run by a group of men, mostly former British SAS and mostly over 60 and all of them enjoying the chance to discuss their glory days in the field just a little too much. There was one younger guy, though, a jungle specialist, who knew far too much about how to deal with a deadly snake bite in the Amazon and had a real bee in his bonnet about the validity of Bear Grylls. These men were all incredibly knowledgeable and we spent the week learning how to cope with everything from violent interviewees to missile strikes.

'The biggest killer for journalists in the field? Car crashes,' they warned. 'Never get in a car you don't trust, and always wear a seatbelt,' and they ran us through a series of mocked-up vehicle disasters with very convincing actors requiring the urgent medical treatment we'd just been taught.

Daniel and I were the only New Zealanders on the course, but there was a journalist and camera operator pairing from Japan who could barely speak English, and a handful of aid workers made up the rest of the group. By day three we were all being kitted out in body armour and joking our way through a helmet fitting, before heading into a field where we learnt to identify landmines and how to respond to a grenade being thrown in our direction. The final day was a test of everything we had learnt that week: a simulation designed to be as realistic as possible so that if the worst ever did eventuate in real life, we would have had some experience under that level of pressure.

'Ha, this is a bit of fun,' I said to Daniel.

'Innit,' he replied, and I wondered how many months I'd have to live in London before I could start saying 'Innit' too.

We were providing first-aid to a group of five or so gunshot victims in the forest when suddenly there was shouting and gunfire and we were stormed by a group of men in balaclavas. They put black bags over our heads, tied our arms behind our backs and marched us into a shipping container. Yelling in our faces in various languages — Arabic and Russian and Turkish at a guess — they started stripping us of anything valuable while forcing us to hold our arms above our heads. I could hear Daniel grumbling: 'Oh do you really have to take my watch?'

We were obviously aware it was fake, but when the cold metal of a gun is pushed against your back or forehead it's hard to think logically. Long before Kent, my siblings would kidnap me, tie me up and hide me in cupboards when their friends were over, so they didn't have to deal with their annoying younger sister all day. Needless to say, this meant I had a bit more experience in this sort of situation than Daniel did, and it showed. One by one we were taken outside for interrogation, and then they started turning us against each other. Kneeling side by side, still with bags over our heads, Daniel and I were grilled by our captors.

'Do you know her?' they asked Daniel, and a gun was pushed against my temple.

He panicked. 'No.'

'Is she a spy?'

'I . . . I don't know?' he replied, sounding even more unconvincing.

And just like that, I was executed.

I don't think we passed that particular test, and I remember the Japanese crew looking at us with sympathy at dinner later that night. Fortunately, it seemed unlikely we would ever be in an environment even close to that, so I wasn't overly bothered by Daniel's lack of loyalty under pressure.

Our training went largely forgotten in the five months that followed. We travelled from Ireland to Scotland to France with the All Blacks and to Glasgow to film with President Obama and Prince William at the climate conference COP26; we went hunting in Finland for the world's largest treasure trove, travelled to Switzerland for an America's Cup announcement and went to Dubai to film with Six60 at the World Expo; and all of that without any need for body armour. It was then, and always would be, the best job in the world; it wasn't that good things came to an end but instead that peace in Europe was about to. And what we learnt in Kent would save our lives.

BEFORE THE WAR BEGAN
January 2022

The murmurings were getting louder, and slowly but surely news of Russia moving troops towards the border of Ukraine, especially via Belarus, was gaining traction in the bulletins. Daniel had been listening to a podcast on the recent history of Ukraine and Russia and sent it to me with the message: 'I reckon you should get across this. Could be quite big.'

The first story we filed about Ukraine was on the 23rd of January 2022. For 67 of the next 81 evening bulletins we filed a story about Ukraine too. After that, I lost count; famously more of a words girl than a numbers one.

Sarah de Croy, who was our direct manager and the Director of Newsgathering, was deeply passionate about foreign news. Despite most of our story requests being huge maybes in terms of logistics and finances, we were spoilt in that the message down the phone from her was almost always 'Well, let's at least try to make it happen.' Sarah Bristow was the Director of News, and I was both mildly scared of her and incredibly in awe of her. A force in the industry, she had given me this job and embraced my style of storytelling when others had told me I would have to change almost completely if I was going to get anywhere worth going. Together, they came to be known affectionately in our bureau as The Sarahs, and absolutely nothing we achieved would have been possible without them. Did they message us far too much when they should have been asleep? Yes, absolutely. But nobody is perfect.

Up until this point, everything in the bureau had been about keeping costs down. Whenever I would price up a trip, I would pick the cheapest accommodation and flights, unbothered by the comfort of either but just wanting The Sarahs to approve it so we could go. When we decided to pitch a trip to Ukraine, I took this same approach and, given that it was Eastern Europe, I thought our low-cost proposal was going to be a no-brainer for them. That was either optimistic or naive, or perhaps both. Their primary concern was not the money but our safety, and it took days of back-and-forth phone calls and tweaking of health and safety plans before things started to gain momentum.

It was late on a Saturday night in London when I finally felt like we were getting close to sign-off. That same night the United States National Security Advisor decided to hold a press conference, and his timing, honestly, could not have been worse. From his podium, flanked by the Stars and Stripes, he warned of the 'very distinct possibility' of a Russian invasion of Ukraine within the next 48 hours, involving a major attack on the capital Kyiv with aerial bombing and missile attacks that would kill civilians. I watched it thinking that it only strengthened my case — that we needed to get there as soon as possible before it all kicked off. But The Sarahs had the opposite reaction. The phone calls that followed felt like we had taken ten steps backwards: the heightened risk had changed all the considerations and everything needed to be reassessed. Daniel was at the pub the entire evening and was very little help, which I've never let him live down.

I didn't sleep at all that night. I filed a story for the bulletin and burnt the rest of the midnight oil updating a health and safety plan and finessing the proposal, while desperately trying to find a body armour supplier that had stock available and at a sensible price, then went straight to do a live cross about the latest at 5 a.m. Daniel arrived at the live cross also low on sleep, but nursing a different type of headache to the one I had developed.

The Sarahs had been in touch with the fancy security team at our parent company, Discovery, who had advised that we really should be staying at the so-called media hotel in Kyiv, which just so happened to be five-star luxury accommodation with rooms well beyond our usual budget. All of the world's networks were basing themselves there and there were rumours about the hotel's coordinates being provided to the respective militaries so they knew to keep their missiles well clear, but it also meant we could easily share information with other journalists regarding risk, safety and movements.

The expense alone was enough to convince me that the trip was never going to happen. Instead, to my surprise, we were sent a list of items we needed to gather in the next 24 hours, like a treasure hunt around London, and if we were successful we would be able to fly to Kyiv. There were GPS trackers and satellite phones to collect, but the toughest task was finding body armour on a weekend. Most places were either closed or already sold out of gear as journalists and aid workers all over the city started to get themselves equipped for deployment, if they hadn't deployed already. So when on Monday morning I found myself standing on the floor of a PPE manufacturer putting more money on the work credit card than I made in a month but with two sets of top-tier kit secured, I was in complete and utter disbelief.

KYIV, UKRAINE
mid-February 2022

On Tuesday we left for Kyiv.

As we walked through duty free at Luton Airport, my phone rang. It was Sarah Bristow.

'How are you feeling?' she asked.

'Yeah, good.' And a polite back-and-forth followed. I was a new correspondent, still desperate to prove myself and at that point even more desperate to get into Ukraine. I didn't want to say the wrong thing.

'Listen, Lisette. You have my absolute permission to do whatever you need to if things ever start to feel not right. Don't even worry about calling. Just do what you need to do.'

The tone of the conversation had taken a turn, and all of a sudden I felt like I shouldn't be pushing through a bunch of British 'Bride Tribes' spritzing themselves with free perfume while I continued this call. I looked through the crowd for Daniel and found him standing at a coffee counter, mouthing at me from afar 'Which one?' while holding up a chocolate croissant and a plain one.

'Have you spoken to your parents? Do they know you're going in?' Sarah continued.

'Oh shit,' I thought to myself, 'he's gonna get the plain one.'

'CHOCOLATE,' I mouthed back with gusto.

I wrapped up the call with Sarah, assuring her that we were fine, everyone had been told, we both felt good, we both felt supported, and I pushed through the hordes of holiday-makers towards Daniel. Before we'd left, we'd each provided The Sarahs with the name and number of the person the newsroom would call first if our deployment ended badly. I didn't want to make a bigger deal out of it than necessary so had been avoiding the conversation with home completely, but the thought did cross my mind in that moment that at least my nominated sister should have a heads-up.

'Have you told your family?' I asked Daniel.

'Yeah . . . have you? I got you plain.'

'No I haven't — should I have?' I replied, taking the croissant and trying to hide my disappointment.

'Well my dad said "You're fucking mad. I'm not happy, Dan. And I'm not telling your mother", so I'm not sure if it was the right or wrong thing to do . . .'

With a stale chocolate-less croissant in one hand and scalding-hot and almost undrinkable coffee in the other, we walked towards the gate destined for Kyiv, where just a handful of others sat, and I wrote a message to the family group chat.

'Hey family. It's not a big deal but because I don't want Mum to have a heart attack when she turns on the news, I thought I better send out a PSA that I'm about to board a flight to Ukraine. I have $6000 worth of body armour in my bag and 24/7 personal security so I'm sure we'll survive whatever Putin throws our way. I'll keep in touch.'

My dad quickly replied: 'Lela. Amazing. Your first foray into a war zone. Do you need a contact?' before proceeding to list every Ukrainian he's ever met.

I remember so clearly boarding our Wizz Air plane. A bright-pink, budget Hungarian airline. I found my middle seat, 11B, and said hello to my window-seat mate to the left. Daniel sat to the right of me, 11C. An hour later 11A was grabbing my arm, convulsing, with saliva spooling out of his mouth and his eyes rolling back. We called for help; the Wizz staff jumped into action and we were moved to the back of the flight while the medical emergency was dealt with. As I sat in my new seat,

I was adamant it was a bad sign. We had barely left London and the trip was already being defined by death.

11A didn't die. I actually saw him walk off the flight into Kyiv, the colour back in his cheeks. He probably looked better than I did by that point, having landed in the Ukrainian capital with four words playing over and over in my head: 'We shouldn't be here.'

It was the 16th of February 2022 when we first set foot in Kyiv. I had no idea, of course, how much this city would one day mean to me. The lady at border security asked me what story we were covering, and I looked at her with a head-tilt, thinking, 'Well, isn't it obvious?'

When we walked through the sliding doors into the arrivals area of the airport, it didn't take me long to spot him. Extremely attractive and dressed to perfection. His suit looked like it was custom-made, and a small Louis Vuitton cross-body bag was slung across his chest. He stood up instantly, cutting a direct path to us.

Artem was the closest I've ever come to discovering James Bond in the real world. The owner of a private security firm in Ukraine, he had been recruited to escort us around Kyiv and ensure we were kept safe. I immediately felt safe. And perhaps a little bit in love? This would become an ongoing and slightly embarrassing theme for me and the security officers we were assigned, and was the cause of a lot of 'Oh here we go again'-esque comments from Daniel, which, honestly, I never appreciated. Is it my fault if I can recognise a handsome man and he can't?

Artem took us to the car, and there we were introduced to Tomlin. He was the opposite of Artem; short, slightly stout, middle-aged, and dark-featured with stubble. He could only speak broken English, but he had the friendliest smile and over the next week, as we drove around the city, I would often catch his eye in the rear-view mirror and we would share a mutual chuckle at whatever fresh madness we had encountered. He drove a black Mercedes Benz G-wagon and it didn't suit him at all, but I loved it. Just an hour earlier, as we flew into Kyiv, I had been expecting the bitter worst. But suddenly I was receiving Hollywood-star treatment. A professional chauffeur and James Bond, both dedicated to us? I could get used to this, I thought.

I was expecting a city on high alert, but apart from there being fewer people on our flight everything appeared as normal. There wasn't any panic; the locals laughed that the only invasion there was going to be was 'from the media' and I started to wonder if this was one of those much-talked-about, and often-denied, media beat-ups.

I tried to get a selfie of the team as we walked to our first location, but Artem kept diving out of shot. It was slightly strange. After the third attempt I looked at him with a raised eyebrow. 'I'm sorry, do you hate photos?'

'I don't take photos. Even on my wedding day.'

'Who is this man?' I whispered to Daniel as Artem walked off ahead.

Tomlin smiled mischievously at my confusion. He clearly knew something I did not.

Over his shoulder Artem called back: 'I like to lay low.'

I decided that too few minutes had passed since meeting him for me to start grilling him for his life story. It would be polite to wait at least a few hours, I reasoned with myself, and I left it at that.

I've lost count of the number of bomb shelters I've spent time in, but you never forget your first. Mine was under a pizza restaurant in central Kyiv and was a Rolls-Royce of shelters, really. Clean and tidy, with plenty of comfortable seating and great lighting. Most were not like that. All over Kyiv, we found them. At the bottom of apartment buildings, inside public buildings, inside bars. The local government had introduced an app that showed you where your nearest shelter was and we decided it would make a good story. Most we visited were derelict and dilapidated and probably not up to standard, which was the point the local media had been making in recent days, but nobody seemed overly worked up about it because any talk of an invasion was just 'media hype'. Right?

Artem suggested we should go to the Arsenalna underground Metro system. The deepest subway in Europe, it was built with war in mind, designed to double as a bomb shelter in the event of an enemy attack. I stared at Artem in disbelief. I could not fathom a government having to design a public rail network with a bunker mentality. It would make a great story, though, so I was eager to get there. A few hours later, as we packed up for the day after filming our piece, I thought (like the complete amateur I was) that I had seen it all. It was mere weeks before harrowing images of scared residents cowering in that very subway were broadcast around the world as the war, and their worlds, closed in around them.

Standing in Saint Michael's Square a couple of long nights later, while waiting for a live cross, I decided to ask the question that had been plaguing me since hour one.

'So what's in the Louis Vuitton?'

A smile emerged on Artem's face, and mine instantly followed.

'You can't tell me?' I pushed.

'My pistol,' he said, holding his bag casually over his shoulder.

I watched Daniel's head spin around.

'Your pistol?'

'Well, no one is going to expect that I've got a pistol in a Louis Vuitton bag, are they? So I can get in anywhere with it.'

'Can we see it?' Daniel asked.

'No.'

The border with Belarus is only about 200 kilometres from Kyiv, and with Russian troops setting up camp there, the intelligence suggested they would invade from that point also. We wanted to see it for ourselves, and Artem agreed it was possible. It would take a few hours, but to this day I've never met anyone who loves driving as much as Tomlin and he was looking forward to the open road.

'Six presidents have sat where you've sat,' he said off-handedly to me as we left and I felt instantly insignificant.

The plan was to meet the locals who live in the villages nearest to the border, the families who would be the first to meet the enemy if this supposed imminent attack ever did eventuate. As we got closer to the border, the mood started to change. In Kyiv nobody was particularly worried about the war, but *here* they were bracing for unwanted visitors. There were army vehicles on the road and the odd tank to the side of it slightly hidden by trees, and in the village of Ripky we found a man making and giving away wreaths. 'To put on the graves of our enemies when they arrive,' he told us and I felt a cold breeze down my neck.

He turned to me. 'Are you scared to be here?' he asked, and I took it as a hint that I should be.

We filmed in the town and then continued to the border, where you could stand in Ukraine and see Belarus.

'Belarus is just 500 metres from here, 30,000 Russian troops are amassing along this border,' I said to the camera, behaving perhaps a little too much like I was on the front line for someone who was absolutely nowhere near a front line.

As we drove homewards, I spotted a war monument that we all agreed would be worth stopping to film for the story. We unpacked the gear and started to set up, but suddenly we had company. A member of the Ukrainian army pulled up in a truck and Artem told us to get in the car. We couldn't hear much, but what we could hear didn't sound good. Eventually the car door opened, Artem got in, turned to Tomlin and said, in an unusually uneasy tone:

'Let's get the fuck out of here.'

The army had been notified by a local resident that a TV crew was sniffing around the border area with a camera, and potentially revealing Ukrainian army positions. They had tracked us down and Artem bore the brunt of the very unimpressed soldier. We were lucky to have been allowed to keep our footage, but I think Artem's military background had softened the seriousness of the offence. Again it was an abrupt change from the feeling in Kyiv. In the north, people were genuinely worried and they weren't taking any risks.

I leant forward from my presidential seat in the car. 'Do you guys honestly think there won't be an invasion?'

'No, there won't. The tanks could never get far enough down this highway before we saw them and stopped them,' Tomlin replied.

'What would you do if it did happen?'

'Well, I would take my wife and son to the Polish border.'

'You've thought about that?'

'Yes, they've packed bags at home. Some petrol, some water, some money, sitting in the garage in case.'

'You've got that all organised already?'

'Yes. And a gun.'

'I would stay and fight,' Artem confirmed.

'But it's not going to happen?' I pushed.

'No, it's not going to happen,' they replied, almost in unison.

There is a period before most live crosses where you're just waiting. Sometimes you've left it far too late and there is no waiting at all; just a lot of swearing as you rush to get the link up in time. But usually everything is sorted and checked around fifteen minutes before you're actually on air. It gives you a chance to speak to the team in New Zealand, and confirm that the presenter in the studio can hear you and vice versa. In the Ukrainian winter this was a particularly uncomfortable wait, but Daniel and I had developed a new favourite game to pass the time. This could essentially be drilled down to 'How much new information can we learn about Artem?'

Standing at the ready in Sophia Square, I was rapidly losing feeling in my feet when I heard Daniel throw a curveball: 'Have you ever been shot?' Again that familiar smile emerged on Artem's face, and again Tomlin chuckled at the reaction on my face.

What followed was a story that to this day I google to assure myself it is true. Artem had, in fact, been caught in a nasty gunfight, shot multiple times and left to die while working as a close protection officer in the Middle East. In what he thought were his final minutes of life, he had shot dead multiple people to protect his clients and he now lived with a permanent hit put on his name. He was providing enough detail that we knew we could ask for more and Daniel and I were peppering him with questions, not overly surprised that our James Bond friend had lived such a life but still shocked at it nonetheless.

'Lisette, it's Sam in the studio — can you hear me?'

The voice of Samantha Hayes popped into my ear and interrupted my line of questioning.

'Yeah, I've got you, Sam . . .' reluctantly pulling my attention away from Artem and turning to the camera. Daniel looked as dumbfounded as me, and Artem and Tomlin were still chuckling. They weren't being flippant about the deadly incident, but they were certainly enjoying the reaction of two Kiwis who were now so obviously roaming in a very foreign world.

As we packed up and headed back to the hotel, we spotted two familiar faces across the square. It was the Japanese crew from our training course, and we smiled widely as we walked over to say hello.

'Hey!'

'Nice to see you!'

Their English had improved a bit but not enough for a full conversation, so we parted ways fairly quickly. What was not lost in translation, however, was the distinct shock on their faces that we had been let loose in Ukraine after our questionable performance in Kent.

On our last day in Kyiv, we had gained permission to visit a training session of the Ukrainian territorial defence; essentially, volunteer soldiers who could be called on to bolster numbers if war began. It was held at a secret location in an abandoned forest on the outskirts of Kyiv and we were sent a GPS location point just hours before we were due to arrive.

As we pulled up and found a park, I couldn't believe what I was seeing. There were people from all walks of life showing up like it was Saturday sport — dressed head to toe in military gear, carrying guns they'd brought from home, along with snacks for lunchtime and an attitude of let's prepare for the worst. They were stay-at-home mums, accountants, IT technicians, teachers, tea-makers. People with no idea how to even hold a gun, now holding one, running army drills and preparing for face-to-face combat. Ukraine was readying an army and everyone here felt worried enough to get training. They were not natural soldiers — they didn't even want to be soldiers, but they did want to do what was best for their country, their children and their grandchildren.

I watched as trainees stood shaking, holding a deadly weapon for the first time; as wobbly-legged recent teens tried to rustle up some bravado in front of the actual soldiers who were yelling commands in their faces. Some were still too nervous to hold a real gun so held wooden cut-outs instead. It was equal parts inspiring and disturbing.

Artem just looked disturbed. 'This is some USSR *bullshit*.'

He was furious with the level of training, with what they were being taught. It was outdated and unhelpful, and these novices would only get in the way on the battlefield, he explained. 'They are going to be lambs to the slaughter,' he said, informed by a knowledge of life at war that we did not pretend to possess.

By afternoon, things were wrapping up in the forest. We had more interviews and footage than we needed, and I was beginning to sense that all the talk of not being worried was disguising some very serious worry. It had been a heavy day, and my usual default in high-intensity situations is to hunt for a laugh.

'Now there's guns everywhere, surely we can see yours, Artem!'

I said it jokingly and didn't expect he would respond, but within a second there it was: the distinctive sound of the chamber of a gun being emptied. With unsettling ease, our James Bond had pulled out his Louis Vuitton secret, taken the necessary safety precautions and was now holding it up to show us.

'Do you want to hold it?'

'Absolutely not,' I said, having always been allergic to guns.

'Absolutely!' said Daniel, with a surprising amount of delight.

That day we departed Ukraine. After filing our last story we went to the airport for what will, no doubt, have been one of the last flights in or out of the country in recent years. I am still, to this day, disappointed that we left before the war started; but if I'm honest with myself, as I left Kyiv I thought the war would never start and I'd never be back. We said goodbye to Tomlin and Artem, and in a sign of how far we had come, we shared a hug. They told us to call us if we did return, promising we could all work together again, and I left Artem with a smile and the parting words: 'Don't do anything silly like go to war.'

He laughed at me.

I remember hearing Daniel say, in a far more knowing tone than mine had been, 'Be safe.'

We boarded another pink plane taking us three hours away to London, and when we landed the big news had broken. The Brits were in panic mode, with headlines everywhere announcing: 'The Queen has Covid.'

PARIS, FRANCE
February 2022

From London's Luton Airport we raced home to re-pack, drove to Windsor Castle to do a live cross about the Queen, then crossed our fingers that it wouldn't kill her as we rushed on to catch a train to Paris. New Zealand's foreign minister Nanaia Mahuta was in France for a series of bilateral meetings and we were expected to be there to cover all her vigorous handshaking. But everything she said was overshadowed by Ukraine.

After two days in the croissant capital it was clear we were on the verge of history. I was struggling to sleep, trawling news websites and constantly messaging anyone who knew anything for the latest information and insight out of Kyiv. I was due to fly to New York on the 25th of February for my best friend Kate's thirtieth birthday and was feeling increasingly sick about it. I was calculating flight times like a possessed travel agent, trying to work out how long it would take me to get from Manhattan to Kyiv if the war started; the numbers weren't pretty, but they were doable and I convinced myself I would go to New York and I would have fun.

I must have got some sleep that night, despite everything, because I woke up to the news that Putin had launched his invasion. My phone was overflowing with messages and within seconds I was crying angry tears. No one in the Auckland newsroom had woken us up, assuming it was best to let us rest after a busy week, and the news had broken on the 6 p.m. bulletin without us. I don't know if it was because I was incredibly overtired or my ego had inflated to dangerous levels, but I threw the second-greatest hissy fit of my professional career (which had nothing on the greatest, yet to come), convinced I had 'missed' the story. There followed a back-and-forth of immensely stressful, tear-stained conversations, which boiled down to the decision to cancel the US holiday.

It is a nasty side-effect of this job that you are constantly letting down your friends and family. Never where you are meant to be, always changing plans last minute and, in the eyes of almost everybody, putting work first. Once the decision was made, I was determined to make it worth it. We would not be staying in London.

Daniel and I spent the evening in my apartment with the TV screen split across six different international networks, watching the coverage wall to wall and working out a pitch of exactly where we needed to be. Fortunately The Sarahs were doing the same, and within hours the plan was set to get to Poland to cover the unfolding refugee crisis. When it was finally approved, around 10 p.m., we had completely forgotten about getting a negative Covid test so we could board the flight, and the fact that Covid was now an afterthought told us everything we needed to know about how significant this war was. A last-minute panic saw us running through the city in search of a 24-hour clinic to get swabbed before heading straight to the airport.

PRZEMYŚL, POLAND
late February 2022

Our first stop was to be the train station in Przemyśl, a town with a name that isn't pronounced even remotely close to how it's written. Trains were travelling there from Ukraine, shipping frightened residents out in their hundreds of thousands. We were due on air for the morning bulletins, but were struggling to find the station and it looked likely we would miss our slot. I was doing a phone interview with one of the Kiwi radio stations while we drove and as we pulled in to the carpark I heard myself absurdly starting to explain how you could even find bomb shelters in strip clubs.

The train station was tiny. Much smaller than I had imagined, especially given the number of people who were passing through it. It was old but tidy, and I think under any other circumstance you might have driven by and commented, 'Oh, that's cute!'

I had barely stepped out of the car and Daniel barely had the camera fired up when my phone rang and I was connected through my earpiece to the studio. Ryan Bridge, the presenter in Auckland, started asking me questions about what was happening where I was, and we walked into the train station, discovering things live on air along with the viewers. My friendship with Ryan has been formed on the basis of frivolous banter and a mutual love of a hearty laugh, but there was none of that on this day. Hundreds of families were sitting on the floor inside the station, scared children sheltering in their mothers' arms, huddled together for warmth and relying on donations for food. There simply wasn't enough room in the foyer, yet the trains just kept arriving with more people.

When we got off air, I looked at a mother cowering in a corner and stupidly asked, 'Are you okay?' She stared back at me with terrified eyes and shook her head. It hit me like a tidal wave. This story was massive. And this was just the beginning.

Early the next morning, it was snowing heavily and freezing cold and we were double-puffered, with scarves and beanies and gloves and thermals on, when we parked up in our rental car at the border crossing to Ukraine. The stream of people was constant. Families with children, with babies, wrapped in heavy blankets, fleeing to safety in Poland. It was minus 6 degrees and I had lasted only 30 minutes outside before I'd had to get back in the car, but these Ukrainians had been walking for their lives for *days*. You could feel the weight of history hanging in the air, and I distinctly remember the moment I realised this would need to be the best story we had ever produced. 'Let's go,' I said to Daniel, pushing open the car door into the blistering cold.

I had never seen such raw desperation with my own eyes. Thousands of people kept arriving across the border, fighting for a spot on the buses that were also constantly arriving to take them to emergency housing. People were crying with relief and horror as they remembered where they'd come from: 'Fire everywhere, it's terrible, it's . . . like a nightmare, like you see a very scary film, a very scary movie,' one woman told us through her tears.

We had been filming all day and were about to leave when I spotted a family of two children and their mother — who looked at me a beat too long, which is often as much of an invitation as a journalist gets. 'Do you speak English?' I asked her, but she shook her head.

'I do!' her daughter interjected, wrapped up in a black

puffer jacket and baby-pink scarf and stepping forward from her mother's side.

'I can speak English!' she said again.

I looked at her mum with a raised eyebrow and motioned 'Can we speak to her?', and the mother managed a very tired, but very loving, nod. The girl proceeded to tell us how her dad had stayed behind to fight. She was speaking with bravery and brilliant English, when suddenly she fell apart. 'Because now is war in Ukraine, and . . .' the tears started flowing and she leant forward, wrapping her arms around me in a hug and burying her face in my jacket. I hugged her back, and we stood like that for what felt like five minutes but was probably only one. I looked at Daniel and I knew he was thinking the same as me. It was our most powerful interview of the day, and would make the story. This young girl would make people care. When we watched the story for the final time that night before sending it back to Auckland, I felt silent tears trickling down my own face.

People back home did care. People cared so much that the decision was instantly obvious to us and The Sarahs: we had to get back to Ukraine. That's how Daniel and I found ourselves standing side by side at ATM machines at a random Polish bank, withdrawing thousands of dollars in cash. Our credit cards would only let us withdraw $300 at a time, so for 30 minutes we stood there going through the withdrawal process on repeat, building a stash of cash the equivalent of $10,000 USD and praying the bank wouldn't suspect fraud and cut us off. We wrapped rubber bands around wads of dirty notes, trying to maintain some order, and stuffed them down our puffer jackets as we hurried back to the car and transferred it all into the glove box like some sort of amateur drug-dealing duo. The money would be used for emergencies, like if the electricity went down and credit cards and eftpos were no longer an option. The reality is, money talks; and the thousands we now had would certainly help us get to safety faster if things went downhill.

We headed to the supermarket next, filling the trolley with dry food that would keep us going. Again the risk of losing electricity if the power stations were bombed was a real one, so we resorted to a gourmet selection of Pringles, muesli bars and scroggin, throwing in two-minute noodles, pasta and tomato sauce in the hope that most nights we would be in a position to cook.

I became obsessed with buying a beanie before leaving. I had never let myself wear a hat on air, convinced it looked too shabby and imagining my mum's musings as she perched on the arm of the couch watching from afar, but the temperature was plummeting day by day and I decided that my presentation standards would have to take a hit.

LVIV, UKRAINE
March 2022

Days before I moved to Europe, I had splashed out on a shiny new three-piece set of suitcases. They were outrageously expensive, extravagant even, and I blew my entire moving allowance on them, but they came with a ten-year warranty and I told myself it was a mature investment for a serious foreign correspondent. As I unloaded the suitcases one by one out of the boot and on to the rough gravel at the Polish border with Ukraine, I found myself wondering if the warranty covered war zones. I wasn't sure, and honestly, I'm still not. But what I knew for certain was that the Lisette who'd bought those suitcases never imagined that within months they'd be filled with two sets of body armour, helmets, multiple military-grade first-aid kits, $10,000 USD worth of cash, GPS tracking devices, satellite phones and enough dry food and water to last two people a fortnight. Life comes at you fast.

The night before, we had been given the all-clear to cross the border. It was our second trip to Ukraine, but our first time entering an active war zone. Everything had changed. Missiles were being fired haphazardly across the country, Russian troops were steadily advancing on Kyiv and nobody knew what President Putin was going to do next. We decided that Lviv would be the best starting point for us. Just two hours from the border with Poland, it would be easy to escape to safety quickly if we needed to, but it would also allow us to get closer to the story than any other Kiwi crew. Like our first trip, we would have a security team and a driver with us the entire time — but this time, given the increased risk, we had been assigned *two* security officers as well as a driver.

When the war started we had fired off a text message to Artem to see if he would be available again and, more importantly, to check if he was doing alright. He simply replied: 'Been hunting in the Kyiv area. Having good results already.' There was no further explanation of what, or who, he had been hunting, exactly, but none was necessary. We knew Artem well enough by this point to know he would have been the first to report for duty when the war started. With Ukraine under attack, the strong and the trained had been called to fight, and it was clear that getting a local security team again was not going to be possible. We had to look elsewhere.

Our phones dinged, and we looked down to see the faces

of Vadim and Marcel, the two Polish men now charged to watch our backs. Along with their mugshots, the email sent from the contracted security team explained that they were ex-military, with good experience, and while they couldn't speak Ukrainian we would meet a Ukrainian driver, a man named Bosko, once we crossed the border and he would be able to translate for us. Together as a team of five we would have our bases covered. There was a meeting point included in the email and we headed in that direction to find our two new Artems. Neither Daniel nor I had mentioned any nerves, but I think we were both looking forward to the added comfort of having some James Bond characters around.

As we arrived at the meeting point, about 100 metres from the border crossing, I saw Marcel. He was small in stature, looking barely older than a teenager, dressed in khaki green and wearing heavy boots that were a little too clean to match the aforementioned 'good experience'. His cheeks were flushed from the cold and he had on a backpack far too big for him. We later discovered it was filled to the brim with dehydrated army rations. Later again we discovered that dehydrated army rations are disgusting.

Marcel seemed on edge already, and we were still in Poland. I shook his gloved hand. 'Marcel? I'm Lisette. How are you?'

'Nervous,' he said, and the way he said it made it sound like an understatement.

'Nervous? Why nervous?'

'Because we're going into a fucking war zone.'

I looked at Daniel, and he looked at me, and the mutual look said something along the lines of 'Thank fuck we got an extra one of these guys.'

And then Vadim turned up.

Dressed head to toe in military camouflage, he also had on

heavy boots — but his looked worn. Well worn. I could only see his eyes. A dark-green beanie was pulled down low over his forehead, and a black buff covered from his neck up over his nose. I'm not entirely sure he even introduced himself, but he grunted a few grunts and I remember letting an audible sigh of relief escape. This man was scary as hell, but I got the feeling he had fired many bullets in the past and would probably take one for me and Daniel if it came to it. Marcel looked even more relieved than us.

'We're gonna be fine,' I thought to myself, and together as a newly formed team of four strangers we trudged off towards the border.

With the airspace above Ukraine now closed, there were no more flights in and out of the country; walking, driving or training across the border were the only options. The train stations were overflowing with refugees and getting insurance for a car going into a war zone is always going to be a tough ask, so our best option was to walk. We weren't the only ones, of course; there were millions of people crossing the border but they were going in the opposite direction. Ukrainians continued to pour into Poland and as we walked towards the border checks, those coming the other way looked at us in confusion. Journalists were gathered in a pack at the entry point to border control, trying to interview anyone going into Ukraine.

'Why are you heading in?' they asked Marcel.

'Are you joining the fight?' they asked Vadim.

'Are you an aid worker?' they asked me.

Daniel gestured to his camera and everyone backed off.

'Oh, you're press,' they muttered, not hiding their disappointment. There was no story here.

But there was about to be.

We kept trudging forward in the frozen conditions until we reached passport control. It was quiet and tense and I'm not sure what I was expecting, but it was set up like any other border crossing around the world. Although maybe a few more guns. No, definitely a few more guns. As always, though, there were booths with officers ready to stamp your passport, and there was the usual split-lane system that you see at airports everywhere: go left for EU Passports, go right for All Passports. It was hardly rush-hour in terms of entry into Ukraine so there was little speed advantage for those who are part of the European bloc, but systems are systems and as a Polish citizen Marcel headed straight for the left lane while we gestured, with dramatised regret, that we'd have to meet him on the other side thanks to our lowly New Zealand citizenships. Vadim had been following behind me and I expected him to break off and follow Marcel through the fast lane, but he didn't. I pointed out to him that he could go through the EU lane with Marcel.

All I got in return was a firm shake of the head.

I was confused. If he was Polish, why wasn't he going through the EU lane? I figured he was sticking with us out of obligation, not wanting to leave us alone.

'You're Polish, right?' I asked.

Again, a firm headshake.

Now I was really confused. My gut did that pesky thing it does when something doesn't feel right and all of a sudden I felt a bit sick.

'What nationality are you?'

'Belarusian.'

Not good. Putin's men had just spent months preparing for war from a base in Belarus, amassing at the Belarus–Ukraine border and launching their attack from that position. The president of Belarus, Alexander Lukashenko, described by many as Europe's last dictator, was Vladimir Putin's most loyal ally. Belarus had played a crucial role in allowing the invasion to occur; they'd actually aided it. I could feel my heart rate rising and my brain was working overtime. Our team had said Vadim was ex-military. That would *really* not be good. But they'd also said he was Polish and he wasn't. So I was hoping they'd got this wrong, too.

'Did you serve?' I asked, as casually as possible.

'Fifteen years Special Forces. But fuck Lukashenko.'

I am proud to say I don't think I let my jaw drop, but I am certain my eyes bulged just a tad. Despite the lukewarm sentiment towards his old boss, we were now trying to get into an active war zone with a man every person in the vicinity would absolutely consider to be the enemy. I leant forward and whispered to Daniel: 'Vadim is ex-Belarusian Special Forces, we need to get away from him.'

At this point 'ex' was feeling optimistic.

Daniel's eyes did what I imagine mine did 30 seconds prior, and we moved with renewed pace towards border patrol to hand over our passports as a pair, leaving Vadim waiting in line alone.

Stamped and through, we met a panicked Marcel. 'Where's Vadim?'

As he asked, we looked back to see our fourth teammate surrounded by Ukrainian officers, the guns now out of their relaxed positions and raised . . . and maybe not just for effect. Yes, in retrospect, there were *definitely* more guns than at your usual border crossing. We quickly relayed our recent learnings to Marcel, and he did not take the news well. At all. I saw the sweat appear within seconds.

'He's a fucking Russian spy!' he exclaimed. 'We're going to

get arrested for sneaking in a Russian spy!' But based on the number of Ukrainian officers now marching Vadim away for questioning, it was clear that any attempt to 'sneak in' had been unsuccessful. Trying to further distance ourselves from the situation, we stepped outside to discuss our next move just as Marcel realised he had been carrying one of Vadim's bags and still had it over his shoulder. I've never seen a man drop a bag so fast, before jumping back 10 metres and starting to pace erratically.

I got on the phone and called the team who had organised our security to explain the situation. Vadim must have provided fake information and documents and the guys on the other end apologised for the situation, but the more pressing issue now was that we were in Ukraine with 50% of the security team we thought we'd have. And the remaining 50% was currently having a panic attack.

'We're comfortable with you proceeding with the trip with just one security officer, if you guys are feeling happy with Marcel. You've met him now, got a feeling for him, what do you think?' HQ said down the line.

I looked over and saw Daniel running Marcel through deep-breathing exercises, and made a quick decision for the both of us.

'Yeah, he knows what he's doing. We're both more than happy to carry on with just Marcel.'

'Cool. Sorry again. We're tracking you from now, so just keep in touch. Bosko is waiting to pick you up.'

We left the bag and Vadim behind.

I couldn't imagine things getting much worse, but when it rains it pours and we were in the eye of a storm. Bosko looked barely

23 years old, but he had the energy of a 45-year-old street-side scammer. He had a gold chain around his neck and the shortest sniff of a moustache, truly the worst moustache I've ever seen. He wore chunky black sneakers, black trackpants, a tiny black scarf and dark-blue puffer jacket that was far too small for him.

Bosko was immediately apologetic about the poor communication over where he would be waiting and quickly walked us to the car, speaking in broken English with us and broken Polish with Marcel. At this point Daniel and I were just trying to convince each other everything was under control, but I was desperately missing Artem and Tomlin. The car we arrived at was small. Far too small for what was going to be a five-person crew before one of our crew got bloody arrested. The car would barely fit our now four-person crew and it almost certainly wasn't going to fit all of our gear.

Bosko looked at us with a sorry face and shrugged unhelpfully, and Daniel and I began to play Tetris with our bags and bodies. In the end, we rammed our luggage into the boot and squashed in the back seat with barely any room to breathe; the car's spare tyre, the tripod and fuel canisters piled up across our laps and blocking us from view of Bosko and Marcel in the front seat, which was probably for the best as Daniel and I exchanged looks of horror. I wasn't entirely sure the car was roadworthy. It looked little better than something we would have called a paddock-basher back home, the kind of worthless hunk of metal that Dad would let us hoon around the farm in before we had our licences. I could hear the voices of our trainers in Kent drilling into us that under no circumstances should we ever get into a car unless we had given it a full safety inspection, and I mentally dismissed them with 'Now's not the time' as Bosko turned on the ignition. As we settled in for our two-hour drive to Lviv, packed in like sardines, Bosko started explaining with pride that he was in fact a car dealer, importing cars from the United States to Ukraine with his uncle, which is where he had got this 'new car' from.

Any self-pity was quickly overshadowed by the scene unfolding around us. As we drove towards Lviv, the roads were lined with refugees awaiting entry into Poland, having made the walk there from god knows what terror. It was 30 minutes into our drive before the lines of people finally finished, but the path they had walked was unmissable. The roadside grass was flattened by the desperate footsteps of the millions of Ukrainians who had trampled their way to safety this past week; nappies, food wrappings, water bottles and clothing littered the route and I couldn't believe how far they had walked.

Russian forces had been met with more resistance than anticipated since the invasion began, and already Moscow seemed to be shifting its strategy. It appeared to no longer be focusing only on military targets, but on civilian ones as well — striking key population centres. A massive convoy of Russian troops north of Kyiv had been largely stalled for days, but the Kremlin was refusing to back down from its initial plan to capture the capital and Western officials were warning there would be an increase in the severity of strikes as Putin tried to bomb Kyiv and other cities into submission. Nowhere felt safe, and families were fleeing from all over the country.

As we drove into Lviv, we started encountering checkpoints and I disappointed myself by reaching for the ultimate cliche: 'This is like something from a movie' — but I still struggle to describe the feeling any better. On either side of the road would be a stack of tyres and sandbags, forming a wall which soldiers were crouched behind holding weapons. Some checkpoints had wooden huts, or huts made of corrugated iron, and there would always be fires lit, for soldiers to stand near to keep warm. You'd pull up to the checkpoint, slowly, and military men with their faces covered with buffs would stare inside a wound-down window and question a suddenly serious Bosko, who would reply with a string of information I couldn't understand other than the words 'journalist' and 'Nova Zelandiya'. We would get the nod from the soldiers, the window would go up as Bosko farewelled them with an almost compulsory 'Slava Ukraini' and we'd drive through. Every time, I held my breath. And every time, Daniel hid his camera, which could easily be mistaken for a weapon.

When we arrived in Lviv, the wartime conditions continued to reveal themselves: the city's statues all covered in white wrappings or sandbagged completely. 'To protect from bombing,' Bosko said matter-of-factly.

It was 8 p.m. when we did our first live cross into the morning news in New Zealand from the city square and within minutes we had attracted attention. Soldiers were at our side, with faces of steel and hands firmly grasping their guns. They said something in Ukrainian and I stared at Bosko as my heart raced.

'Documents,' he said. We retrieved our passports and press accreditation and showed the soldiers, who snatched them with suspicion and eyed them — and us — for far too long to feel good about. They spoke again to Bosko and left us to it, having reminded him of the curfew in place around the city. No one was allowed out of their houses between 10 p.m. and 6 a.m. and we were getting close.

Having settled into our accommodation, with Bosko and Marcel in a separate apartment, Daniel and I looked at each other and took a huge breath. We had been running on adrenaline until this point, charging through the steps that would get us right here, to the moment where we could stop and make a plan for how the hell we were going to get through the next few days with these two schoolboys in tow.

I took a packet of pasta and a jar of tomato sauce from our bag of supplies and made us the worst dinner. It was the opposite of comfort food, and the situation was about to become even more uncomfortable. We were a couple of spoonfuls into our stodge when we heard it. It started low and grew in volume and pitch, and over the top of the blaring siren came the voice of a Ukrainian man repeating calm instructions. An air-raid siren completely consumes you; you can feel it under your skin, and while Lviv was so far west that it had been largely ignored in the invasion and we knew we were safe, my voice of reason was fighting a losing battle after a day of checkpoints and soldiers.

In a small town hall the next morning we met a group of women, wives, daughters and mothers who were dedicating hours on end to stringing pieces of green and brown fabric together. The camouflage netting would be used to cover tanks to help conceal their positions in satellite imagery taken by the Russians. As the women worked, they sang. It was a song of strength and freedom that ended with a chant of those increasingly familiar words: 'Slava Ukraini' — 'Glory to Ukraine'. I couldn't believe how much the lives of these families had transformed in just a matter of days. The men were sent to war, and their loved ones abandoned their day jobs to either flee the country or join the war effort by making items like these nets.

Air-raid sirens continued to sound throughout the day and we would all collectively drop what we were doing and rush down to the bomb shelters together. Crammed into those tiny spaces, it was an equaliser like I had never experienced before. Everyone shared reassuring smiles, trying to ease each other into some sort of fake comfort, before the siren stopped, the all-clear was given and everyone returned to the task at hand. One of those tasks was making Molotov cocktails, and we were on our way to a local brewery to film the process when Bosko pointed out a huge billboard on the roadside.

'It says "Fuck off Putin",' he said, and he and Marcel descended into the laughter of teenagers. It *was* quite funny. Locals had been putting the signs up all over town and people tooted support whenever they drove past them, adding to the growing sense of camaraderie and defiance in the country.

Bosko and Marcel had hit it off quickly, a blessing really because I think Bosko's relaxed approach to things was helping with Marcel's anxiety. They were both also smoking constantly and I think that was helping too. They had taken to referring to each other as 'my friend', and in their strong Eastern European accents it was highly entertaining and somewhat endearing; but if you chuckled when they said it they would add it the end of every sentence for the next fifteen minutes like children who'd made their parents laugh. This was exponentially less entertaining and less endearing, so Daniel and I had stopped reacting.

Marcel hadn't operated in a war zone before; he had trained with the Polish army but didn't serve for long before moving into a job providing security on ships, guarding against pirates. That job in itself boggled my sheltered brain, but also helped to explain why coming to Ukraine had been such a stressful job for him. Bosko, on the other hand, with no military training at all, wouldn't have wanted to be anywhere else. A classic wheeler and dealer, his uncle, the one he had the slightly questionable car import business with, had seen an opening in the market when the war started: driving news crews around. The uncle couldn't keep up with demand so had started passing work Bosko's way. Bosko wasn't going to be conscripted yet due to his age, but also because he had a neck injury which made him a less than ideal candidate. He was upset about that, to be fair, and wanted to do his part, so figured this would be his wartime contribution; for now, at least. He was incredibly well-meaning, and was always making phone calls to friends or family who he thought might be a good interview subject for us. They never were, and after all his phone talking he would inevitably insist on stopping for a cigarette or a kebab, which cost us valuable time, but we grew quite fond of his efforts.

We arrived at the brewery and walked up to the security point. As we showed our accreditation, we were kindly asked to remove all weapons before walking through the scanner. Daniel and I chuckled at the suggestion. 'No weapons here,' we said as we walked through, but we turned around to see Bosko and Marcel emptying their pockets of an extensive collection of knives. Having been transformed into a Molotov cocktail factory, the brewery was working overtime to deliver to all of the checkpoints around the city, arming the soldiers in case of trouble. They were also releasing the recipe publicly to encourage people to make their own at home. We saw the flyers plastered on poles all over the city, right next to the posters urging people to give blood immediately to send with medics to the front line.

As we waited at the kebab shack on the side of the road for our post-shoot snack, I felt the chilling touch of a gun against me. My heart skipped a beat and I spun around, far too quickly, to find myself face-to-face with a soldier.

He mumbled something apologetic-sounding in Ukrainian and I instantly felt like an idiot for jumping. He was just waiting in line for a kebab too. I'd been accidentally grazed by his gun. As if it were a handbag.

The Lviv train station made the Polish one look like a holiday camp. A major transport hub, it was huge but still crowded. The square in front of it was swarming with military, aid workers and on-edge refugees. There was a man playing John Lennon's 'Imagine' on a piano; one mother was swaying from side to side beside him, holding her toddler in her arms and doing her best to pretend everything was going to be alright. The station was overflowing with families fighting for a spot on a train to the West. The underground network of corridors was also full; people had been waiting down there for ten hours at a time, unwilling to give up their spot in line to go to the bathroom or eat. It was filthy and the smell was horrific. When a train pulled up to the platform above, there would be an underground surge for a spot. The thousands would all push towards the stairs and run to make it on to the train. It wasn't a ticketed system, but a case of if you could fit, you could stay. Those who made it on would start praying and crying, thanking god for saving them a spot. Those who didn't would descend into prayer of a different type, knowing they would have to hang in there longer still before their help arrived.

It was utterly harrowing, and the stories of the hell they had survived further east only added to the nightmarish picture. 'Two bombs come down and our house was shaking. We doesn't have a bomb shelter. I say to our friends in all countries, help for us, help for Ukraine! Because the Russian people kill us about nothing!' one woman cried into Daniel's lens.

While Marcel panicked about the number of people, and Bosko took some more calls and had another cigarette, Daniel and I were charged with adrenaline. We stood on the platform filming as mums ran to the train dragging their children along behind them hand-in-hand. In these situations, Daniel would have his headphones on and I would hold the microphone so I could speak to him from afar and point out any shots I thought were worth grabbing that he might not have seen. This is notoriously annoying for camera operators, who have almost always already seen the shot and got it, or have found something far better to film; but most do it anyway to appease the micro-managing journalists they enjoy working with . . . deep down.

On this particular day, I spotted a girl crying hysterically as she tried to get a spot on a train, and I said down the microphone: 'Dan . . . the girl in the puffer jacket and AirPods!'

He turned around to me: 'Lisette, what sort of fucking description is that?! It's a sea of puffer jackets and you want me to locate the person with an AirPod?!'

And then we laughed. Standing there amid overwhelming trauma, unlike anything we had ever been exposed to before, trying not to cry was becoming harder by the second. The situation wasn't funny at all, but we had been so immersed in sadness for so many days and were so incredibly tired that a burst of laughter suddenly provided a temporary escape and we couldn't resist it. The only saving grace is that everyone was so focused on their own mission that day that I don't think we offended anyone; they probably didn't even notice us and that five-second dose of laughter got us through the rest of the day.

Outside we met a man of fighting age who was waiting for his call to duty, and I asked him how he thought it would end.

‘I think that Putin fucking die in his bunker and we will dance on his grave,’ he told us.

As we drove away from the train station, I could see Marcel on his phone flicking through pictures of scantily clad females. I guess we all had different coping mechanisms.

The next morning I was woken up by the sound of my phone ringing. Shit. We’d slept in. The team in Auckland were ringing to connect us to the studio for our live cross, and I was still in my pyjamas. I yelled at Daniel to wake up, answered the phone and assured them we’d be on air in time but would just need a few extra minutes before we could do the sound check. I grabbed the beanie I’d bought a week ago in Poland and thanked past me for being so insistent on getting it. Shoving it on my head, I no longer needed to worry about doing my hair, and six minutes later Daniel and I were standing in snow outside our apartment and I was live on air, with a huge chunk of sleep still in the corner of one of my eyes.

We left Ukraine that day, and Marcel and Bosko shared a hug.

‘Goodbye, my friend.’

‘Goodbye, my friend!’

‘Keep up the English,’ I encouraged Bosko.

‘I’ll be in touch about you getting me a car,’ Daniel joked.

‘Okay, okay, my friends,’ Bosko said, smiling. He kissed the cross on the chain around his neck and started rummaging in his back pocket for his cigarettes as we headed off on our walk across the border.

There was still a long line of people trying to get through to Poland; the surge of refugees had slowed but it hadn’t stopped. We joined the queue behind a husband and wife as they walked forward together in silence. She was pushing suitcases, with a baby on her front and a bag on her back, but her husband was lifting the weight of the bag from below so she wasn't really carrying it at all. They were minutes from saying goodbye to each other for who knows how long, and I heard myself mumble: 'What world are we living in?'

Marcel was less affected. I saw him smile and say something to one of the female border guards.

'Do you know her?' I asked.

'No, my friend,' he replied with a sly smile.

'What did you say to her?'

'That she has very nice eyes,' and his own twinkled mischievously.

It's fair to say Marcel had warmed to life in Ukraine.

PRZEMYŚL, POLAND
March 2022

Safely back in Poland, we headed to the only hotel in the area that had capacity for us. It was an extravagant ski resort about an hour from the border. Settled on a snowy hill, surrounded by ski fields complete with chair lifts, the grounds included separate indoor pool complexes, ice skating rinks, pens filled with animals for children to go goo-goo over, and multiple restaurants and bars. We arrived mid-afternoon and figured that the bosses would let us stay there a night as a treat before packing us off to London once again. I had a hot shower, tried to catch my brain up with where my life was at, and had almost fallen asleep in my hotel robe when my phone rang. The Sarahs.

I called Daniel into my room and through the speaker phone they told us they were in no rush to get us back to London. 'You guys need to have some good sleep, book yourselves a massage at the hotel, have some good food and try to relax,' they said.

'Lisette, are you listening?' Sarah Bristow fake-growled. 'Under no circumstances are you to file a story for at least a day, okay?'

I looked at Daniel in disbelief.

'How long are we staying here?' I managed.

'We just need to assess the options. We need to see how we can keep the coverage going. But you need a break first.'

We found ourselves strangely promising to have the next couple of days off and hung up the phone. I couldn't believe it. We were being told by our bosses to rest up in one of the most amazing resorts I had ever stepped foot in. We were overtired and slightly giddy as we made our way to the hotel bar, eager to follow instructions and let our hair down. It probably took just one drink for giddy to turn into tipsy and we spent hours in the bowling alley that night, me guttering almost every ball and Daniel getting pretty much straight strikes as we pretended the horrors of the neighbouring country didn't exist. The wholesome family ski holidays taking place around us were probably very confused about how we fitted into the picture of the luxury resort, but we weren't deterred. We hadn't had to use our body armour yet and by 2 a.m. we had convinced ourselves it was a good idea to put it on as we played Monopoly Deal in my room. But the next day, after a long sleep-in, we were done pretending and ready to go again.

We set up an office in the hotel cafe and got planning. We started collating an extensive pitch to convince the bosses to let us do a full tour of the countries where refugees would be heading. We'd already done Poland, obviously, but what about

Romania, Slovakia, Moldova? As we costed up flights, cars and accommodation in a spreadsheet, and listed our different story angles and our health and safety plans, Daniel looked up and said: 'I just want to go back.'

'Same.'

'Why don't we?'

'Well, where would we go?'

'Odessa,' he replied without missing a beat.

This Ukrainian city is a pearl of the Black Sea. Sitting on the coast to the south it was once a much-loved Russian holiday spot due to its beautiful beaches. Putin's men had been steadily advancing in from the east and down along the southern coast, capturing critical territory including Kherson and the port city of Mariupol, which suffered an apocalyptical attack and remains, to this day, under Russian control. Putin had already annexed the Crimea peninsula in 2014, so if his forces were also to gain control of Odessa then Ukraine would become landlocked. But the Russians hadn't arrived there yet. They were still fighting in the next city along, Mykolaiv, just 100 kilometres away, and at least for now Odessa was one of the last cities on this stretch that stood untouched.

'It's a long shot — they'll say it's too dangerous,' I said.

'We could go in from Moldova.'

I was keen, and we were pitching to go to Moldova anyway, so there seemed no harm in tacking on Odessa as the last stop of our tour. 'I'll add it to the document and if they're not interested, then we can easily just chop it off and end in Moldova.'

'Yeah, good plan. You just never know.'

He was right, of course; we'd never thought we'd get to Ukraine the first time and now we'd been twice.

I finished the pitch document and sent it off to the powers

that be. A few hours later, New Zealand woke up and my phone rang. The Sarahs.

'Great document, thank you. Let's get you guys straight to Odessa.'

I've never asked them to confirm the fact, but when the phone call ended, Daniel and I looked at each other and laughed.

'So that was their plan all along!'

From the start the resort had felt too good to be true, and in the years that have followed we've joked that it was the ultimate honey trap. The Sarahs were always so mindful of not making us do anything we weren't comfortable with that I wouldn't be surprised if they had been waiting for us to ask to go back in, not wanting to suggest it first themselves and risk making it feel like pressure. Regardless, the ball was rolling now. The Moldovan airspace was closed due to its proximity to Ukraine, so we would have to fly to Romania and drive from there to Moldova, and then on to Ukraine. It was a total logistical nightmare — but we were getting used to those.

ODESSA, UKRAINE
mid-March 2022

Our Romanian driver dropped us off at our accommodation in Moldova and farewelled us with a gift, a few notes of local currency. 'Keep it, like a souvenir,' he said. 'It's worth nothing, but you could use it for toilet paper if your motel has none.'

This didn't fill us with confidence. Moldova is the poorest country in Europe and fairly dangerous in its own right. There is a pro-Russia breakaway region within the country called Transnistria, which we were told with some force to avoid at all costs, so instead we headed to film a story at the refugee centre in the capital, Chişinău. In a remarkable show of generosity, Moldova — which barely has enough to look after its own people — had opened its doors and set up several camps for displaced Ukrainians. Their generosity didn't stop there. We were due to travel to the border the next morning, but we still didn't know how we were going to get there. We asked our motel receptionist if she knew any taxis that would take us, and she started insisting that she would drive us to the border herself if she could find someone to cover her on reception. Given that it was 200 kilometres away this was an outrageous offer, so we tried to talk her down. In the end, we reached a compromise and she arranged for her friend to drive us.

When we met our Moldovan saviour not long after the crack of dawn, he spent at least the first fifteen minutes of the drive shaking his head at our plan to enter Ukraine. We were getting used to that reaction by now, but it always came as an unsettling reminder that perhaps our own anxiety levels should be a little bit higher. The big drives always provided crucial sleeping time for us and it is a superpower of mine that I can nod off anywhere, anytime. I can't tell if it's because I'm perpetually tired or because I'm well-hardened from years of having to sleep in Mum and Dad's wardrobe on family holidays while all my older siblings baggsied the beds. Possibly a bit of both. On this day, though, I struggled to doze off quite as quickly as normal. It was my niece's first day at school and I was suddenly very homesick. That morning, my phone had buzzed with photos of her, my bright-eyed goddaughter, in her school uniform and it reminded me of how desperately far we were from New Zealand. A year prior I didn't even know where Moldova *was*.

When we arrived at the border, it was a familiar sight. Minimal traffic going into Ukraine and an awful lot coming out. We thanked our driver, who wished us well, and we hauled all of our bags out of the car and started trudging towards the guards to start the exit from Moldova. But it wasn't going to be easy. Camera gear is registered with what is called a carnet, which needs to be stamped when you travel between countries. I describe it, probably poorly, as a camera's passport. Because of the camera's value it would be taxed if you were importing it, and the carnet shows that it is under your ownership and you intend to leave the country with it again, therefore getting the customs tax waived. If you don't get it stamped, the border security staff start to huff and puff and can issue you a huge fine. I make no secret of the fact that I hate carnets. They add hours to your travel time, especially in Europe and the Middle East where the language barriers are immense and the behaviour of border staff can be questionable. At every airport and train station, you spend at least fifteen minutes waiting for someone to show up to fill out the paperwork, then another fifteen waiting for them to actually do it. And that's on a good day.

On this particular day, the carnet almost sank us. The day prior, as we had driven from Romania into Moldova, we had crossed the border by car and had forgotten to get the carnet stamped out of and into the respective countries. Daniel later claimed that as we crossed the border he had known he needed to get the carnet done but was so sick of me complaining about how long it took that he decided not to poke the sleeping bear snoring beside him. As Romania is part of the EU and Moldova is not, this was a major mistake. The Moldovan security man, with his pot belly and scruffy beard, knew it too and was demanding to see our paperwork.

‘Big big no no,’ the scruffy man said, and I realised in horror that we were not going to get past him; he was either going to confiscate all of our equipment or slap us with a monumental fine. I could already hear myself making the phone call to The Sarahs, trying to explain how we ended up abandoned at the Ukrainian border with no story, no transport, no camera and thousands of dollars worth of fresh debt.

I was about to start trying to talk our way out of the situation when Daniel looked at me with eyes that said ‘Can you just keep quiet for once?’ I knew it was the right call, but the next half-hour was excruciating. The scruffy man made Daniel follow him to the other side of the checkpoint, and I could see him berating Daniel in front of a group of border force officers. They were all shaking their heads and putting out energy that wasn’t *quite* as aggressive as what Vadim had faced but not far off. I felt my panic rising, but quickly realised that I was probably not all that far off Marcel behaviour and needed to get a grip. I stayed where I was and hoped like hell Methven had taught Daniel enough southern charm to get us out of this. He is adamant to this day that he was making progress, and had managed to convince the scruffy man to let us go through, but he also admits it was somewhat fortunate that the Moldovan president suddenly arrived at the crossing point at that moment. Suddenly the border force had something more pressing to deal with, and promptly told Daniel to get a move on.

‘Look out for warships,’ one of them yelled after us.

‘Enjoy your stay in Ukraine,’ yelled another. As if it were a holiday.

We’d been incredibly lucky, but we weren’t going to sit around to discuss it. Grabbing our bags, we moved with pace through the Moldovan checkpoint, desperate to get to the

Ukrainian side and on with our assignment.

Our passports were stamped with far more ease at the Ukrainian checkpoint, but as we were walking onwards to find our driver an officer started yelling after us in Ukrainian. 'What now?!' I grumbled, growing increasingly frustrated with the hold-ups. The officer seemed to be concerned that Daniel was already filming at the checkpoint, which is essentially asking for an arrest warrant. Of course he hadn't been, but we were bracing for another tense discussion when all of a sudden I felt a rush of air and movement all around me. I was surrounded by huge men, dressed head to toe in combat black. They looked like SWAT officers, and they grabbed our bags, dismissed the angry border force man and whisked us towards two huge trucks. So little had been said, and they'd moved with such pace, that all of a sudden Daniel and I found ourselves in the back of one of the trucks, along with one of the best-looking men I have ever seen, driving at 180 kilometres an hour through the Ukrainian countryside with a man who made The Rock look dainty squashed into the other front seat.

'Have we been kidnapped?' I said quietly to Daniel, trying to catch my breath.

'What the hell was that?' he replied.

It was, of course, and we did quickly realise this, our new security team. We knew immediately that we were in safe hands. We also knew we were much closer to the war now. These men were not here to joke or laugh, they were not inexperienced boys; they meant business.

Ukraine looked different, too. As we drove, we saw trenches dug into the farmland, soldiers were in place waiting for the worst and there were tanks everywhere camouflaged into the trees. There were far more checkpoints and the conversations were more tense, but everyone clearly knew our guys because as soon as they set eyes on our driver they'd wave us through. There were hedgehogs on the roads — big metal rods over a metre long and thick like planks of wood, crossed over each other and placed where Russian tanks would want to go but wouldn't be able to now.

Once we arrived at the accommodation, I got settled in the penthouse apartment on level 7, and sent Daniel down to level 2 with the guys. 'You don't appreciate the views like me,' I justified.

Andrei, one of the security guys, wanted a team meeting and it was clear he was in charge. He oozed wisdom. Not a big man, but he looked as tough as nails. Probably in his fifties, he spoke quietly — but no one would dare talk over him so he had no need to raise his voice. He laid down the ground rules. There was a tougher curfew in Odessa: we couldn't risk being outside out of hours or the police would think the worst. Andrei lit a cigarette and his crew all followed suit.

'Let's go see the bomb shelter,' he said. There wasn't one in the hotel, so we'd have to go next door when the siren sounded and needed to know where it was. We made the 100-metre journey down the street and Andrei took us down to the shelter through a door that was clearly marked. It was cozy and I hoped we wouldn't see much of it, though it felt inevitable that we would.

Finally, Andrei introduced Dmitry. I'd guess he was about my age, with short-shaved blonde hair and a chiselled jaw. He had blue eyes that brought out the blue of the band wrapped around his arm on top of his black jacket. They all had the blue band. What were those blue bands? And I heard myself ask the question.

'We're friendly forces,' Andrei said. 'Everyone sees this, and they know we are friendly forces.' His explanation went some way towards me understanding how we had been getting through checkpoints so quickly. Dmitry wasn't very talkative, but he didn't have a wedding ring on, which gave me more hope than Artem ever did. 'Dmitry will be our driver,' Andrei said. 'He's a firefighter so he has the emergency sticker on his truck and that way we can go anywhere without any questions. It's perfect for you,' he continued, unravelling the checkpoint mystery in a single sentence. Tapping the truck lightly, Dmitry smiled and I returned it. 'That is perfect,' I said, already imagining myself as Mrs August in the Odessan Firefighters and Plus-ones calendar.

'Lisette . . .' Daniel said in a warning tone, 'come on — he can't even leave the country!'

As we left the shelter it was already getting dark and Andrei again began with his curfew lecture. We could leave at night for the shelter, of course, but we'd be best in a group and we'd need to have our press accreditation on us at all times. A police car slowed next to us and rolled down the window in suspicion, before saying something that made everyone except Daniel and me start to laugh. We looked at each other in confusion: what could possibly be so funny? As the officers drove off, Andrei turned to us, taking a big drag of his cigarette and still smirking. 'They thought your camera was a javelin,' he chuckled to Daniel, who promptly dropped the camera from its normal position on his shoulder to hang by his side instead.

That night, my old deskmate Tom McRae, who is a very funny man and was one of the brilliant newsreaders at Newshub at the time, messaged to check how our journey into Odessa had gone.

'I hope you're keeping a diary or notes on this whole thing,' he wrote after I filled him in on the latest. 'Will make a big chunk of your autobiography.'

'Ha,' I replied, assuming of course that he was joking.

'I'm being serious,' he sent back a moment later — to which I responded, just as quickly, 'My autobiography will read "I was too busy doing my actual job to think about this book, so I'll remember what I can and make up the rest to ensure a good story!" '

I wouldn't want to inflate Tom's ego too much by admitting that he gives good advice, but that night I did start writing things down, which has really helped limit the amount that needed to be made up . . . although the bit about him being 'brilliant' might need fact-checking.

My sleeping superpower was almost a problem in Ukraine. I am such a deep sleeper that I always went to bed feeling just a little bit worried that the air-raid siren wouldn't be loud enough to wake me. So when I heard pounding on the door at three in the morning, I knew exactly what had happened. The siren was blaring and I jumped out of bed to get the door.

'I know, I know, I'm sorry.'

'We need to go to the shelter,' Dmitry said, and I cursed myself for letting him see my bed-hair so soon into our love story.

'Two seconds,' I said, scrambling to find some decent clothes to wear, struggling to find a bloody sock, stubbing my toe on the bed and cursing again before finally following him to the shelter. Everyone else was there already and I cursed for a third time; this time for letting the team down. I didn't want to be the liability of the group and from then on, while I didn't have a plan to combat my deep sleep just yet, every night I laid out my shelter clothes before I got into bed: boots, socks, jeans, bra, black thermal, puffer and beanie all sprawled out on the floor in front of the door ready to step into on my way out to the shelter.

This bunker had two rooms and the walls were covered in Soviet Union-era posters, with step-by-step instructions on how to tend to battlefield wounds. The door to the outside world was thick, solid metal that I could barely close on my own. Dmitry took over as I struggled, and as he bolted it shut in one easy movement I thought of the silly finance boys in London that I'd dated in the past who couldn't even change a car tyre.

There were mattresses in the far room and there were people lying on them with their pets, ready to hunker down for as long as it took. The first room, where we were, had chairs, not mattresses, and green walls. It also had a kitchenette. Andrei looked at me with a slight nod, but didn't say anything.

I turned to Daniel. 'Sorry I slept through — how long have you been here?'

'Five minutes or so.'

A short man appeared from the far room. Rugged up in warm clothing and with a rosy face, he looked so friendly I almost asked him for a hug. I could have used one. Instead, he lifted the kettle he was carrying in my direction, offering me a hot drink.

'Oh, no, thank you,' I replied, still wondering if a hug was an option.

He was the shelter keeper, Andrei explained. Responsible for the key that opened and locked the shelter, and so he had to be the first one there every time. It was also his job to keep it clean and tidy and, it seemed, to provide tea, coffee and comforting smiles. Due to its position within the country, Odessa deals with regular air-raid alerts. Most missiles fired from the Black Sea have to pass over Odessa to get further north, so will trigger the alert even if they are not destined to land there. The constant stream of night-time attacks was a deliberate strategy of Russia's, of course, a way to torture the population by keeping them sleep-deprived and on edge.

Two hours passed and I was starting to think we were going to have to do our live cross into the news from the bunker, making a mental note that in future I needed to bring a hairbrush and makeup with me, when word came that the alert was lifted and it was safe to return to our rooms. By this point my personal alarm was due to go off in 40 minutes to get ready for our cross, but I'll take 40 minutes of sleep over none, and my superpower paid me back for the earlier faux pas by allowing me at least 39 minutes conked out.

We were set up in the square for our live cross an hour later, smugly talking about how well the timing had worked out, when the air-raid siren sounded again.

'Ahh damn.'

'Spoke too soon.'

Racing back to the shelter, with just ten minutes to go before we were due on air, we had very little hope of getting back above ground for the live cross; and given that there was no cell signal underground, it was unlikely we were going to make our slot.

It wasn't until the shelter keeper was speaking to Andrei and pointing to a box on the wall that I realised they had bloody Wi-Fi down there.

'It is 2022, after all,' Daniel reasoned. We were connected in an instant, and I ended up doing a cross into the news bulletin from underground using Zoom on my phone.

'Lisette joins us now from a bunker in Odessa . . .' Mike McRoberts said in my ear, and honestly I was more shocked by the link actually working than the sentence itself.

On our first full day in Odessa I felt like a ping pong ball — going underground and above, underground and above, as the sirens kept sounding. The entire central city was a fortress braced for invasion. Huge barricades of tyres and concrete slabs several metres high blocked access to major landmarks, but also, most crucially, protected the access to the country's biggest port. For both sides of the war, it is a significant place. During World War II as part of the Soviet Union, Odessa fought so hard that it was honoured by the Kremlin with the title 'Hero City'. It was actually founded by the Russian empress Catherine the Great, but as we walked through the city filming, it was clear that the Ukrainians were protecting the history they were most proud of. A statue of Catherine in the heart of Odessa stood exposed to shelling, while hundreds of sandbags were piled high to protect statues of Ukrainian icons.

Soldiers were everywhere. It felt like ten times as many as there had been in Lviv and they all looked so angry. Their eyes didn't blink, instead scanning the area constantly for Russian visitors. Putin had his warships sitting nearby, just off the coast, and there were Ukrainian tanks hidden in the bushes across the beachfront pointing out at them in response. 'If they will come here, I think this will be a mistake,' one of the soldiers told me. As we spoke, the siren sounded for the third time that day and Andrei ushered us towards the nearest bomb shelter. It was dimly lit and it wasn't until we were downstairs and huddled together in a small room that I noticed the neon-red sign reading 'Night Cats'.

A lady appeared out of nowhere. 'You are welcome, but please be . . .' and held her finger to her lips. Andrei winked at me and pointed to the sign directly above my head. 'Men's Club', it read. We shared a chuckle and I remember thinking that my earlier assertion on national television that the entire city was now fully focused on war was not entirely true after all.

By the time we made it back to our accommodation, the curfew was about to be enforced and there was nowhere to get food. I opened up my suitcase and rummaged through the rations in search of inspiration. The facilities in our rooms were limited, no stove top or microwave, so it was clear I was going to have to get creative. While Daniel edited the story I began my own project: boiling pasta in the kettle on repeat until it slowly started to soften. As I stirred in a bottle of cold tomato sauce and tipped the pasta into two separate glasses, I wasn't feeling very confident but we were both too hungry to care.

'You'll have to drink it because there are no spoons,' I told Daniel on delivery. He gave rave reviews.

I heard it the next time. The siren sounded and I jumped out of bed in an instant. I pulled my clothes on and with my makeup and hairbrush in tow, I was out the door and rushing downstairs to the meeting point, ready to go with the crew to the shelter. But when I burst into the foyer, no one was there. I was furious at myself: I'd done it again. I'd slept through the alarm and they'd all gone without me.

My head was pounding from the wail of the siren and I knew I had no choice but to go alone. Heading out into the midnight darkness, I had been jogging towards the shelter for two minutes when I realised I had no idea where I was going. The siren was so deafening that I couldn't get my thoughts in order and it was so dark I could barely see.

'Where the hell am I?' I thought, fighting against near-crippling fear. 'And where the fuck is the fucking shelter!?' I felt like I could hear an actual ticking time bomb growing louder and louder, and I was on the brink of tears when I decided the only option was to run back to the hotel.

'But there's no shelter there!' my brain shouted back at me, and I spun around in a hopeless circle. When I saw the police car, I froze. It was past curfew, and I was out by myself — and I had forgotten all of my documents. It was War Zone 101 and I had failed all of Andrei's three rules. Don't go out after curfew, don't go anywhere alone, don't go anywhere without your passport or press accreditation. I was terrified of the police officers even when I was in a group and with my documents in daylight, and my highly wired, extremely tired brain quickly weighed up the perceived options: stay looking for the shelter and the cops will either shoot at you or arrest you; or run to the hotel where there is no shelter and die from the incoming missile. I could see the light of the hotel foyer up ahead and found myself sprinting towards it. I had never been so frightened in my life and as I burst in through the doors I was breathless. And mortified. There they were: Andrei, Dmitry and Daniel, stepping out of the lift.

'What . . .?' I could barely speak.

'Ahh, you beat us down!' Andrei said, looking impressed. 'You are the best soldier!'

I smiled weakly but didn't say a thing, desperately trying to get control of my heart rate and not wanting to embarrass myself or jeopardise my newly awarded title of 'best soldier' by admitting the truth. Daniel looked at me with a raised eyebrow and it was obvious he knew there was more to the story.

'You heard Andrei — I'm the best soldier,' I said.

In the blur of my terror, it had felt like I was outside by myself for half an hour, but it must have been a few minutes at most. Now, as we moved towards the shelter together, I couldn't believe how easy it was to locate. The siren had got the better of me again and I was humiliated, but I also had a live cross to prepare for.

We said good morning to the shelter keeper and again he motioned to the kettle, offering a coffee.

'Actually, can I borrow that?' I asked. He couldn't understand English, but he read body language well enough to happily pass me the kettle. Placing it in front of me on the table and reaching for my makeup bag, I started applying various layers of foundation and concealer on my face, using the kettle as a mirror while the shelter keeper watched with amusement. I looked up just as Dmitry came through from the back room.

'You look nice,' he said.

'So do you,' I replied, thanking god for the freshly applied concealer that was now disguising a hot flush.

'Oh *would* you two get your own bunker?' Daniel muttered.

'I would love to, but there's missiles coming so we're stuck here with you,' I replied.

There was a spring in my step after my bunker flirtation and as we sat down for breakfast I decided I could probably get away with a bit of prying.

'Where are you from?' I asked Dmitry.

'The east,' he replied.

'East, east?' I asked.

'Donetsk.'

Right. So, east east.

His family was still there. His parents and his two younger sisters, he explained. It was an area that had been haunted by fighting ever since the annexation of Crimea in 2014. They had been on the front line of the Russian aggression for years now, and his hometown was under Russian occupation.

I looked at this man, eating an omelette calmly in front of

me while his family's freedom was stifled and his own future was so unknown. I had spent the past few days with Dmitry and he had been calm the entire time, never giving any indication of the true stress and fear he surely must have been experiencing.

'They didn't try to leave when the war started?' I asked.

'No. It is their home. Only cowards leave.'

Andrei nodded in agreement.

'Some men, they try to sneak out of Ukraine in women's clothing,' Andrei said.

'Cowards,' Dmitry spat again.

Andrei nodded a second time.

'We have to fight for our freedom. We have to fight for our land, and some of these men only want to look after themselves.'

New Zealanders have no idea how lucky we are, I thought to myself.

Not everyone in Ukraine wanted to pick up a gun and fight. There were many thousands who did and wouldn't have had it any other way, but the declaration of war didn't automatically trigger an affinity to weapons and death in every Ukrainian man. Those who were of fighting age couldn't leave the country, but there were plenty who were not called to the front line, either not needed yet or not properly trained to be of any help amid the ferocity of the battle.

As we walked down to the beach mid-morning, we found hundreds of men armed with spades rather than guns. They were relentlessly digging sand, filling empty bags, and stacking them on a truck that would then drive off to build a new fortress at the entrance of the city. It was an eerily beautiful sight. With the Black Sea behind them, where Russian warships lurked, these men were working tirelessly and singing together the chant of national resilience: 'Slava Ukraini, Heroiam slava!' 'Glory to Ukraine! Glory to the heroes!' They were praying that the rough weather continued so the Russians at sea would get seasick, and would run their ration supplies dry before making it to the beaches of Odessa, but they were going to be ready either way.

Ever since arriving in the coastal city, I had been trying to get access to the catacombs: a warren of limestone tunnels, 2500 kilometres long and 40 metres underground. During World War II, when the city was under siege by the Nazis, Soviet rebels used the tunnels as a secret headquarters and Odessans were now returning to the bunkers seeking safety from the Russians. I wasn't sure how to go about getting into the tunnels — it was hard to know what an entrance looked like — but I had told Andrei and Dmitry that we'd love to go down there and they'd promised they'd ask around. I'd been updated by them throughout the week that they were still trying but so far hadn't had any luck. The catacombs were locked most of the time due to how easy it was for people to get lost in the labyrinth, and most Odessans had never ventured into the underground world out of fear.

After our live cross that morning, Andrei told me he had heard from a friend who had a key to a nuclear bunker we could go see instead. It wasn't the catacombs but it sounded interesting enough, and with no other leads we decided to go for it. We arrived at a strangely derelict intersection of roads; to one side, under a big tree, a man was waiting with a dog. I realised as we approached that this was Andrei's contact. They shook hands and shared a customary cigarette while Daniel and I looked around wondering what was about to happen. Very little had been said when the man took off his gloves and started digging around his pocket for something. He pulled out a small key and walked a few steps behind the tree, where a slab of metal, maybe a metre square, lay on the ground. I saw then there was a padlock and realised this must be the bunker, but as he leant over, popped the lock and opened the hatch, I knew I was staring into the historic catacombs of Odessa.

The open hatch revealed a dark, deep staircase that extended further than I could see. The dog went first and I was happy to follow its lead. It was strangely damp and the camera lens instantly started fogging up from the moisture.

History had been fossilised down there, with remnants of the Soviet Union at every turn as if the platoon was about to return to its old military encampment at any minute. Lightbulbs were strung across the ceiling and there were weapons and helmets leaning against the limestone walls. The tunnels were spacious, a few metres wide and high, with different walkways to go down everywhere you looked. Some opened up into rooms that had inbuilt wall seats and tables like dining areas; others resembled sculleries, piled up with bottles of water and pots and pans. There were some areas designed as bedrooms, with inflatable beds already pumped up and waiting for a tired and scared someone to rest their head.

It was unlike anything I had pictured, more sophisticated and more extensive than anything I had imagined, and as we turned the corner I saw a middle-aged man arranging dry food and water in an alcove off to the side — and he was carrying an unimaginable burden. His wife was nine months' pregnant.

'We come down here every night,' he explained, with welling eyes that set off mine. 'She will have the baby here, so

I need to make it as comfortable as possible for her. We won't be able to have a doctor, so . . .' and he trailed off, pointing to the stash of basic medicine he had piled up to the side of the already deflating mattress.

'Did you think about getting her out of Ukraine?' I asked, as softly as possible.

'She could leave, but where would she go? She would have a newborn, all alone. Homeless, and in a foreign country. And for how long?'

He paused. 'If she is here, at least I can look after her.'

I searched, but couldn't find a single word of comfort to offer that man. On every anniversary of the war since, and on many unremarkable days in between, I have thought of his family and hoped with all my heart that all three of them are alive, safe and together. Their baby would be around three now, born into a family of so much love but also into a world of war. It was painfully cruel.

We were reaching new levels of exhaustion in Odessa. I had lost track of how many 20+ hour days in a row we had worked, and living in a permanent state of high alert was not as easy as I was pretending it was. As I tried to script my story that night, I could not keep my eyes open. I finally decided to set a two-minute timer and fell straight to sleep. I woke up two minutes later feeling genuinely better.

For those of you who are interested in feeling sorry for us, or are understandably confused by the time zones, below is an average day's schedule in Ukraine:

05:30 — Wake up, attempt to make myself look presentable (please pretend it isn't obvious I do my own hair and makeup).
06:00 — Drive to our live location, set up equipment and do technical checks with the Auckland studio.
06:30 — On air for *Prime News* (famously 'First at 5:30').
07:00 — On air for *Newshub Live at 6pm* (say a Hail Mary and try to make sense).
07:30 — Pack up the equipment and grab a quick breakfast while calling The Sarahs for a check-in ('Yes, survived another night!').
08:30 — Begin shooting our next story.
10:30 — Set up for live cross into *Newshub Late*.
11:00 — On air for *Newshub Late*.
11:30 — Carry on filming the story of the day.
17:30 — Film pre-recorded pieces for *Newshub Live at 11:30* and *Newshub Live at 4:30*.
18:00 — Return to the hotel and start transcribing the day's footage.
19:30 — Set up for the morning news live cross and begin radio interviews.
20:00 — On air for *AM*.
20:15 — Start writing our 6 p.m. story.
21:00 — Call with The Sarahs to recap the day ('Yes, survived another day!').
21:30 — Finish writing the story and hand over to Daniel to start editing. Start planning the next day, filling the crew in on the plan and updating our health and safety document.
01:00 — Finish the edit and send it back to New Zealand.
01:30 — Shower, get into bed and brace for at least two trips to the bomb shelter between now and 5:30.

And that was if everything went to plan. It very rarely did.

I had barely shut my eyes that night when the banging on my door started. The self-loathing was instant. How could I have slept through *another* air-raid siren? It was getting ridiculous. I raced to the door and flung it open to begin my apology, but never got the chance.

'Get out! Get down! Get out!' A Ukrainian man I'd never seen before was yelling the instruction at me repeatedly, but I didn't need to be told. The smoke hit me in the face and I felt the fire before I could see it. The heat was overwhelming — the flames were licking the wall on the other side of the corridor. All of a sudden I had a damp white cloth shoved over my nose and mouth and the man was pushing me down low to the floor in the direction of the fire exit. 'Get out!' he screamed after me.

As I crawled through the corridor and into the concrete staircase, a stream of heavily armed soldiers and firefighters came running past. My eyes were stinging from smoke. The sprinklers had been activated and there were hoses spilling water all the way up the staircase but I couldn't stop coughing into the white cloth. The sirens were still screaming, and based on the number of guns I had seen in the past 30 seconds it didn't take long to work out what had happened. Our hotel had been bombed.

The smoke started to lessen as I made my way down the stairs, and I could hear myself swearing over and over, shaking uncontrollably. I burst into the foyer and out on to the street and around me, everywhere, there was chaos. The hotel was surrounded by military vehicles and emergency services. A man was lying on the ground on his stomach in front of the hotel, surrounded by at least seven Ukrainian soldiers who had pinned his arms behind his back and were pointing guns at his head.

Where the fuck was everyone? I couldn't see anyone from our team and suddenly felt sick. I was kneeling on a patch of grass next to a group of police cars, with lights flashing all around me, when finally I saw Daniel, Andrei and Dmitry coming towards me, digesting the scene. Andrei diverted off towards a group of soldiers and Dmitry gave me a look of 'Alright?' before lighting a cigarette and joining Andrei in the search for answers.

Daniel, reaching my side, had a bloody *smile* forming on his face. 'Bit of excitement, aye?' He slapped my arm like we'd just been on a rollercoaster ride. I stared at him in shock.

'A bit of excitement?' I asked, trying to steady my nerves and wipe away my tears.

'Oh, shit. What happened?' he asked.

'The whole building is on *fire,* Daniel, we've been bombed, we almost *died*!' I said, far too loudly and, you could say, borderline hysterical.

'No we haven't, Lisette. My floor was fine.'

I was confused and still in shock when Andrei and Dmitry came over.

'The man in the room opposite yours had some kind of episode and lit the place on fire,' Andrei explained.

The sale of alcohol had been widely prohibited in Ukraine since the war started, in a bid to keep people sober, especially members of the military. It unfolded that my hotel neighbour was an alcoholic and had been suffering from severe withdrawals, with hallucinations resulting in him taking to his hotel bedroom with a lighter in the middle of the night. It was someone in the hotel opposite ours who first spotted the flames from across the street, breaking through a window on the top floor. I was the only other person staying on that level, and given that the rest of our team were several floors below, they had fortunately had a very different experience to mine.

Two hours later, with the firefighters happy that the danger was dealt to, we were allowed back into our rooms.

'We need to move you,' Dmitry said to me. 'I'll come with you to get your things.' Not for the first time on this trip I wished Dmitry wasn't seeing me in such a tragic state, and I definitely didn't want him seeing what a mess my room was. Keeping a tidy house hadn't been high on my priority list, and there were about ten too many empty chip packets and half-eaten chocolate bars on the table. He insisted, putting his hand on my shoulder, and I knew there was no going back. Annoyingly, Daniel and Andrei decided to join, which kind of ruined the moment. As we climbed the stairs, the guys were making casual conversation and I think they were still struggling to grasp why I was so rattled, but when we opened the fire exit door on to my floor, every one of them stood still. The entire left-hand side of the corridor was blackened, the ceiling too, and the floor was drowned in water. You could see how close the fire had been to getting to my door. I heard Daniel whisper 'Oh fuck.'

'See! I told you!' I said, storming into my room, feeling vindicated despite discovering that everything I owned now absolutely stank of smoke. Fortunately all of the expensive camera equipment and laptops were kept down in Daniel's room so we hadn't lost anything vital, but all four of us were silent as we began packing up my worse-for-wear belongings. That was until I heard Dmitry say, 'Do you want to keep this KitKat?'

It was 5 a.m. before I got settled in my new room, and in 30 minutes or so we were due to get sorted for our first live cross of the day. The heater wasn't working and my teeth were chattering as I lay down for a quick nap. By the time we were standing on the beach of Odessa set up for our live, I was completely fried and only still standing because I knew that after these two crosses, we would be in a car driving back across the border.

News of the fire had made it back to the Auckland newsroom, and as we waited for our cross we joked with the presenters that Daniel hadn't made it out and Andrei had taken over the camera duties. Things were surprisingly jovial when Dmitry suddenly took off down the beachfront towards a man skulking by the surf club. I looked at Andrei, who had tensed all over, and we cut the laughter with the studio immediately. From our spot we watched as Dmitry grabbed the back of the man's shirt and engaged in an intense conversation.

After a minute of interrogation, Dmitry let the man go and walked back over to us. 'All fine,' he said to Andrei.

'What was that about?' I asked.

'That man has a "Z" on his jacket. But it is just a brand.'

The city was not only bracing for the arrival of Russian troops, but people were also hyper-aware of the number of Russian sympathisers there were in this area, and anyone who gave any indication of support for Putin's cause was promptly dealt to. The letter 'Z' had become a militarist symbol for Russia, sprayed in white paint over tanks and military machinery and used by civilians to indicate support for the invasion. Accidentally wearing a 'Z' was a mix-up you'd work hard to avoid.

A journalist, Mary Anne Gill, from the *Cambridge News* back home wanted to interview us for a piece in the local newspaper that morning. I could imagine my mum buying the paper in the town supermarket with a proud look on her face and didn't want to deprive her of the motherly bragging rights at checkout, so agreed to do the interview. I barely remember what I said, but I know I was close to tears the entire time for no obvious reason; apart from, of course, the several glaringly obvious reasons. When I read the article a couple of weeks later, the opening line read: 'It's 7:50 a.m. in Ukraine and Lisette Reymer's eyes are bloodshot; her body language oozes fatigue.' I was clearly no longer able to even pretend I had it together, and it was a good thing we were on our way back to Moldova an hour later.

It was a long journey home, back the way we came: Moldova, Romania, Poland — but Warsaw this time, not Kraków — and we got the carnet stamped properly at every step. I think we did most of it without talking, fading between sleep and silent processing. I was getting sicker by the second, my body finally calling time on our escapades, but there was no paracetamol or lozenge in the world that chirped me up quicker than the Instagram notification that beeped at me on that journey:

'Dmitry has requested to follow you.'

LONDON, UNITED KINGDOM
April 2022

'Oh thank god you're alive!' Sam the concierge greeted me as I arrived back at the apartment. 'Don't do that again!' he instructed, feigning a heart attack.

'Okay, I promise!' I said, not meaning a word of it.

I still hadn't heard from my mum, who is notoriously bad at communication, but Sam seemed to have been refreshing YouTube for our stories every day, desperate for regular proof of life. It was incredibly sweet. I should add, because I can hear her complaining to Dad in real time as she reads this — 'Oh that's not fair, Garry, listen to what she's written!' — that my mum has since revealed the reason she chose not to message me when we were in Ukraine.

'Because, Lisette,' she explained in a fluster, 'I was worried the phone would beep and you'd panic and stand on one of those nasty landmines!' It was an extreme theory, for sure, but it came from a good place, not one of parental negligence. We also later learnt that Daniel's mum, Di, and mine had been messaging each other, running a very niche support group for worried Kiwi mothers of children reporting from war zones. They were the only members.

Our phones were filled with lovely messages when we got back to London, but the common theme was one of warning. Journalism can be addictive, and there's a rush you get from a live cross or telling a big story that is supercharged when you're doing it from a high-risk environment. It can start to make other days, and other stories, feel a bit dull. We had agreed to counselling sessions through work as a requirement for our deployment, but I don't think we ever slowed down enough in 2022 to truly appreciate where the concern was coming from. I had a two-week window when we got home to move out of my apartment and find a new one before our next overseas assignment, and that kept me distracted enough to avoid really processing anything; this time around at least.

'Thanks for everything, Sam,' I said as I rolled my suitcases out of the foyer a few days later, complete with my newly acquired bag of body armour.

'Stay away from war zones, would ya, and don't be a stranger,' he said with a tilt of his cheesecutter.

I was only moving down the road, but it was going to be a big change. A four-bedroom apartment shared with three others, all of us strangers, and all of us living incredibly different lives. There was a girl from Essex who ended up siphoning money out of the flat account to fund her shopping addiction; a chef from North England who would cook full roast meals in the kitchen at 2 a.m., waking everyone up; an Irish gas analyst who ended up making so much money trading off the war that she never had to flat again; and me paying full London rent for a room I was very rarely home to enjoy.

'I like the redhead at the desk,' the chef reported back after a night of stalking on Newshub online.

GALLIPOLI, TURKEY
late April 2022

I wasn't even in a war zone the first time I almost died on the job. Yes, there has been more than one time. More than twice, even. But the first was in Turkey.

As a wannabe Europe Correspondent you would always dream of covering the Anzac Day commemorations at Gallipoli, knowing it was at least one assignment you could count on getting approval for from the producers. When we arrived in İstanbul I was instantly enamoured with the city. It was loud and colourful and vibrant. Everyone was tooting and everyone was busy and there were flags everywhere. Small ones strung up as bunting over shop windows, and huge ones billowing on towering poles. We jumped in a car and began the drive to Gallipoli, a three-hour journey that flew by as I marvelled at how each new flag seemed to be getting bigger than the last and we serenaded the open road with our own personal never-ending Eagles concert.

We arrived in a small town called Eceabat just as dusk fell. Only a fifteen-minute drive from Anzac Cove, it's the most convenient place to stay but it is a basic town, with more stray dogs than residents and they certainly act like they own it. We were welcomed into our accommodation by a stench that made my eyes weep, and when I got in the shower I felt a cool breeze from above and looked up to see the night sky greeting me through a massive hole in the wall. Well, that's why it was cheap, I thought to myself.

Gallipoli is a beautiful place and as we drove around the winding coastline the next morning, I felt myself getting emotional. It is stunning, but its history haunts it. Thoughts of how many people have died fighting for this piece of sea and land invade your mind, and the peace they now rest in is eerie. As we filmed the rehearsals for the dawn service I found myself growing increasingly uncomfortable. The Anzacs invaded this land, and now we were back here to honour their sacrifice in front of the descendants of the people they attacked. It felt wrong. I couldn't fathom, 100 years from now, Russians travelling to Kyiv to honour their brave soldiers who fought there. In the end, after cornering a local historian and grilling him for far longer than he probably had hoped for, I came to see the beauty in the way Turkey has embraced New Zealand and Australia. Together our three countries are able to acknowledge the shared pain and suffering of a time when war was a default option. It shouldn't be an option at all anymore.

What wannabe Europe Correspondents don't realise about the Anzac Day assignment is that it is one of the most taxing you will ever have. Kiwis start arriving at the Gallipoli grounds around 10 p.m. to set up camp ahead of the dawn service. So it's not until the evening of the 24th of April that you even start filming. After interviewing the happy campers, and just as the cold really starts to set in and everyone else dozes off in their sleeping bags, you start the overnight effort to script and edit as much of your story as possible for New Zealand's 6 p.m. bulletin. At dawn the service begins; you chug your fifth coffee, rub your hands together aggressively to stop them losing all feeling from the cold, and keep scripting as the ceremony takes place, adding in all the key moments.

With the dawn service complete at Anzac Cove, you hurry to do some more interviews and finish the story to send home to New Zealand before the deadline of the bulletin, which you are also crossing live into. As soon as that story goes to air in

New Zealand you begin your day all over again: the Chunuk Bair memorial service is just beginning, which you also need to file a story on. You blub like a proud Kiwi baby watching the New Zealand Defence Force haka and by midday, when the service finishes, the hot Turkish sun is burning you to a crisp, your eyes are stinging from tiredness, you haven't eaten anything except salt and vinegar Pringles in sixteen hours, and you still have a story to write and edit.

And here is where things started to get dicey. On this particular trip Daniel and I were booked to stay in Eceabat for another night, but given the situation with the hole in the wall and the smell of sewage filling our bedrooms, we decided that instead, if we were feeling up to it, we would make the trip back to İstanbul in search of nicer accommodation. Having finished the shoot at Chunuk Bair, we agreed that a fresh ocean swim would refresh us and we'd be good to go. When we emerged from the Aegean Sea we felt like new humans.

'Amazing what it can do, isn't it?!' I gushed.

'I don't even like the beach but I feel alive again,' Daniel agreed, puffing out his chest.

We picked up two cans of Red Bull from the petrol station, filled the car with gas and began the three-hour journey back to İstanbul feeling fresh as two daisies and excited to get to clean linen and finish our Chunuk Bair edit without having to put pegs on our noses to survive. The daisies wilted incredibly fast. Within 45 minutes Daniel had pulled over, too tired to drive any further.

'I just can't keep my eyes open,' he said, exasperated, as if there was no explanation for it.

I took a turn at the wheel, feeling like the team hero, while Daniel got some much-needed shut-eye — but an hour later I was the one rubbing my eyes, this time in shock. I recognised the bridge up ahead but I didn't want to admit it. Eventually the panic got the better of me.

'Daniel! Wake up!' I said, leaning over to shake my co-pilot out of his slumber. 'Something has gone terribly wrong. We're back at the bloody bridge!'

It was a rude awakening, for sure.

'You've driven us backwards up the fucking highway, Lisette! We're ten minutes from Gallipoli!'

He returned to the wheel after that. And I took a turn sleeping. But an hour later it happened again.

'Lisette! Wake up!' Daniel was grumbling. 'We're back at the bloody bridge again! We must be missing a turn-off or something!'

We ended up trading places and driving back and forth for the next six hours, the drive time extended dramatically by a series of exhaustion-fuelled mistakes and close shaves as our eyelids drooped. It was a horrendous idea to keep driving and the regret was far more uncomfortable than my night's sleeping on a pullout couch in Eceabat had been, but through some miracle we arrived in İstanbul in one piece.

By that point we were also running incredibly late for our evening live cross and still hadn't eaten. As we set up the camera in the square by the famous Blue Mosque, a random man, who looked suspiciously homeless, offered us a piece of grilled corn. To this day I can't work out why on earth we thought it was okay to eat corn from a stranger, and it boggles me even further that five minutes later I was live on air talking some sense; although that detail is obviously debatable.

By the time we got packed up it was 8 p.m., and now into our thirty-sixth hour of no sleep we were desperate to finish our edit and get to bed. It was midnight before we sent the package to New Zealand. We slept until midday, then boarded a flight to London feeling genuinely lucky to have survived the day.

I covered the Anzac service another two times during my stint in Europe, and both times the accommodation was truly horrific, possibly worse. But never did I ever contemplate that drive again.

BUCHA, UKRAINE
May 2022

We weren't back in London two weeks before we were off again: from war memorials to war. Bucha, a city just 30 kilometres north of Kyiv, had been liberated and the stories coming out of it were harrowing.

When Russian forces stormed into Ukraine from Belarus, capturing Bucha on the way to Kyiv had been a significant part of a larger tactic to encircle the capital and topple the government. Putin's men ended up occupying Bucha for a month. Peace talks were still being attempted at this stage of the war, and Moscow eventually committed to scaling back activity near Kyiv, in a move intended to increase trust and progress towards a deal. When this withdrawal began, Ukrainian forces moved into Bucha and regained control — and the war crimes discovered there were revealed to global outcry.

There were heart-wrenching reports of Russian soldiers killing people in the streets, of mass graves, and of summary executions where soldiers would kill civilians at checkpoints based on a text message on a phone. I was determined to get there.

We had been in touch with Ron Mark, the former New Zealand Defence Minister, who was going to be travelling into Ukraine with another Kiwi, Owen Pomana, as part of a wider charity group. They were our way back into the country. Their group was heading to Kyiv but via Dnipro, a large city in central Ukraine that was under attack and hungry for the supplies Owen had gathered together using Kiwi donations. Our producers were sold on the Kiwi angle.

Ukraine is huge. It would take twenty hours non-stop to drive across it, and so it made more sense to cross the border from a country to the south of Ukraine rather than making the long drive in from Poland. We'd done a similar thing going to Odessa from Moldova. This time we decided to enter through Romania. In just a few hours we could get from the Siret border crossing to Dunaivtsi, the charity's meeting point in Ukraine, and then we'd begin the longer trek to Dnipro the following day as part of the aid convoy.

Meeting our team was becoming my favourite part of every trip, and we had arranged for our new security officer to stop by our motel in Romania for a pre-trip briefing. Lukasz was Polish and had served eighteen years in the Special Forces, with most of that spent in Afghanistan and Iraq. He was no Dmitry, but he was impressive. Tattoos covered his arms and he wore a tight T-shirt, jeans and the uniform chunky boot. He had only left the Special Forces five months ago, so this was the beginning of his private security career.

From the outset, Lukasz seemed all business, no pleasure; but that was fairly standard with these guys. Meanwhile my phone was dinging with my incredibly unprofessional friends demanding details: 'Let us know if you get another hottie.' Relenting with little persuasion, I snapped a picture on the sly and sent it through — 'Confirmed' — just as Lukasz reached for Daniel's phone to examine a map. The timing could not have been worse. Daniel was a member of the group chat I was messaging, and I froze, waiting for Lukasz to see a picture of himself pop up on the phone he was now holding. Thankfully I was saved by Daniel's lack of notifications; but the universe was clearly telling me off for being so inappropriate and the message was received.

Our driver was Ukrainian, so we would walk over the border

together as three and meet him there. I vowed not to objectify our next team member.

Just thinking of Petro makes me laugh. Tall and lanky, in his forties, he had a thinning crop of dark hair and a huge 'I'll do you a deal, great deal, just leave it with me' type of energy. I don't think I ever saw him without a cigarette in his hand or hanging haphazardly out of his mouth. He spoke very little English, but he had a sparkle in his eye that told us he was going to be trouble. He was the grown-up version of Bosko, and the anti-Lukasz: all pleasure, no business.

We shook hands with our new driver, who held mine just a little bit too long, before walking over to his car: a four-wheel-drive that was tidy enough but nothing fancy, and certainly a long way from Tomlin's VIP collection of vehicles. I got in the back seat and shut my door with my usual vigour, and Petro quickly came around, opening it again. 'New car, new car,' he said with a pleading face, closing the door gently this time and throwing up praying hands afterwards. Finally getting behind the wheel, he offered us all a water before turning on the ignition, and I got the sense he was following a YouTube instruction video on how to be a chauffeur. Lukasz looked at Daniel and me with a smirk and we all got settled in.

This was going to be interesting. It was also going to involve some linguistic gymnastics. Petro could speak Ukrainian and Polish, and so for the next week he would translate Ukrainian into Polish for Lukasz, who would then translate from Polish to English for us. It was confirmed early on in that first drive together that Petro, as predicted, had only been working with members of the media since the war started. Previously he had been a police officer, with no explanation readily available as to why that particular career had come to an end. As Lukasz translated for us, Petro, with one hand holding a cigarette and the steering wheel, reached for his phone with the other and trawled through his recent photos until he came across one of himself and Hollywood actress Angelina Jolie. 'Aha!' he exclaimed proudly, pointing to us and then back to the photo. He had, it turned out, been the A-lister's driver when she visited Lviv in recent weeks. I would have paid good money to have seen her face when Petro turned up to collect her.

Within half an hour of driving, the engine warning light came on and we pulled over while Petro fiddled around under the bonnet of his 'new car'. It was warming up in Ukraine now, the seasons changing, and as I sat in the long roadside grass a huge Red Cross truck raced past us. I found myself wondering if we should have hitched a ride with them. The car caused us trouble for the entire drive, and we stopped repeatedly before Lukasz insisted that we just ignore the light and keep driving; the constant warning *beep* that accompanied the light was significantly harder to ignore, but we had places to be.

When we finally arrived at the aid centre in Dunaivtsi, Owen and Ron were hard at work among a hive of activity. A group of around 50 people were moving fruit, vegetables, flour, rice, bedding, clothing and other basic necessities out of small vans and into big trucks that would be sent off to war-zone hotspots, including Dnipro, the next morning.

'Where we're going is hell,' Ron Mark told us — but I don't think even the devil is that mean.

Daniel and I were in our hotel room that evening beginning the writing and editing process when Lukasz burst into my room. 'I need to speak to you,' he said, sounding scarily stern.

'Okay, what's up?' I replied.

'I just saw a man in the foyer of the hotel and he started asking me questions about what we were doing here and wanting details about Petro.'

'Right . . .'

'I recognise him from the aid centre, so I asked him why he was at the hotel and he said he was going to the gym, but he was not in gym clothing.'

'Okay . . . and you are worried about him?'

'I think it is suspicious. Why is he here? I think we need to change hotels.'

I did a quick google and couldn't find any other accommodation nearby; we were, after all, in a very remote town in a war-torn country. The night was getting on and moving hotels could cost us hours; it was the last thing I wanted to do. Daniel pulled the footage from the day up on the laptop and we asked Lukasz to point out the man in question if he saw him in the footage.

'That one,' he said, pointing to a man carrying a box of fruit behind a child I was interviewing at the time. I took a photo and messaged it to one of the organisers at the aid centre. 'Do you know this man in the white shirt very well?' I wrote.

'Not very well . . . Why do you ask?' came the reply.

'Our security officer has just raised a concern. He was at our hotel a short time ago asking direct questions about our movements, and he had been asking some interesting questions earlier today too of our security and particularly of our driver.'

'Be cautious.'

The hairs went up on my neck.

'What do you think the level of risk is?' I asked Lukasz.

'Seven out of ten,' he replied.

Shit. For some reason six out of ten would have seemed ten times better.

'There are no other hotel options anywhere nearby. What if we all slept in the same room and just stayed incredibly vigilant, and we'll be out of here first thing in the morning?' I said, searching for a compromise despite there very much looking to be no room for one.

'I'm not worried about us, it's Petro that is at risk,' Lukasz replied.

'Oh.'

'But I am paid to look after you, not him, so I don't mind if we stay,' he said.

'Well, we're a team,' Daniel and I replied together.

'Have you spoken to Petro?' I asked Lukasz.

'No.'

We called in our driver, who was outside having a cigarette and wheeling and dealing on the phone as he had been for 80% of the day, and explained the situation. The man had been asking probing questions about Petro, specifically his history as a police officer.

'How do you feel?' we asked him.

'Pffft, fine! Fine! Fine!' he exclaimed with gusto, while lifting his T-shirt slightly to reveal a Glock tucked casually into his waistband.

'Fine?' I asked, to be sure, choosing to ignore his casual disclosure of a deadly weapon.

'Fine!' he replied, and smiling from ear to ear, he asked: 'Now, whiskey time?'

Ukraine was in the midst of an acute fuel crisis, with all but a handful of pumps nationwide closed to the public. Russia had been deliberately targeting fuel infrastructure, and stocks were running dangerously low. On the 550-kilometre road from Lviv to Kyiv there were only two working petrol stations, and any we saw open here in the south had a huge queue stretching for kilometres. The shortage was so serious that there was also a limit on how much you could buy at one time. People were waiting hours to buy just 10 litres of petrol. We had known that this was going to make our lives difficult on this trip, but it was proving to be totally debilitating. Military and aid vehicles were, understandably, the priority, but as Petro was explaining to Lukasz, it meant we were essentially stranded and would almost certainly not be able to get to Dnipro with this charity convoy.

Our story looked dead in the water, but Petro seemed to have contacts all over the country and his many phone calls had resulted in a plan of sorts. I wasn't convinced that Petro was all that reliable, but his was the only plan we had so we decided it would have to do. The bosses were not overly interested in us being in Ukraine with limited ability to get ourselves out again, so we were well aware that we were working on borrowed time and the pressure was on to make something out of nothing. We were going to divert to Lviv, where Petro had managed to wrangle us four canisters of fuel, and we'd take these with us to Kyiv to use to get around the city.

The drive to Lviv was long. We stopped at every petrol station we saw, but they never had a drop of fuel available. What they did have were hotdogs, and we had one at every garage; stress eating at its finest. The lack of fuel also meant we couldn't have any air conditioning on in the car, and packed into the back it was becoming suffocating. As we waited, out of sheer hope, in the queue at one gas station, I sat outside on the grass soaking up the fresh air and sunshine, a hundred metres or so from the car where I saw Daniel and Lukasz start laughing. Feeling like I was missing out, I walked back over.

'What's so funny?' I asked as Lukasz went to check on Petro inside.

'Lukasz just took one look at you sunbathing and goes, "War is hell".'

By the time we made it to Lviv I was eager to get some fresh footage in the camera and we headed straight to the location of a recent missile strike where seven people had died. Conveniently, the bombsite happened to be next to a mechanics, and Petro took the opportunity to get his 'luxury' car looked at. I was relieved to finally have a professional on the tools, even if it did delay us.

It turned out that Petro had roped in his dad to find us some petrol, and before we knew it we were in his parents' backyard, dropping off our personal suitcases at their home to make room for the canisters of reserve fuel Papa Petro had rustled up out of nowhere. Petro clearly came from a long line of hustlers, but we were grateful for the fuel so didn't ask too many questions. He was, of course, very concerned about the petrol stinking out his car, so proceeded to wrap the canisters up in an obscene number of black rubbish bags. The fumes still made me dizzy.

The drive from Lviv to Kyiv takes seven hours without stopping, which is long enough as it is, but Petro managed to drag it out by insisting on multiple meal breaks. 'Whiskey time?' he'd continue to joke, with a persistence that suggested it wasn't actually a joke. I was worried about having enough content for a story that night, but Petro would just pretend he couldn't hear me, turn up his Ukrainian music and veer off to a restaurant whenever he spotted one that took his fancy. Ukrainians refuse to eat a meal without having a beetroot soup called borscht first, so these breaks were not quick ones. Daniel and I would have been happy enough to continue on a steady diet of hotdogs if it meant getting to our destination faster, but Petro's driving was questionable enough when he was well rested and we conceded that the breaks were probably for the best.

The drive time was filled with Petro's endless stream of phone calls, and halfway to Kyiv, several calls in, he dialled up a new friend while excitedly pointing to us. The call was answered in Ukrainian and then that unmistakable voice filled the car:

'Hello, my friends!'

'Bosko!' we exclaimed. Lukasz turned around from the passenger seat in confusion and Petro started laughing, utterly delighted with himself. It turned out that Bosko had supplied Petro with his car, and now everything made sense.

An hour out of the capital, reality hit. In our recent conversations the war had been almost overshadowed by the fuel shortage but we were quickly reminded of the real story.

It was actually a petrol station that first caught our attention — but not for the prospect of fuel. It looked like it had been caught in a tornado. Parts of the building were strewn all over the forecourt and there were huge divots where shrapnel had touched down. Looming behind it was a ginormous warehouse, the size of several rugby fields, and it had been completely obliterated. Just a skeleton of what it once was and surrounded by crumpled iron, everywhere. We started walking the perimeter and rounded the corner to find a row of around twenty trucks completely burnt to a crisp, all backed up to their loading docks, the goods they were due to deliver still inside. One trailer was full of charred motorbikes.

We were getting a tour from a man who had worked there in happier times when Lukasz started pointing out the different missile craters and chunks of warheads he was picking up off the ground. He had been a missile expert in the Special Forces, but 'I was never at the landing end,' he explained. He was behaving like a child at Christmas, inspecting them all with interest and moving from one to the next at pace. Having spotted a particularly big crater in the paddock next door, he jumped the fence and got to work, analysing it for clues of what weapon was responsible. Our tour guide immediately intervened, bringing Lukasz's attention to the various unexploded missiles in the area. 'I wish he had told me sooner,' Lukasz said, far too casually, as he climbed back on to our side of the fence.

The closer we got to Kyiv, the worse it became. Burnt-out Russian tanks were abandoned down the highway, with Russian uniforms discarded on the ground around them, boots and all. At every tank there was a Ukrainian, or two or three or four, treating it like a tourist attraction; stopping to take selfies and celebrate pushing Putin's men off their land. They told us stories of living under Russian occupation, of their houses being shot at: 'They are not soldiers. They are orcs. Only orcs behave like that.' I made a mental note not to complain about Petro's meal breaks in the future; there was never going to be a shortage of material on this trip, and our story that night was one of our best yet.

By the time we arrived in Kyiv the fuel shortage was more dire than ever, and we were working overtime to conserve what we had left. We were walking everywhere, lugging our equipment kilometres down the road every morning from our hotel to our live position and back again. On our second morning in Kyiv, as we walked back to our hotel, a jeweller standing outside his shop smiled at us and said hello.

'We have to change our walking route,' Lukasz said. 'If the jeweller is recognising us already then who knows who else has caught on to our movements.'

'Are you serious?' I asked, almost laughing.

'It's dangerous,' he said, sounding tense.

'Do you think you're a bit paranoid?' I asked, after a couple of minutes of walking in silence.

'Good question,' he replied, lost in thought. 'My girlfriend thinks I am,' he eventually added.

I supposed it was an occupational hazard, and given he had only recently left the Special Forces he was probably still readjusting to the real world, but I really hoped he would take some time off after this trip. He needed it.

We had a meeting in the city with the mayor at mid-morning and I was dreading the walk. It would have been a five-minute drive, but Lukasz was insistent that we didn't have enough spare fuel to drive there. In my desperation I swallowed my pride and rang the meeting organisers to see if there was any chance they could pick us up on the way past. By some miracle they agreed to send someone they kept calling 'the Terp' to collect us. It wasn't until I got off the call, relieved, that I realised he must be an interpreter.

He was dressed in a suit, spoke perfect English and seemed very official, with a car befitting of Tomlin's collection. Daniel and I were in the back seat making polite small talk when Lukasz's well-trained eye noticed something our civilian eyes had not.

'Where did you get a full tank of gas?' he asked.

‘I have a special card that is given to leaders of aid organisations. It allows me to access the city’s reserves.’

‘Can we use it?’ Lukasz said, trying his luck.

‘Mmm, maybe,’ said the Terp, with a smirk.

The meeting was a bust. We had been promised the mayor but the mayor didn’t show, and I was beginning to wonder if it was all a lie to get us there in the first place and film their semi-propaganda. The day was getting away on us and we were trapped in this seemingly endless meeting. I’m impatient at the best of times, but there’s nothing I hate more than wasting time and I was growing incredibly agitated. I was about to call it when Lukasz came over.

‘Let’s get out of here, I don’t like this,’ he said.

‘What?’

‘My phone battery is draining too fast. Something is wrong.’

I thought he was being over the top again, but agreed we were well overdue leaving so happily pulled the pin on our participation. It was already early afternoon and we had filmed nothing of any value. Central-city Kyiv was not where the story was; the Russians hadn’t made it there. The big story was in Bucha, just a 40-minute drive away.

I begged Lukasz: ‘We *have* to go.’

‘If we go, we won’t have enough fuel to get out of Ukraine in a hurry if we need to,’ he retorted. ‘Petro is working on it.’

Petro was, of course, on the blower, but I doubted very much he was making any progress. In fact, I was certain he was still making calls about the new car part the mechanic had told him he needed.

‘He knows a guy who has been siphoning fuel out of people’s cars, and he’s agreed to bring it to us from Lviv. But it will be four times the normal price,’ Lukasz told me.

‘And still seven hours away,’ I added, knowing that the

ethical issues with that particular scenario were even greater than our time restraints. I was growing increasingly frustrated with the situation and was convinced Lukasz was playing it too safe.

'The risk is too great,' he kept saying.

'We are in a war zone. There is always going to be risk,' I fought back. 'But we are here to get the story and right now we don't *have* a story, so we need to go to Bucha!'

Frustrated, I banged out a message to the Terp, asking if there was any way we could use his magic card, but he was probably still in the meeting and I didn't get a reply. Worse yet, we were running out of daylight, which meant we were running out of time to film anything. It was too dangerous to be out working after dark, and we had to plan any travel around being back at the hotel by the time the curfew was in place. It was a race against time to both find petrol and film something worthwhile, and I was gearing up to launch a full verbal assault on Lukasz when Petro interrupted, speaking to Lukasz while still holding his phone to his cheek.

'Okay, something crazy has just happened,' Lukasz translated for us. 'We will have 60 litres in 30 minutes.'

My jaw dropped. Petro kept talking into the phone, while fist-bumping towards us, celebrating his win. I hugged him, and as he hung up the phone he announced with genuine enthusiasm: 'Whiskey time!'

I still have no idea how he pulled it off. We had been begging petrol stations for fuel, offering as much as $100 for a litre, and had ended up with zilch; and now, all of a sudden, Petro had unlocked 60 litres? When we pulled into a random carpark on the side of the road 30 minutes later, I was so nervous it could have been a Class A drug deal. Our hero was there waiting for us already, with a stack of red plastic containers filled with fuel lined up at his feet. He helped us fill our tank and gave us the leftovers for our stocks, and he only asked for $100. He was a borderline-mad conspiracy theorist and even more paranoid than Lukasz, so had been stashing fuel in his garage for months in preparation. We paid him double, because it was the least we could do, and left in a hurry for Bucha.

In Bucha, a small city of 40,000 people, over a thousand had been killed. The people there had seen the worst of the war, the worst of the Russians: mass rape, mass murder, mass torture.

As we drove into the city, my first thought was 'It doesn't look that bad' and then I felt sick for ever thinking that. We turned a corner and the city turned black. Incessant bombing had left behind a mess of bricks and belongings, house after house burnt to nothing. We saw a man standing in the backyard of one of the properties, and he showed us where he had hidden with his family when the Russians started blindly shooting at his home. His wife and children were now living with a stranger in France, he explained. 'I had to get them to safety. Somewhere they could begin to heal.' The Russians ended up taking over his home and using it as a headquarters. Five of his neighbours were killed before they had a chance to escape. 'I must have had a guardian angel, we were lucky,' he said, and I double-checked the translation. 'Lucky' meant something different where I came from.

Lukasz had heard of a village called Moshchun, just twenty minutes down the road, which was considered a gateway to Kyiv and so had been caught in one of the fiercest battles of the war so far. He wanted to go so he could geek out on all the military hardware he had been told had been left deserted in the fields; and while I found it hard to believe that things could get much worse than Bucha, we agreed to head in that direction.

As we drove towards Moshchun the road turned to gravel and started weaving us through a large forest. It was getting on in the afternoon and the light was turning into a golden haze; but it was more haunting than beautiful. Up ahead I could see a checkpoint, and I see it to this day, as clear as if I was right there all over again. Ukrainian soldiers stood by fires, one burning on either side of the road. Their huts were concealed slightly by the forest around them but their extensive gun collection was not concealed at all. The smoke was rising through the trees, and hanging from the branches above were the uniforms of Russian soldiers, stuffed like scarecrows and with nooses around their necks. I gasped, and saw Daniel instinctively push the camera down lower so as not to attract any unwanted attention as Petro rolled down the window, spoke to one of the soldiers and we all showed our accreditation.

I had no idea what was going to happen next, but one of the soldiers jumped on a bicycle, motioning for us to follow him as he took off down the road, into the town. It wasn't a town, though, not at all. It was a disordered footprint of a town that once was. Every house was all but flattened, so destroyed you could barely tell one from another. The walls that were still standing were riddled with bullet holes, and it reminded me of the ugliest truth of all: there hadn't been a natural disaster here, this was not the scene of a tsunami, or a wildfire, or a hurricane. This was a man-made tragedy.

The soldier explained how they had fought the Russians there head-on, and how he'd watched as a paramedic rushed into the paddock where we stood to tend to a wounded soldier.

'She was blown up into two pieces, in front of me,' he said.

Even Petro had gone quiet. I didn't know whether to cry or vomit, but as Daniel turned the camera on me I crouched down next to a burnt-out Russian tank and started rifling through the rubbish left strewn around it.

'Russian belongings are everywhere,' I said, 'food rations, leftovers, frying pans and clothes . . . scattered everywhere.' In this one village it was estimated that $60 million NZD worth of damage had been done and I felt like that was conservative. In the distance I could see an elderly woman walking slowly through the wreckage of a house. She could have been in her eighties, and she looked at me with the saddest eyes I have ever seen. She had been evacuated through a green corridor when the fighting intensified; and when she'd returned, her home of 70 years was gone. 'I'm too old for crying,' she told us, as she blinked away the tears.

The sun was disappearing fast and Lukasz was beside himself trying to keep us moving, so we said our goodbyes and piled into the car. 'Surely we have time to swing by Irpin?' I said to Lukasz, referencing the famous bridge that had been blown up by the Ukrainians to stop the Russian advance. You could almost see the frustration steaming out of his ears, which was as expected given that he was becoming more tightly wound by the minute. 'It's just a joke!' I said. 'Thank you for today.'

Beyond all odds, we had managed to tell the story we had come for, and despite a 1 a.m. live cross for our weekend political show *The Nation* and an overnight shift of air-raid sirens and trips to the bomb shelter, the minutes I did sleep that night were sound ones.

On the drive back to Lviv to collect our belongings before crossing the border into Poland, Lukasz and Petro were talking among themselves while Daniel and I dozed in the back, when I heard Lukasz start laughing. The pair could not have been more opposite and I was curious about what had prompted this mutual entertainment.

'Petro is just telling me he has seven girlfriends and two ex-wives,' Lukasz laughed.

'No wonder he is always on the phone,' concluded Daniel with a chuckle.

Petro was loving the attention and started pulling up photo evidence of his various lovers. I think it's safe to say that 75% of the photos he was showing off to his passengers were sent to him on the assumption they were for his eyes only.

'Fuck! Petro!' yelled Lukasz suddenly, no longer laughing.

'It's fiiiine,' calmed Petro. But as Daniel and I looked up at the highway, we quickly agreed with Lukasz that it wasn't fine.

'You're on the fucking wrong side of the fucking road,' Lukasz was shouting as a huge truck came screaming towards us. He reached over and grabbed the wheel, directing us off the road while Petro made noises that sounded a lot like 'What? It's all under control!' Lukasz was ropeable, perhaps a little bit with himself for the temporary lapse in business mode, but mostly at Petro, who was growing more ludicrous and reckless by the hour.

We course-corrected and drove on, and I must have fallen asleep in the back seat because I remember waking up and thinking 'That went fast' before quickly realising we were not at the border. Instead, we were in a suburban cul-de-sac.

'Surprise!' Petro said, and Lukasz was already protesting: 'We don't have time for a surprise, keep driving!'

But Petro had other plans. He parked up outside a house,

jumped out of the car to light a cigarette and lounged against his door as if he had nowhere better to be. He was clearly waiting for something, or someone, and I had to wipe my eyes to make sure I was seeing clearly when this person emerged. But there was no mistaking that voice:

'Hello, my friends!'

Petro had diverted us half an hour off-course to stop by Bosko's house for a catch-up! Daniel and I got out of the car for the obligatory hugs, but while we were pleased to see him we were exhausted, and with many hours of driving still between us and our heads being on actual pillows, we could have done without the unsanctioned stopover. Lukasz didn't even pretend to be pleased. 'Petro! Get in the fucking car! We have to go!'

Petro and Bosko were, of course, in full flight, sharing a cigarette, offering us one and trading tales of their time with their friends the Kiwi journalists. Bosko had a list of new English words he wanted to clarify the pronunciation of with us, and as he ran through them I could see a vein growing more and more pronounced on poor Lukasz's forehead. It was definitely time to go.

By the time we arrived at the border late that afternoon, I was more frightened of the internal war between Lukasz and Petro than the one Putin was raging. We said goodbye to our eccentric driver, and as we walked across the border I saw Lukasz physically relax, relieved to be back in Poland where people followed rules and there was order to life.

'Whiskey time,' I said.

KRAKÓW, POLAND
May 2022

On arrival in Poland we resumed our traditional therapy. Selecting a seat at a restaurant in the square nearest our hotel, we spent the next six hours watching the British stag parties disintegrate from obnoxious to incoherent and making bets on which man in a waistcoat and top hat would be the first to manage to convince a tourist to take an overpriced horse carriage ride around the Old Town. In between, we would debrief the stories we had told, the people we had met, the things we had seen, and order a constant stream of $3 Polish gins throughout. It wasn't medically approved therapy and as we stumbled to our hotel it's fair to say it wasn't the healthiest approach, but it worked for us. We would cry on and off for hours, both from laughter and from the realisation of what it was we had covered. To be fair it was always me doing the crying, but Daniel always ended up more intoxicated and honestly I would love to know which of us the Polish wait-staff considered to be more of a liability.

On this particular evening we received a call from The Sarahs, asking us to extend our trip and travel on to Finland and Sweden to cover the developing news of their intention to join NATO. The decision of these countries to join the security pact, both having been famously militarily neutral for decades, was a sign of the times and showed yet again the wide-ranging impact of the war.

As with all such phone calls, it was an instant 'yes' from us, followed by a mad panic to make it happen. I'm telling you now, you haven't lived until you've tried to negotiate the EasyJet website to book flights after six gins and no sleep for a week. Aware that it was likely we would end up telling a story involving the president and prime minister of these countries, it was clear that my 'war uniform' of black jeans, black chunky boots and a puffer jacket was not going to be up to standard. Fast forward two hours and I was singing to the Eagles in a Polish-Irish pub, with a bag of new Zara blazers and TV-appropriate shirts at my side, after another few gins that I definitely did not need. Fast forward another two hours and we were back at the hotel, it was 2 a.m. and I had left $250 worth of brand-new clothing in that Polish-Irish pub, never to be seen again.

Fast forward two more hours and my alarm was attacking my peace, sanity and eardrums. We had a flight to Stockholm to catch. I messaged Daniel our routine 'All good?' and jumped in the shower to try to wash away the bad decisions and figure out what on earth I was going to wear for the day ahead.

As I hurriedly packed my bag, I realised my WhatsApp message was still unread and Daniel was definitely not 'all good'. I zipped up my trusty suitcase, walked out the door and started knocking on Daniel's. No answer.

'Daniel!'

No answer.

'Daniel! Wake *up*!' I said, raising my voice and intensifying my knocking in equal amounts.

I probably stood there for 30 seconds making far too much noise, my phone buzzing with messages from our Uber telling me he had arrived, before Daniel finally emerged, half-naked, at the door.

'Where are we going?' he said, on high alert but also deathly hungover.

'The airport,' I said. 'Hurry up, we've got two minutes,' my own head pounding.

'What do I need?' he asked.

'Everything! Come on, we've got to go.'

'But what do I need, Lisette!' he said with growing frustration.

'Daniel, you need everything!' I said, pushing into his room and starting to throw all of his belongings into his suitcase.

'But what camera do I need and are we taking body armour?' he asked.

I stopped and looked at him, and it clicked. And I saw it register on his face too.

'We're going to Sweden, remember? Our flight leaves in three hours and our Uber is already here. Let's go.'

Five minutes later, in the car with our heart rates dropping, I turned to him.

'You thought we were still in Ukraine, didn't you?'

'Yeah,' he said.

We always underestimated the stress we were under in Ukraine, how constantly on alert we really were. We got so 'used' to going into an active war zone that we managed to trick ourselves into thinking it was normal. Just another trip. But it wasn't. The alcohol obviously hadn't helped this particular situation, and the lack of sleep was also not ideal, but when Daniel heard me banging on his door in the middle of the night his assumption was that he had slept through an air-raid siren. He'd thought I was telling him the airport had been bombed and we had to go film there.

Whenever I returned from a trip to Ukraine, I would, for weeks, react to everyday emergency-service sirens as if they were air-raid sirens, and I would hate it when people knocked on doors around me. It triggered an instinctive panic response, as if a timer had just been switched on and I had X number of minutes to get somewhere or do something.

Fortunately, Daniel and I were both still a bit delirious, or drunk, or both, and were able to laugh at the confusion, but I think we both quietly thought in the days that followed that our boozy therapy sessions were possibly not the only ones we needed.

STOCKHOLM, SWEDEN & HELSINKI, FINLAND
May 2022

Sweden was a blur. I know very few of you will care for the ongoing saga of my outfit, but for those of you who do: I ended up wearing the same black long-sleeved skivvy I had been wearing under my body armour. It was borderline see-through and to this day I watch the story I filmed outside the Swedish parliament and cringe at the fact you can see my bra. I was so tired that when the president's motorcade came by and Daniel prompted me with 'Rolling!', I just stared at the camera and said, 'I've got nothing.' Supreme journalism.

Everyone we met in Sweden was on edge about the decision to join NATO. Having worn their neutrality proudly for so many decades, no one was excited about giving it up but most agreed it had to be done. When we arrived in Helsinki the feeling among locals was entirely different. A paranoid nation, with the memory of Russia's 1939 invasion fresh in their family histories, Finland was desperate for security.

If you share 1300 kilometres of border with an aggressor, you are always going to prepare for the worst; but Finland takes it to the extreme. We were invited to tour the city's underground shelter, and having now spent time in bomb shelters myself I thought I knew what to expect. But this wasn't your typical bomb shelter; it was a hidden city. We took a lift 30 metres down and found ourselves in an alternative universe. It was modern and slick, built into the city's two-million-year-old bedrock. The shelter was gas-proof, blast-proof, nuclear-proof; whatever you need to be proofed from, it was proofing. It was even disguised as a happy place to spend your time, with a playground, gym, cafeteria and sports courts all right there, underground.

Along the edges of the corridor there were flat-packed metal bed frames ready to be assembled in haste, and yellow squares lined the floor like an extravagant game of hopscotch was about to be played with thousands of people.

'What are they for?' I asked.

'Each square represents where a portable toilet cubicle will go,' I was informed.

The plumbing was already installed and ready to be turned on. 'We have drinking water, we have additional power systems, we have ventilation,' Anna Lehtiranta from the Helsinki Rescue Department continued. 'We are all ready here waiting for something that we do not expect to happen.'

It would house 6000 people if needed, and there were 60 of these bunkers in Helsinki alone, along with more than 5000 smaller ones. Overall there was room underground for 900,000 people, 300,000 more than the city's population. That afternoon, my head was still spinning with the numbers as we drove to the Russian border. The highway to St Petersburg was abandoned, the traffic stifled by war. I would have given anything to have been able to cross over and experience Russia, but the visas for journalists were absurdly complex and notoriously difficult to get approved. It also just so happened to be the only place The Sarahs had ruled an absolute no-go from a safety perspective, although we continued to ask the question. We filmed our piece at the border and entertained ourselves with what-if scenarios instead, fantasising about a world where we would just try to drive through to Russia right then and there.

Hours later, we were sitting in our hotel editing our piece when a text popped up from my best friend Kate (who by now, I'm pretty sure, had forgiven me for missing her thirtieth). She's a very fancy international news producer and always one step ahead of me, and on this particular occasion she had beaten me to the breaking news headline.

'Oh my god. Sanctioned! Nice to be noticed, I suppose,' she wrote.

I clicked the link she had shared and there it was: my name. Number 24 on an updated list on the Russian Foreign Affairs website. I had just been sanctioned by the Kremlin for my Russophobic agenda and would never be allowed into the country. To this day I have mixed feelings about it. As much as I desperately want to experience Russia for myself, being in Putin's good books would have disturbed me as much as being on his naughty list did.

I was, in truth, too relaxed about it. I had company — there were other New Zealanders on the list and journalists from all over the world had already been named — but a phone call from the powers that be suggesting I didn't make any big public comment about it because others who had been sanctioned had security concerns for their families made me think twice about my nonchalance.

LONDON, UNITED KINGDOM
June 2022

By the time we had a chance to check a calendar, it was the end of May and London was in full peacock mode, showing off its summer best. The parks all over the city were filling up with happy faces and far too many people wearing swimwear in an area where the closest thing to a nice body of water was a jug of Pimm's.

The London summer is Mother Nature's way of apologising for the grim February she makes you endure. The long days make up for the brutally short ones, and when you're standing outside a bustling pub, with live music playing and a pint of cold cider in hand in the still-warm daylight at 9 p.m., you're convinced the winter was worth it and you mentally commit to doing another.

The summer of 2022 was particularly extraordinary, and not just because it was my first proper northern hemisphere experience: something historic was occurring. New Zealand cricket legend Brendon McCullum had just signed on as coach of England's Test team . . . and to add to the excitement it was also Queen Elizabeth's Platinum Jubilee. There was a slight clash in dates with the two stories, and Daniel was eager for us to forget the Queen while I was eager to forgo the cricket. We ended up compromising and covering both, darting between press conferences at Lord's, famously known as the Home of Cricket, and parties at Buckingham Palace, famously known as the Home of the British Royal Family.

There was a healing joy that came from shedding our puffer jackets and beanies and filming in the sunshine around so much happiness. The Platinum Jubilee was set to be a four-day celebration of the Queen's 70 years of service, a milestone no other British monarch had achieved. From Thursday to Sunday there was a string of festivities planned in her honour and the city was wallpapered in Union Jacks. It was jubilant in every way. The mile-long Mall that leads up to the palace was lined with tents, full of die-hard royalists camping overnight to get the best view of Trooping the Colour, an annual birthday parade that had been supersized for the occasion. Everyone was dressed up: in crowns, in Queen masks, and in red, white and blue sequins. One particularly patriotic woman revealed her custom-made Union Jack underwear to the camera, which we probably could have done without. I hadn't experienced royal fever before, but now we were in the thick of it with a million people surrounding Buckingham Palace, climbing gates and trees to ensure they had a top spot from which to wave at the Queen when she appeared on the balcony for the famous aircraft flypast. 'It's probably the most British day you could have,' one man told me, and I didn't doubt it.

As the Queen aged, there was more and more talk of her failing health and people were genuinely relieved to see her in person. Her eventual death had haunted journalists for decades; there's a long line of Europe Correspondents before me who had anxiously studied the details of her life in preparation for the coverage of that historic moment. I too followed that tradition, never going anywhere without a pack of homemade flashcards with 'Queen facts' on them in my handbag, and always having a black blazer nearby for when the news broke. I can't tell you how many times I got that damn blazer dry-cleaned without ever having worn it, petrified that it wouldn't be in perfect condition when the time came but only ever dirtying it from lugging it around with me out of paranoia.

In recent months the health updates we were receiving from the palace had become increasingly concerning and even leaving the UK was beginning to result in nervous murmurings from the bosses. Nobody wanted to be caught out, and I would have more than a few nightmares about lying on a beach in Croatia when the code words came through — 'London Bridge is down' — and forever being known as the Europe Correspondent who missed the Queen's death. I think the majority of the millions who gathered for the celebrations that weekend knew that this would be her last jubilee, possibly her last birthday, and while it never felt sad it did feel like everyone wanted to show the Queen how loved she was while she was still alive to see it. When the Red Arrows flew up the Mall and over Buckingham Palace in formation, creating the number 70 in the sky, the Queen beamed and the crowd cheered even louder. It felt like a temporary antidote to all the sadness in the world, and I was delighted.

'Ahhh . . . England just lost a wicket!' Daniel exclaimed.

A huge grandstand had been set up facing Buckingham Palace for the weekend, where invited guests and VIPs would be able to sit to watch the concert on Saturday night and have the best view of the various events planned. The left-hand side of the grandstand was reserved for celebrities and members of the public who had tickets, and the right-hand side was even more exclusive, requiring extreme levels of accreditation and police clearance that had been sorted months in advance. On that side was the Royal Box, where the royal family would sit, and next to that was a huge portion of risers dedicated to the media networks, who set up extensive temporary studios with the palace as a backdrop. We had been doing our live crosses from a spot at the top of these risers, and had been able to leave the bulk of our gear there throughout the day, which made it much easier for us to get around and film amid the swarming crowds.

With Trooping the Colour wrapped up, we had gone to collect our equipment from the riser and were making our way down again when we heard police motorbikes. I saw the flash of a shiny burgundy car with that small but instantly identifiable flag on its roof, and I squealed at Daniel in a panic: 'The Prince is coming!' Charles and Camilla lived a few hundred metres up The Mall at Clarence House, and looked to be sneaking out of Buckingham Palace via the cordoned off area, past the Royal Box, up to their front gate. We dropped the extra gear and ran down the final stairs of scaffolding to the ground, finding ourselves right next to the car where the future King and Queen sat. There was a huge green fence separating us from the public still celebrating on The Mall and it was too high for them to notice what was happening on our side.

Daniel hoisted up the camera to get a shot of the royals as they drove past, but they didn't drive past. The car stopped, and right in front of us, as the fence was pulled open, Charles and Camilla stepped out of the car and walked out into the public eye to meet and shake hands with those still partying on The Mall. There was no other media around. I saw one of the security officers look at us, then turn to a royal aide and say 'BBC' with approval, before ushering us through the fence as part of the royal contingent. We spent the next ten minutes side by side with the royal couple, Daniel filming with unprecedented access and the crowd growing hysterical as they tried to get a photo for their personal collections; and me standing by in shock, too overwhelmed to even think about doing the same.

For the next two days the Queen wasn't seen in public, with the palace issuing a statement saying she had been experiencing some discomfort and was needing to rest. It wasn't overly unexpected, but it was yet another hint of her deteriorating health.

On the final Jubilee day there was a pageant planned, and it was borderline insane. It was the most outrageously over-the-top procession of floats and dancers and military members and gymnasts and celebrities and puppets and vintage cars, and every section of the three-hour parade was themed to represent a different decade of the Queen's reign. At one point we found ourselves in a new cordoned-off area where the tail-end of the procession was waiting to take off. 'I think that's Bear Grylls,' I said to Daniel.

'Yeah, chewing on some jerky in a Jeep, how on-brand,' he replied, as we waltzed over, asked for an interview, got the interview and carried on our way.

Everyone was in such good spirits, and even Daniel had stopped streaming the cricket to soak up what was occurring around him. No one, not even the cricket-lovers in the crowd, wanted to miss the pinnacle moment of the parade: the part where the Gold State Coach came by — a royal treasure which has been used at every coronation since 1831. We knew the Queen wasn't going to be riding in it given that its lack of suspension makes it notoriously uncomfortable, but I was still a bit disappointed when it passed by empty; all the royal talk was making me believe in fairytales again.

At the conclusion of the parade, the police removed the barriers and the crowd collapsed on to The Mall, running up to the gates of Buckingham Palace to secure a good spot for British pop star Ed Sheeran's promised performance. We were right under the Queen's balcony when the doors opened and she appeared, surprising everyone. The 96-year-old monarch, dressed in the most perfect green outfit, started waving to the crowd; and just like that my faith in fairytales was restored. We were in the perfect place to film a piece to camera and Daniel pushed record, expertly framing the Queen up on the balcony before zooming out to reveal me in the crowd. 'The Queen famously said, you have to be seen to be believed; today she has been seen, believed, loved, and celebrated,' I finished, just as the party smoke cannons went off around us.

'That was bloody perfect,' Daniel shouted, 'You're even wearing the same green as her!' We interviewed crying royalists around us, and as the crowd started dissipating we decided to call it a day.

'I think we just saw the Queen at her last ever public appearance,' Daniel said.

'Yeah, I think you're right.'

But given that she'd made it to the balcony we figured she would survive the week at least, so I booked a flight to Greece that night for a holiday and flew out the next morning, geeky flashcards and black blazer in tow.

MADRID, SPAIN & BRUSSELS, BELGIUM
late June 2022

The New Zealand prime minister was coming to Europe for a whirlwind tour, although they're always whirlwind trips, those political ones. Highly choreographed and jam-packed with handshakes and photo opportunities, you hold on for dear life and try to enjoy the cold mini pies and quiches you steal off plates meant for more important people.

Jacinda Ardern's first stop was Madrid, where she was attending the NATO summit. Every year on the first Monday in May, celebrities of all sorts are invited to the Met Gala in New York, wearing outrageous outfits and sending fans into a tizz. A NATO summit is for me the Met Gala of the political world. Not because of the outfits on display, although I would challenge any Met Gala suit to rival what President Macron of France serves on the NATO blue carpet, but because suddenly a huge portion of the most powerful world leaders are gathered in one place, in one room, at the same time. We're talking the US president, the Turkish president, the French president, the UK prime minister, German chancellor, Canadian prime minister, etc., etc. Seeing them interact with each other, watching the different friendships and power dynamics at play and guessing what they're all discussing, makes it political-nerd Disneyland.

They spend two days meeting, in big breakout groups, and in one-on-one bilaterals which are the most incredible of all. It's like political speed-dating. Small pop-up boardrooms are arranged one beside another down a maze of corridors, and world leaders have an itinerary of rooms to go to at different times where they will meet another leader. There is usually a stash of giant world flags down the side of the main corridor, and stressed officials dart in and out of their rooms, taking out the flags of the leaders that just met and quickly replacing them with the flags of the next two who are on their way. Once the flags are arranged at the head of the table in the room, journalists are invited in to set up — we're there for the initial meet and greet but are booted out before the serious conversations take place. We squash up in a corner of the room, with cameras at the ready, waiting to see which of the world leaders shows up first. One will arrive through one door with their posse and awkwardly make a joke to the journalists as they wait for their date to arrive, and then the second leader will arrive in a bustle through an opposite door and apologise for having kept the other waiting. They shake hands and pose for a photo with their flags, and just like a scene from *The Bachelor* or *The Bachelorette* one will often offer the other a gift, such as a football or an All Black jersey, to help break the ice. The recipient is always very grateful and everyone smiles, and then as the 30 seconds of small talk starts to wane the media officers step in and start to usher the media out.

Before all the NATO excitement got underway on day one, we did a live cross into the 6 p.m. bulletin. Daniel was responsible for filming a pre-event with Jacinda Ardern after our live and only he was accredited for the event, so I got on with other work until he had finished. When we met up again, I asked if I could watch the footage.

'Sure,' he said, perching next to me and pushing play on his morning's work.

I saw it straight away.

'Um, do you notice anything?'

'No?'

'You don't see anything here?' I said, looking down at myself and back to the screen in front of me with Ardern front and centre.

'What are you talking about?'

'We are wearing the *same dress*, Daniel!'

'Oh, you are too,' replied the newly declared Least Observant Camera Operator in History, before adding, 'Maybe she won't notice either?'

She clocked it immediately.

I didn't have time to change before the prime minister's press conference and as she walked towards the press pack I saw her start to laugh.

'It's a great dress,' I offered.

'Nice, nice choice, yeah,' she replied in good humour. 'We won't talk about it. I've got a jacket over the top, but do we need to confer for the rest of the trip?'

Later that day we did try to film a piece where I spoke to the camera as Ardern worked in the background, as journalists often do in television packages. The doubled-up dress looked absurd and the clip was unusable, but everyone got a great second laugh out of the situation so it wasn't a complete waste of time. It was too late, though, for the original press conference exchange, which was caught on video and already out in the world. It ended up gaining the predictable 'who wore it first, who wore it best, journo stole my look' traction and one radio station dedicated a full segment to discussing why on earth I didn't change my dress — as if it were a cardinal sin to wear what the prime minister was wearing, *and* as if I carried around a spare in my handbag (with my dead-Queen blazer I was already at max capacity).

In my defence, it was a blue dress and I had honestly been counting on Ardern to wear red. Regardless, the 'scandal' was all very Met Gala.

Having travelled from Madrid to Brussels to secure a free trade deal with the EU, Ardern's last stop on tour was England, where she was due to meet with then British Prime Minister Boris Johnson. Downing Street is one of my favourite places in London. The street itself is blocked off so the public can't walk up to the door, and instead a steady stream of tourists stand at the metal gates and look up the 200-metre cul-de-sac to steal a glimpse of the famous Number 10 on the right-hand side. Accredited media can access the street, passing through the well-armed police guard at the gate and through heavy-duty security scanners. Opposite the door, on the other side of the street, is a specific pen set up for journalists to work from, and on important days there is towering scaffolding to climb up, so hundreds of us can fit crammed in together with all of our cameras and questions and litres of coffee.

British prime ministers have lived at Downing Street since 1735 and to stand opposite Number 10, picturing the likes of Margaret Thatcher and Winston Churchill walking through that same door, was always very surreal. Larry the cat has lived there since 2011. The seventeen-year-old tabby started life as a stray but is now considered a civil servant, so has a home on Downing Street regardless of who is in government. He's served for six different prime ministers to date, and seeing him patrolling the street, as well as scaring off foxes at all hours of the day, was also quite surreal. Larry is such a fixture that if the door to Number 10 doesn't open for him within a minute or two of him arriving out front, a journalist will more often than not go up and knock on the door on behalf of Larry, and he is promptly let in.

We spent many early mornings alone on the street with just Larry for company, looking up at the famous building while waiting for a live cross, and wondering what was going through the mind of the embattled prime minister inside. Nothing entertained me more than when the postman would come up the street and casually drop off the day's newspapers at the doorstep, their headlines screaming about the resident's incompetence. Our media accreditation only got us so far, though: up to the door, but not through it — and Ardern was our golden ticket into the famous house of power. I was having all sorts of outrageous imaginings of walking in to find Boris Johnson doing the Hugh Grant *Love Actually* dance down the staircase, but it wasn't quite like that in the end.

When Ardern arrived, Boris Johnson walked out through the door to meet her, and they both smiled and posed for a photograph while the British media yelled at him 'Prime Minister, is your leadership lacking?' He was embroiled in a scandal at the time, although he mostly always was and so the smiling and posing continued undeterred.

As soon as they went inside the main door, we were unleashed. The entire contingent of Kiwi journalists who had been travelling with Ardern suddenly ran like headless chickens across the street, through the side door of Downing Street, up a series of stairs and down a dimly lit corridor into a grand sitting room, where the pair would soon arrive via a much more distinguished entrance. I tripped my way up the stairs and was so worried that my puffing was going to get caught on the microphone when I made it to the meeting room that I can barely recall a thing about the experience, but these three things I know for sure: there was a ridiculously large chandelier, Ardern and I wore different dresses, and less than a week later Boris Johnson would be forced to move out.

CHUR, SWITZERLAND
July 2022

I have always had a soft spot for the story that comes at the end of each bulletin. The 'kicker', as it's known, is the dessert you get for agreeing to eat your vegetables. It's not the most important part of your diet, sure, but we all deserve a treat.

Daniel and I had been asked by *The Project* to go to a town in Switzerland called Chur, on a specific mission to try to convince the mayor there to agree to be sister-cities with Whangārei. In Switzerland the views are extraordinary and they're free, but everything else is completely unaffordable, so it was a country I was always more than happy to visit on the work credit card instead of my own. We were looking forward to an easy-going trip with low pressure and plenty of delicious chocolate.

By the time we got to our accommodation, though, things were starting to get tense. Boris Johnson, who had partied his way through Covid, had just been served resignation letters from two of his most senior Cabinet ministers and was now fighting for his political life. The chancellor and the health secretary had quit based on the prime minister's lack of standards and integrity; and *I* was going to quit over the stress of being in an obscure town in Switzerland while Downing Street was hitting the headlines. The Europe patch is a big one and obviously there will often be more than one big story happening at the same time; you can't be everywhere at once, but there is a unique type of discomfort that sets in when every other foreign correspondent in London is descending on Number 10 to cover unfolding political history while you're racing around a random location hundreds of kilometres away teaching a very confused Swiss population how to do the 'chur' head-nod.

We only lasted the morning. We booked a new, much earlier flight home and we shot our entire story in Chur in a couple of hours before beginning the journey back to Downing Street. Boris was gone by the time we touched down in London and as we waited for our bags to turn up on the belt I was completely unbearable to be around.

'Why did we ever think we could get away with this? It was too good to be true,' I whined as Daniel grew increasingly fed up with my complaining.

'There's nothing we can do about it. We'll get there when we get there.'

But by that point I was pretty convinced the whining would help.

Love him or hate him, Boris Johnson knew his way around a speech. He was often utterly outrageous but it was almost always entertaining. My caveat for that statement is that it would be at least 95% less entertaining if he was *your* prime minister. I was fuming to have missed his resignation address, but we did make it back in time for New Zealand's 6 p.m. bulletin so I decided to stay in the job after all.

BIRMINGHAM, UNITED KINGDOM
late July 2022

Boris's career wasn't the only thing going up in flames. London was also literally on fire. The city had recorded its hottest day on record, 40.02 degrees, and if you need a reminder of how I cope with heat, please refer to the Tokyo section. The UK heatwave of 2022 was just an incredibly unpleasant, and sweaty, story to cover. London is built to keep heat in, not to air-condition, and there was no escaping the sweltering conditions. It was bleak enough that Daniel voluntarily splashed out the equivalent of $30 on two soft-serve Mr Whippy ice creams, desperate for some cooling relief on the job. Everyone was sleeping with frozen water bottles in their beds, and the fires breaking out in London were proof of how serious the situation had become. The wildfires were, however, far worse in Europe, especially France, and in a frantic attempt to escape the scorching hell of the UK I pitched a trip to go cover it in a different country.

'I just need to get out of this city, Sarah,' I essentially begged Bristow.

'Because it's too hot?'

'Yeah, I'm not coping.'

'And you think going to France to cover the wildfires is going to be a cooler choice?'

She had a point, but if I was going to suffer heatstroke again it might as well be somewhere exotic with baguettes (and the best story possible). Unfortunately, all the flights had sold out by the time we got the green light to go, so my grand plan never materialised. It was probably for the best, as it would have been a very short stint squeezed in before heading to Birmingham for the start of the Commonwealth Games.

I think it was raining the day the rest of the Newshub team arrived from New Zealand.

'What do you call this?' they started. 'All we hear from you for ten days is heatwave this, heatwave that, and we arrive to bloody rain?'

'You just can't trust the media,' they joked.

'I'm in a *trenchcoat*!' one of my wonderful friends and

fellow reporter, Alice Wilkins, said in despair when I first saw her, and boy was it good to see her.

Events like the Commonwealth Games would see our bureau of two suddenly supersized by familiar faces and homely accents. There were six from the newsroom who came over, and as a group of eight we spent the next two weeks racing around Birmingham covering the Kiwi successes and pretending we were in *Peaky Blinders*. I was less interested in a cheesecutter than I was in perfecting my Brummie accent, and by the end of the coverage I had convinced myself that I could get away with saying 'ting' instead of 'thing', just like the locals.

'Bit of a change from a war zone!' one of the New Zealand coaches yelled at Daniel and me outside Kiwi House, where all the family and fans camped out. He wasn't wrong. Telling celebratory stories was uplifting, and we probably needed it more than we realised. I turned 28 on the final day of the games and, just like in Tokyo, we had a fitting celebration planned — not just for my birthday (although my Leo tendencies were pushing for that to be the focus), but mostly to mark the end of a big three-week effort.

It was getting into the wee hours of the morning when Mike McRoberts called it a night, responsibly heading back to the hotel knowing he had one last live broadcast to do in the morning. Daniel had committed to doing the camera work and Mike patted him on the back on the way out the door.

'Right, see you in a few hours.'

'I won't let you down,' Daniel replied.

'I know you won't,' Mike said with a chuckle. I thought it was a bold call.

My alarm went off at 6 a.m. and I rolled over to fire off a message to Daniel.

'Are you up?' I asked, knowing the answer and leaving it barely five seconds before ringing him. After a few too many beats, a groggy voice answered 'Hello?'

'You're due downstairs in ten minutes with McRoberts.'

'Got it.'

And I rolled over and went back to sleep for two hours while Daniel and Mike did all the hard work.

At breakfast that morning, Alex Parsons, another cameraman who I knew was hoping to take over the Europe job when the time came, had a jolt of realisation that Daniel had managed to work that morning despite the late finish.

'Impressive turnaround, mate,' Alex said to Dan.

'Yeah, well, Lisette did have to wake me up,' he confessed with a laugh.

'True?'

'I was never going to make that live cross without assistance, Alex,' Daniel replied, and the laughter continued.

'It was the least I could do,' I added.

Alex nodded his approval and I had a feeling then that he would be a full-time member of the team sooner rather than later.

DOWNING STREET, LONDON
early September 2022

It is British protocol that the outgoing prime minister needs to officially resign to the Queen, and the incoming prime minister needs to be invited to form a government by Her Majesty straight afterwards. Downing Street was abuzz with a sense of occasion. All of the media were ready and waiting to capture Boris Johnson's final departure from Number 10, the new prime minister Liz Truss's arrival, and Larry the cat's reaction to it all. A not insignificant number of protestors were camped at the gates playing their favourite 'Bye Bye Boris' version of 'Bye Bye Baby' by the Bay City Rollers, through a terrible sound system, which made me cringe a little bit but also bop along against my better judgement.

Due to the Queen's deteriorating health, both Boris Johnson and Liz Truss were going to make the trip to visit her at Balmoral Castle in Scotland, as opposed to her meeting them at Buckingham Palace in London, and that was enough to raise alarm bells. It also meant a long time waiting around. Boris Johnson made his final speech and left Downing Street early in the morning, with cameras following his every move. Journalists then crowded around tiny screens commentating livestreams for the next few hours of his flight to Scotland, his drive to the castle, his walk into the castle, and then his exit. There was a lot of time to fill and everyone was running so low on things to talk about that I could have sworn at one point they resorted to a livestream of Larry.

We were camped out at Number 10 waiting for Liz Truss to arrive at her new residence and make her first address, which would provide me with an opportunity to film a fifteen-second bit to camera as she walked in behind. We tracked the livestream of her motorcade arriving at Downing Street, and as the car pulled up Daniel said to me: 'No sudden movements or you'll spook her . . .'

I stifled a laugh, and started talking just as the new prime minister got out of the car right beside me and walked perfectly through our shot up to the podium to make her inaugural speech. An eight-hour wait to generate fifteen seconds of TV sounds like a grim trade-off, but at the time it felt totally worth it.

When official photos were released later that day of the two Liz's meeting and shaking hands, they were scrutinised intensely. The Queen looked frail and had severe bruising on her hand, and I sat zoomed in on it for far too many minutes looking for clues. Liz Truss's first meeting with the Queen would turn out to be her last, because Queen Elizabeth died two days later.

We were filming a story at a recruitment drive for nurses when the update came through. We had been focusing on a Kiwi group who were trying to get young British nurses to move to New Zealand to work there. It was a good story, but I was so obsessed with the Queen's health by that point that I spent most of the day causally working it into interviews, asking as many nurses as I could what they thought the bruising on her hand meant. The general consensus was that there weren't many weeks left — but no one was talking days, let alone hours, and then the official message flashed up on our phones.

The Queen was under medical supervision and the family were on their way to Balmoral Castle.

ROYAL RESIDENCES, UNITED KINGDOM
September 2022

'I can't believe you're gonna bloody get the Queen's death too,' I said to Daniel.

He was due to finish up as Europe cameraman at the end of the year, and we had been joking for months that he was going to have to leave without the royal flush of big stories; but now here we were racing to Buckingham Palace.

'Nice little story on the way out the door for me,' he replied with a smirk. Playing it down was the best way to manage our spiking adrenaline; we were both acutely aware that if we screwed this story up, it would likely be all we'd be remembered for.

It's hard to explain what the feeling was that day. It was a mixture of excitement, relief and mad, mad panic. The excitement came from being at the centre of one of the biggest news events in decades, the relief came from the fact we were in London and relatively well placed to begin our coverage, and the mad panic came from desperately wanting to do it justice. We parked on the grass berm at Canada Gate outside Buckingham Palace, joining the dozens of other TV crews already setting up. It was heaving with rain and we sheltered in the car, frantically writing various different scripts with the latest information we had, not knowing when we were going to get an update.

At that time it was around 3 p.m. in the afternoon in London and the Auckland newsroom had been activated: woken up in the middle of their night and rushed into the office to get organised before *AM* came on air. Melissa Chan-Green is a walking encyclopaedia of the royals, and had once shown me the stack of research notes she had prepared during her time as Europe Correspondent. It made my prep look like it had been done by a kindergartener. She was a presenter of *AM* at the time, and I was more nervous about what she would think of my coverage than anyone else, even though I've never heard her say a critical thing about anyone (except maybe someone who said something critical about the royals), so my worry was probably misplaced.

'Hope you're alive,' my Irish housemate, Eavan, messaged, more concerned with my wellbeing than that of the Queen because no one with her passport was ever going to feel particularly low about the death of an English monarch. I was due to be on air at 5:30 a.m. in New Zealand, and the clock was ticking ever closer without any word from the palace. I had my camel coat on, but if you looked down the line of journalists set up in front of Buckingham Palace I was far from the only one who had a black alternative hanging on a light stand nearby. Mine was the first live cross of the bulletin as *AM* came on air, and Bernadine Oliver-Kerby had started reading the news in the studio. She was seconds away from 'Europe Correspondent Lisette Reymer joins us now . . .' when suddenly an Iraqi journalist jumped in front of my eyeline and started mouthing 'She's dead! She's dead! She's dead!' London Bridge had fallen, and I turned around just as the Union Jack was lowered down the palace flagpole.

Queen Elizabeth II was dead.

Only a moment passed before I was lunging for my black coat and stripping the camel one off, with such ferocity that everyone watching me from the Auckland control room knew exactly what had happened.

'You've got this,' Daniel said.

Operation London Bridge was a well-rehearsed process and it played out with staggering efficiency. During that very first live cross, officials started swarming around trying to pull me off air as they began activating the pre-established plan to move all of the journalists from our usual position to a new one, to make way for the scaffolding that was to be built that very night and used for the next two weeks by the world's biggest networks. The area around Buckingham Palace was soon overrun with people, the internet access was growing dicier by the second, the phone networks were jammed and it was still pouring with rain. We were going live as often as connectivity would allow, and running around in between trying to film and interview the flower-gripping grievers who were arriving at the gates of the palace. It wasn't just flowers they were laying in sympathy — there were so many Paddingtons you'd think it was the fictional bear who had died, and marmalade sandwiches quickly became a top tribute too, prompting officials to ask people to stop with the sammies because it was going to have a negative impact on the wildlife in the surrounding parks.

The rain was adding to the sombre mood and as evening set in, bright lights started beaming down The Mall, drawing everyone's attention. The famous Black Cab drivers had arranged their own salute, and were now all lined up in formation down the famous mile-long stretch to the palace. Parked up, with their lights on and their doors open, the drivers stood beside their cabs, some standing on their door frames, and looked towards the palace with their hands on their hearts as the rain glinted in their headlights. It was, for me, the most touching moment of the evening and so perfectly, brilliantly British.

'Rest in peace, ma'am,' some said quietly, as in their own time they each got back in their iconic cars and disassembled.

It was going to be a long night and we weren't counting on getting any food or sleep, but one of my great friends and former Newshub-turned-BBC journalist, Ed O'Driscoll, was sick of covering such a big story from his newsroom and wanted to be out in the thick of it, so after his shift he braved the crowds to witness history and visit us. Crucially, as far as

Daniel and I were concerned, Ed was our gateway to snacks.

'I'll bring water and lots of food. Let me know if you need anything else,' he messaged me at 8:22 p.m.

'Signal is ducked,' I replied at 8:50 p.m., my freezing wet fingers censoring my growing frustration.

I'm still not sure how he found us among the thousands, but by some sheer miracle, at 9:30 p.m. I saw Ed approaching with an umbrella and a supermarket bag filled with water and muesli bars in hand. I was still too high on adrenaline to eat, and by the time I reached for a muesli bar at 1 a.m. Daniel had hoovered them all up, but the water had been a game-changer. Ed stayed with us all night, helping to carry our gear around as we searched for a signal, trying to move our rental car from its highly illegal park, and pointing out, as politely as possible, before one live cross: 'You could probably use a hairbrush, Lisette.' He wasn't wrong. The downpour had wreaked havoc with my mascara too.

I have receipt evidence that it was 2:35 a.m. when I ordered Ed a cab. Daniel and I continued our live crosses for another hour and crawled into our homes at 4 a.m.

Sleep would have been an obvious option at this point, but instead I lay on my bed and opened an online shopping cart for my favourite shop and got to work selecting any black clothing item that took my tired fancy. At 4:30 a.m. I pushed 'Checkout' and paid extra for overnight delivery. If I was going to wear black and not sleep for two weeks straight, I was going to at least feel as good as possible.

At 5.50 a.m. we were back at Buckingham Palace, setting up for a live cross into the 6 p.m. news, me in my soon-to-be-upgraded black jacket. My nieces already thought I lived in Buckingham Palace, and this certainly wasn't going to help.

The floral tributes had spread into The Green Park, the

bouquets and messages covering a huge area by the time a reinforcement crew of presenters, reporters, producers and camera operators from home made it to our hemisphere. The distance between New Zealand and London was painfully clear in between as we tried to cover the story as a two-man team. What most journalists don't want to admit is that covering royal events is hell. There are tens of thousands of people crammed into a small area, waiting, waiting, waiting for a glimpse of a crown or, in this case, a coffin. It is impossible to get anywhere fast, roads are often closed all around, and you can end up standing for hours in a mosh-pit-type environment holding your place against the pushers and shovers to ensure a good shot, only for someone in front to stand up last-minute in front of the camera or lift their child on to their shoulders. Alternatively, at the point Daniel lifts up his camera to begin filming, you have to deal with the disappointment on the faces of children who have waited equally as patiently only to now have a big chunk of camera block their view of the prince and princess. 'We love our job, we love our job, we love our job,' we would walk around chanting to ourselves, while 'hypothetically' discussing other options for employment.

Every day of Operation London Bridge had an official, predetermined code: D-Day for the day she died, D+1 for the day after her death, counting up until D+10 which was to be the day of her state funeral. By D+3 we had descended into a weird news coverage bubble where everyone else's lives had returned to relative normal, with work and social gatherings, while ours were still obsessively tied to the movements of the mourning King and the dead Queen. The only way my housemates could tell I had been home was if the drying rack in the lounge was covered in freshly washed black clothing. On D+5 I bumped into Eavan in the corridor at home as she returned from a big night out at around 5 a.m. and I was getting ready for another early-morning live cross. She wiped her makeup off as I continued slapping mine on.

'How is it still *going*?!' she exclaimed in her thick Irish accent, fuelled, at a safe guess, by a healthy dose of Baby Guinnesses.

'Yeah I know,' I said with a chuckle.

'How are *you* still going?' she exclaimed even louder.

'That I don't know.'

After the Queen's coffin arrived at RAF Northolt in West London, hordes of people lined the streets to throw roses on the royal hearse as it drove by. Adults were weeping, recalling memories of Princess Diana's coffin arriving at the same airport; and there were young children braving the rain to be part of this moment in history. When we drove back to London it was getting dark, and the highway was lit up with hundreds of glowing billboards, one after another, dedicated to Her Majesty. I could barely believe she was actually gone.

The British love the royals, queuing and tea in the extreme and, I would say, in that order. So an invite to queue to see the Queen lying in state at Westminster Hall was like a bonus Christmas to them. They came in their hundreds of thousands along with flasks of tea to get them through. Elizabeth lay in state for four full days, and that was long enough to turn the Q word into a lifelong trigger for me. Consequently, I'm taking liberties now and I'm going to refer to it as a 'line' going forward. The line was 16 kilometres long at its peak, and people were standing in it, shuffling forward one painful step at a time, for 24 hours at least. Ridiculously, there was even an official line to join the actual line. It snaked its way through London, past all the major landmarks and, in truth, it was quite extraordinary. Strangers would become friends by the end of it, trading stories of their favourite memories of the Queen, sharing picnic food, and taking turns holding their place in the line for bathroom and coffee runs. People were laughing a lot, and crying even more, but there was a beautiful camaraderie in it.

There was nothing beautiful, however, about walking 16 kilometres with 30 kilograms of camera gear and having to negotiate the various road closures around the city that were set up for security purposes. I would like to take this opportunity to publicly apologise to anyone I hit with the tripod over the course of those four days; I promise it wasn't a deliberate act of violence. With the tripod slung over my shoulder as we charged through the crowds, there were a few inevitable casualties where my desperate attempt to get from A to B came at a cost for the diddy-daddlers blocking the footpath. On one of the days, David Beckham joined the line and I was particularly put out that for all our hours spent talking to people in that damn line, I never bumped into Becks. Posh was not spotted in the line at all. We did, however, stumble across our Japanese friends from the hostile training course, who threw us a sympathetic smile from beneath their own exhaustion.

'Nice to see you again,' they said.

'Why didn't they give us some tips to survive *this*?' we replied as we charged on.

We were on a whirlwind tour of royal residences, from Buckingham Palace, to Windsor Castle, to Sandringham and back again; and everywhere we went the florists were out of stock, the palace and castle gates adorned with beautiful bright petals and sketches and paintings of the Queen. Windsor was where our journey with the Queen would end.

Daniel and I arrived in the castle town ahead of the funeral

TOP Clinging to my lifeline (portable fan) before a live cross at the Tokyo Olympics as I struggle to survive the stifling heat. JOHN FLEMING

BOTTOM Blissfully unaware of what was to come . . . My first time wearing protective gear, while learning the ropes with Daniel at our hostile environments training course in Kent, UK.

TOP LEFT Sitting in the car in Poland counting our emergency cash before heading into Ukraine. This wasn't even half of our stash.

BOTTOM Odessa was a fortress; barricaded with sandbags, tyres and metal anti-tank defences, ready for the Russians to arrive.

TOP RIGHT Ten kilometres from the Russian border, walking through the landmine-riddled town of Tsupivka, Ukraine with artillery sounding all around us.
DANIEL PANNETT

TOP LEFT Clothing laid out ahead of the overnight race to the bombshelter, as per my warzone bedtime ritual.

BOTTOM A sleepless night in the shelter, waiting for the missiles to stop flying overhead so we could cross live into the 6 p.m. bulletin from above ground. Wishful thinking.

TOP RIGHT Sixty metres underground in the famous catacombs of Odessa, where we met a man preparing an air mattress for his wife to give birth on.

TOP Daniel getting a shot of a Russian tank abandoned on the highway to Kyiv after the initial withdrawal of Putin's men.

BOTTOM Filming in the corridor of an obliterated high school in Kharkiv.

TOP LEFT A master at work: Alex filming the unfathomable devastation following the Turkey earthquakes.

BOTTOM Alex and I having survived our first encounter with tear gas on the streets of Paris, after fierce riots erupted over France's retirement age.

TOP RIGHT Standing in the rubble for the morning live cross after a night camping out in our car amid constant aftershocks.
ALEX PARSONS

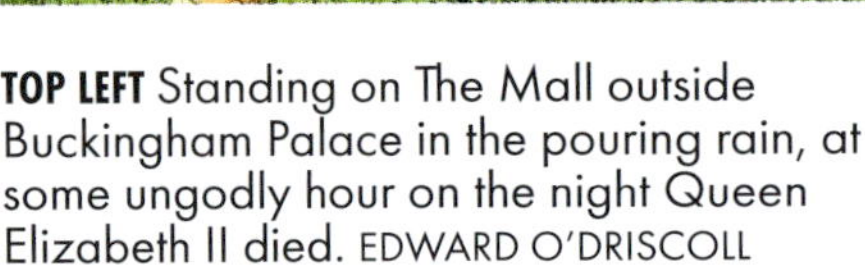

TOP LEFT Standing on The Mall outside Buckingham Palace in the pouring rain, at some ungodly hour on the night Queen Elizabeth II died. EDWARD O'DRISCOLL

BOTTOM LEFT Making new friends in Ethiopia, who distracted me from my crippling fever and nausea. ALEX PARSONS

TOP RIGHT God Save The King! Set up for a live cross outside Westminster Abbey the morning of King Charles III's coronation. ALEX PARSONS

BOTTOM RIGHT A few gins deep, having just arrived in Poland from Ukraine, and watching a live stream of Liz Truss resigning as British PM. Back to work . . . DANIEL PANNETT

TOP She wore it best — it's fine, I know she did. The great faux pas of my time in Europe, wearing matching dresses with Prime Minister Jacinda Ardern while in Madrid, Spain for a NATO summit.

BOTTOM LEFT Waiting to conduct an interview on the edge of the West Bank. ALEX PARSONS

BOTTOM RIGHT Reunited with my brilliant friend Daniel to cover the America's Cup in Barcelona; far less body armour required for this gig than our usual missions.

Going out with a mic drop and immense gratitude on the Europe Bureau's last ever morning news cross to New Zealand from London. ALEX PARSONS

and checked into our latest temporary home. 'You can take the bunk beds, Daniel, as a special treat,' somehow ending up with the master suite for myself.

'So generous, Lisette, thank you,' he replied.

We stocked the fridge with wine, because by that point we needed it, and prepared for the final hurrah. Two weeks of running on a few hours of sleep a night, interviewing people crying every day, and only wearing black was starting to take its toll.

'I'll hardly recognise you when you get back into your colourful frocks,' Daniel joked.

'Imagine when the bags under my eyes are gone too — that'll really shock you.'

The funeral was going to be our final and biggest big day, with thousands descending on Windsor Castle to get a final glimpse of the Queen's last minutes in the public eye. The Long Walk is a four-kilometre avenue lined on either side with lawn and beautiful big trees, and it stretches through the park up to the castle gates. There were huge crowds of people on each side, with children clambering on to their parents' shoulders, and everywhere you could see the historic memory being pocketed for years to come. We spent most of the morning watching proceedings on the big screens as the funeral service took place in the city and the coffin made the slow journey to Windsor Castle, but when the procession finally rounded the corner on to The Long Walk, everyone went quiet. There was a smattering of polite claps, and roses were thrown out over the coffin as it went by. People everywhere silently wept. When 'God Save the King' played for the first time, and King Charles himself looked overcome, there were very few dry eyes left.

A lot of the parents I met during this time would point

to their children with tiaras and princess dresses on and comment how happy they were that their children would always be able to say that Queen Elizabeth was their first Queen. To me, Elizabeth II was the ultimate time traveller. I had always felt she was our tie to history; as if there were an invisible thread that connected us, through her, to the days of Winston Churchill and JFK, Martin Luther King and Elvis Presley, World War II, the moon landing, the fall of the Berlin Wall. She had been there for all of it, met everyone, and she made it all feel closer. Seeing her coffin and being part of the coverage of her death underlined for me that we were entering a new era. Of all of the 'I remember whens' that I plan to roll out in decades to come to rolled eyes and cries of 'We've *heard* this story!', I think the Queen's death will get the most use.

Lovely Lizzy died on the 8th of September, our last day of coverage was the 20th; and as we drove back to London from Windsor Castle Daniel and I discussed the plan for the next fortnight or so.

'Some sleep would be good,' he said.

'Agreed. We're too late for the world rowing champs now so I'll cancel all those bookings. But the bosses are asking if we still wanna do the Joseph Parker fight this week?'

'Yeah, that's Manchester right?'

'Yeah, I reckon that'll be fine?'

'Yeah, and then I reckon we need to get back to Ukraine.'

We slept for two days, wrote up our pitch to get to the front line on the train to Manchester to cover Parker's fight-night, got the tick of approval from The Sarahs . . . and before we knew it we were back at the Polish border.

FRONT LINE, UKRAINE
October 2022

Aleks was very short, but very strong and very fit. He wore khaki pants and a tidy quarter-zip jersey, with a practical boot, and I warmed to him instantly. He looked late-forties and had a trustworthy face with bright blue eyes that I doubted could ever look afraid. He was the perfect mix of being prepared for action while also recognising that he was not a soldier in the trenches so there was no need to go full Rambo. He was Polish and spoke near-fluent English, though for some reason he would never say 'yes' but always 'exactly right', with a thick accent and a generous smile. Aleks was a former Special Forces diver who had spent 20+ years laying bombs under ships and I couldn't help but think he would be the coolest dad at school pickup. He was going to lead our security team for the next trip, our most ambitious yet, and I was relieved to have him on board.

We also had a driver, Oleks, a former police officer and a very large man, who couldn't speak a word of English but did mumble a few French words in our direction from time to time. He would take us over the border into Ukraine. On first impression you would never mess with him, but after ten minutes in a car with him it became clear that he was actually a massive teddy bear. Aleks and Oleks were a great duo to be working with, and it was just as well because we'd also had word that due to the increased risk of this trip we'd have an extra security person joining the team; and that extra person was to be an old friend of ours, Petro.

'He's actually more of a hindrance than a help,' I tried to explain to the bosses, 'and he definitely shouldn't be doing any driving.'

'He's not driving. He'll just take you as far as Kyiv and from there you'll have a new driver and Petro will just be extra security,' they insisted.

'The guy barely knows how to hold his Glock! He's a liability!' I retorted, but I wasn't getting anywhere. The call came from higher up that an added security officer, even if it was Petro, was better than just having one, and we finalised the details of where to meet him once we had crossed the border.

The night before we left for Ukraine, Daniel and I ate our usual last supper meal at McDonald's and discussed the trip ahead.

'What are you most worried about?' I asked him.

'Stepping on a landmine and losing my leg while filming.'

'Yes, because you just kind of lose yourself a bit when you're looking through the camera.'

'Exactly.'

'I'll keep an eye out.'

'I know. Thanks. What about you?'

'I keep imagining a Russian soldier holding a gun up to my face and just shooting at me.'

'Well, that shouldn't happen.'

'No, I know. But that's what I'm most scared of.'

'Understood. I'll keep an eye out,' he promised in return, with a teasing smile.

That night, as I struggled more to digest the McDonald's than my fear, I resorted to my unintentional tradition of watching old episodes of *Keeping Up with the Kardashians* until I nodded off.

Passports in hand, we drove across the gravel between the two countries' border forces, heading out of Poland and into

Ukraine. As we got closer, a red light switched on and the Ukrainian officers came running out of their booths yelling at us to get back.

'Well, that's not normal,' I said, stating the unhelpful obvious. Unbeknown to us, at that exact moment Putin had unleashed an onslaught of missiles on Ukraine, the largest attack on the country since the initial days of the war. Almost a dozen cities had been targeted in the barrage, with strikes at the heart of Kyiv and in areas far from the front line. Putin claimed the attack was retaliation for a Ukrainian blast that had recently destroyed sections of a significant bridge linking Russia to the annexed Crimean peninsula. But Russia had been losing ground on the battlefield for weeks at this point, and the attack also appeared to be an attempt by Putin to silence those in Russia who had been critical of his progress.

As a result of the sudden and deadly flurry of missiles, the Ukrainian border was instantly shut down; partly for safety but also because their technology was being interfered with.

'Well, that's it,' I said to Daniel, 'our trip's over before it's even begun.'

The updates were coming through thick and fast now; the digital map of Ukraine we were consulting was flashing red with air-raid sirens going off, missiles detected and alerts detailing casualties, interceptions and direct hits. The border force officers were trying to get us to return to Poland, but Oleks got out of the car and walked towards them instead. I am still unsure what he said or, honestly, how much he paid, but somehow we were the only vehicle allowed to cross the border at that moment. Ukraine has previously been labelled the most corrupt nation in Europe, and on earlier trips into the country we had heard, through whispers, that before the war some border staff would accept bribes to speed up the customs process. It had been called off when the conflict started out of respect and civil duty, but several months into the war we were given the heads-up: 'Bribes are back on.'

We never did test this theory, and I never asked Oleks what he did to get through the border that day. I didn't have the vocabulary, or the tact. I only knew 'Bonjour' in French and still not a lick of Polish or Ukrainian.

Now that our journey hadn't been completely halted by Putin's onslaught, the attack was suddenly the best thing that could have happened to our trip. After months of the war featuring somewhere in the middle to bottom of the news bulletin — if at all — the story had just rocketed up to the lead spot for every network in the world, and we were right at the heart of it. While international networks were struggling to get into the country, we were already there. From a news point of view, we were in the perfect place at the perfect time.

'Hello, my friends!'

Petro greeted us on the Ukrainian side of the border with open arms and his trademark smile, but the war had clearly changed him. It was more noticeable with him than anyone else we had dealings with. The months of conflict had taken his free spirit and reckless style, and flipped it. He was more cautious and more paranoid; his car had been upgraded to something more reliable, his outfit was more professional, though he seemed to be smoking more than ever. He was dressed head to toe in black, and even his Glock was in a proper holster worn proudly around his waist. As we piled our bags into his boot, I noticed he had also acquired a helmet and vest, which he had never bothered with in the past. I wondered, and still do, what he had witnessed in those months between our trips.

We said goodbye to Oleks who was heading back to Poland,

and Daniel, myself, Aleks and Petro continued on. When we arrived in Lviv, we went straight to our normal hotel to check in. Electricity was completely cut off as a result of the strikes on infrastructure, and people were on edge. The cellphone networks were also down and so communication was fraught. Families who were split up didn't know if their loved ones were safe, and students at university in Lviv hadn't been able to contact their parents in the hotspots to check they were okay. For the first time we were wearing our protective gear in Lviv, and it felt like there really were no more safe havens in the country. Our stocks of cash would have to fund our existence until the card machines were back up and operating, and Daniel would joke, 'Just some walking-about money' while fanning a wad of 500 hryvnia bills and stuffing them in a puffer-vest pocket before we headed out anywhere. There was virtually nothing to eat, but Petro managed to find a place that had some cold beetroot soup up for grabs and he was far too excited about it.

We drove on to Kyiv the next morning, to where a missile had struck a playground in the central city. It had left a huge crater, as deep as I am tall (about 180 cm), and when we arrived it was cordoned off, but barely. The local children were playing in it as if it was a great new backyard attraction, and I watched as two young boys held plastic guns and pretended to fire at each other from either side of the crater. Ten metres away, a perfectly good playground stood unused. The faces of the parents watching alongside me told the real story. They were gripping their prams with intensity, struggling to compute how this was real life.

'We had been playing here an hour before,' one mother told me, pointing to her son and referencing the playground. 'It's one of our favourites.' My mind was crowded with images of my own nieces and nephews playing on the local slides and monkey bars around New Zealand, and it seemed completely incomprehensible that their innocent and happy childhoods could ever be so cruelly shattered as they had been here.

It was getting late and dark, so we set up to quickly film some pieces to camera.

'Step back a bit,' Daniel instructed from behind the lens, and I shuffled back.

'To the right,' he added, and I shuffled again.

'Nah, actually take a decent step right,' he went again, still playing around to get the shot framed just right.

I moved as instructed and felt the ground give way beneath my right foot. I dropped, at high speed, down a manhole that had been covered in debris, stifling a squeal in an attempt not to draw any extra attention to myself — as if that were possible given I was now essentially doing the splits, which, let me assure you, is not something I am capable of doing. The metal lid to the manhole was now lopsided, crushing the one leg and half of my torso that was dangling underground, while my other leg was poking up out the top and my arms flailed around for help. It was unbelievably embarrassing to come to the site of a missile strike and almost die falling down a manhole. Aleks rushed to lift the metal covering off and free my leg, while Daniel yanked at my arm and got me out before I fell down the hole completely.

'Right, are you ready?' Daniel asked, hoisting the camera up again. 'Because the light is almost gone . . .'

'Yep, shall I take a step to the left instead, maybe?'

Jakub took over the driving in Kyiv. He was tall, dark and talkative, and very proud of his armoured vehicle. He had every reason to be. It was like something Jay-Z and Beyoncé would use. The back seats were cream leather and on either side there were holders for flasks, glasses and cocktail shakers, with flashing lights on the ceiling and huge speakers all around. The doors were incredibly heavy and the glass was six centimetres thick. I think I said the words 'I feel invincible.'

Anthony Connell, a New Zealander I had been introduced to, was running a de-mining programme in the north, and I had arranged for us to spend the day with him and his teams, travelling around liberated areas and watching the mine clearance process. Jakub drove to a town not far from Chernihiv where families were wanting to return to their homes now that the Russians had withdrawn, but couldn't due to the risk of unexploded ordinance or landmines left to torture them. In some areas, Russian soldiers had booby-trapped homes on their way out; a final act of spite and destruction. It was a stark reminder of the impact of war, that long after the final missile was launched the suffering and disruption to life would continue.

A car in front of us kept braking suddenly, and although there was a safe distance between us and them Jakub kept shaking his head.

'It's so dangerous of them,' he explained. 'This truck is so heavy, five tonnes, it takes so long to slow down.' Heavy or not, Daniel and I were loving every minute, travelling in luxury we'd never experienced before, let alone in Ukraine. I was almost a bit sad when the drive was over and we got out to start filming.

'We've had reports of something down this gully,' one of the de-mining team, Ryan Napier, explained to us as we all pulled on our protective gear.

'Very nice,' Aleks said, looking at my helmet.

'It's a fancy Special Forces one, I think, with covers for the ears,' I replied, like an idiot explaining the difference between a lion and a giraffe to a zookeeper.

'Exactly right,' he replied, and I was so chuffed he was impressed with my kit that I disregarded his sly 'You don't say' smile.

We were standing on a road with houses just 50 metres away from us on either side, and two young children came riding past us on their bikes, rubbernecking at what we were doing. We descended down the side of the road, pushing through the foliage of the gully, until we found it: a huge rocket embedded in the ground right in front of us.

'Anyone who says they're not nervous when doing a job like this is probably lying,' Ryan said, and I took that as permission to move very slowly from then on. The rocket had been fired and had hit the ground at high speed, but clearly hadn't exploded as intended. Now it sat exposed, and still a major threat. If it was to be interfered with, touched or moved, it could still activate as intended, and the intent was deadly.

De-mining teams would be called to rockets like this one to assess it and attempt to disable or dispose of it, and if they couldn't do so immediately they would clearly cordon it off until they could return with the necessary equipment. It was no wonder that so many people were too frightened to return to their homes, and it was awful to see how the Russians could still hold so many lives to ransom, even in liberated areas.

As we moved from place to place, we passed the trenches of warfare — long dugouts stretching through paddocks, with logs piled on top of each other and built into the sides like retaining walls. The Ukrainian trenches were shockingly close to the Russian positions, and it became clear why there were so many explosives in this area. Our final stop of the day was a sunflower field. It was extensive and ready for harvest, but no tractor would go anywhere near it out of fear of the lethal threat hidden within. Desperate to sell their crops for some much-needed cash, some farmers had been bravely mowing their fields with bulletproof vests on, as if that would be enough to save them if they hit a surprise gift from the enemy; but for many it was a suicidal roll of the dice they couldn't afford either.

As we pulled up to the edge of the field, Ryan got out to do an initial inspection. He returned after half an hour and called off the operation without inviting us any closer.

'It's far more dangerous than we thought; there are scattered mines everywhere in there.' They would need to return with a more specialist team for something this extreme.

There was so much work to be done, but by its very nature it was a painstakingly slow task; not something that could be rushed, not something you wanted to risk getting wrong.

'How bloody shit is Russia?' one of the workmen said to me.

I had been messaging with a man named Nikita, who had been recommended to me by other networks on the ground in Ukraine. Nikita was someone we could hire as a local producer; a role known as a 'fixer', which does pretty much sum it up. A fixer can make your life a thousand times easier, even just by making calls on your behalf so you don't have to struggle through the language barrier. They are also armed with invaluable local knowledge. For example, if you wanted to film at a school they would know where all of the schools were and which would be the best one to film at; they might also have a number for the principal or know someone whose children went to the school so you could get the number through them. They would also know things like how to get to the school via a different road when you discovered that the main bridge to it had been bombed, or, if they're really good, they'd already know the bridge had been bombed and would have taken you the right way from the beginning. A fixer also helps to break down the cultural barrier, and in the east of Ukraine, where a lot of Russian sympathisers live, this is crucial.

I'd had a brief phone call with Nikita to discuss our plans for heading towards the front line the next day, and I was confident we were on the same page. 'It's very noisy there,' he kept repeating, warning of the constant bombs, 'but that is where the story is. I will show you some good places and we will talk to the right people.'

'Great, that's what we're after.'

'Okay. And you are feeling brave?'

'Yes, all good to go; we'll leave at 8 a.m.?'

'Okay see you then, Miss Lisette,' in his thick accent that to my novice ear sounded a little more Russian than Ukrainian.

The phone rang that night while we were editing our story. It was the usual gang of The Sarahs plus our friends at CNN who always had an overview of our plans and offered advice and support where possible. At this point Newshub and CNN were owned by the same parent company, and obviously the CNN crew were far more comfortable operating in hostile environments than we were. In the spirit of newsroom camaraderie they were very generous with their support, regularly sharing their contacts and knowledge, and we relied on them heavily for guidance before and during deployments. We had a call like this every night; a check-in to debrief any issues from the day we'd just had, and to try to iron out any potential issues for the day to come. Tomorrow was a big day, so this was always going to be a long phone call and I fired up

Zoom with a hot coffee in hand while Daniel carried on with the edit.

'You do the talking and fill me in after,' he said, as was our usual approach.

The plan for the next day was to head to Kharkiv, a city in the far east. From there we would be able to travel around to various hotspots, to report on recently liberated towns, like Izyum, and get closer to the front line than we had been before. Kharkiv would be our base. It was the second-biggest city in Ukraine, a regional capital, and while it had dealt with a lot of bombing it had resisted Russian occupation. It seemed the safest place to work from for the week. Nikita was eager to get to the east, the area he knew best and where he knew the best stories were, and I was right there with him. Even Aleks and Petro were making noises about us being too far away from the action currently; but as well-meaning as it was, they didn't seem to realise that in order for us to get anywhere 'exciting' I had to jump through a lot of hoops with the group on the other end of this Zoom: who were now demanding details and plans.

I ran through our proposed movements to murmurs of approval, and despite a red flag raised over the fact we should probably have *two* armoured vehicles with us in case something went wrong with the one we currently had, it all seemed to be okay. I dismissed the concerns about cars, thinking that even one armoured vehicle was a bit over the top, and the call ended. But within five minutes, the phone rang. The Sarahs.

'We've had a conversation, and we don't want you going tomorrow,' Sarah Bristow said.

'What do you mean?'

'We think you need a better plan — more thorough, with more detail around exactly where you're going and what your purpose for being there is,' she continued.

I reacted poorly. I had spent hours planning this trip, I thought pretty thoroughly, but there is only so much detail you can provide when talking about finding a story in a war zone.

'Well, I can hardly give you street names and pre-arrange interviews with people whose houses are going to be bombed between now and then . . .' I responded with far too much attitude. I could picture the frustrated faces of the security guys when I'd have to tell them we were staying longer in Kyiv, and I couldn't bear it. They'd be rightfully snarky over the lack of need for a security team if we were nowhere near the action, and I was also sick of trying to find a story in a city that was literally hours and hours away from the front line. It felt disingenuous, and was actually harder work than going to the centre of the action where the stories were overwhelming in their numbers.

'I think you just need to spend the day tomorrow working with the fixer and putting together a plan so that when we speak next, it's clear where exactly you are going, how long you'll spend there and what you want to achieve there.'

My eyes were stinging with tears, but only from exasperation. I didn't want to stay in Kyiv any longer. I wanted to get to the story in the east, tell it, and get out of the country without wasting any more valuable time.

'This is ridiculous and should have been raised days ago if there was a concern,' I snapped back; and as I did, I knew I was overstepping with the sass.

'Lisette, you are in a war zone . . . you need to have a proper plan.'

I had to resist the urge to slam the lid of the laptop down and end the meeting right there and then. Out of everyone on the call I thought it fair to assume that we were the most aware of where we were, what with the constant trips to bomb shelters and having just spent the day face-to-face with unexploded rockets, but I was also rattled by the implication that I was being reckless or hasty in any way. In retrospect, I've realised that often those in New Zealand were actually far more hyper-aware of the risks than we were, whether that was family members or The Sarahs. While we had slowly started to adjust to our environment, for them there was still nothing 'normal' about all of this and there really shouldn't have been for us either.

'Fine, we'll talk tomorrow,' I said, eventually hanging up the call.

Daniel looked up from the edit.

'I think I went too far . . .' I said, looking back at him for reassurance.

'Yeah, probably,' he said in response.

He might as well have pushed the nuclear button himself. His casual comment triggered the previously mentioned biggest tantrum of my career. A full noise explosion of frustration. 'Well you could have had my back!'

I knew I'd pushed too hard, first with the bosses and now with Daniel, but the only thing that had the power to calm me down and take a few deep breaths that evening was my upcoming live cross into New Zealand's morning news.

The next day, my bad attitude cooling and tears dry, Nikita arrived — ready and set for the front line.

'Change of plan,' I said after introducing myself.

'What is that?'

'Take a seat, get a coffee; we'll be here for a while.'

For the next five hours we worked with Nikita to make the most painfully detailed, colour-coordinated schedule you've ever seen. Every minute of every day for the next week was broken down.

'Then we'll leave for breakfast . . . and how long will it take for us to drive to the first petrol station?' I would say out loud as I jotted it all into the document.

'We're not in the army. We are not your soldiers,' Nikita would argue, and he was right of course — but I wasn't going to give The Sarahs another reason to delay us. By the end of the day, Nikita was furious with me, fed up with my demand for detail and possibly contemplating quitting the job altogether. We had also entered into a strange silent competition, seemingly hell-bent on drinking each other under the table with coffee.

It was early afternoon before Daniel and I rallied to start filming the day's story. There had been drone and missile strikes in the centre of the city, only about ten minutes from us, and we decided to head in that direction. We left Nikita to have some much-needed time alone and jumped into the car with Jakub and Aleks to head to the site for some filming. A mostly glass skyrise building that had been hit was in complete disarray, with its windows blown out and its metal skeleton left blackened and burnt, and we followed the dried droplets of blood to the heart of the blast. The entire complex was deserted, of course, and cars had been left to the rats; their windscreens shattered, with pieces of metal and hunks of tree strewn across their roofs and bonnets and shrapnel slicing into the bodywork. It looked more like the scene of a tsunami than a bomb blast.

'This is great,' I said.

'Yeah, fucking incredible,' Daniel agreed, both momentarily trading our humanity for work mode, which was always far easier to do when there were only broken buildings, and not faces, all around.

Our enthusiasm was cut short by the sound of an air-raid siren.

‘Oh you’ve got to be kidding me,’ I said. The warning of another incoming missile should perhaps have elicited more fear than it did, but I was mostly frustrated at the fresh delay to our already arduous day.

‘Let’s just crank this out quickly and then we can bail to the shelter,’ Daniel said, and I couldn’t have agreed more. We didn’t have much more to film and then we’d have everything we needed to start scripting and editing. The risk seemed worth it and Aleks nodded his permission. I think we were all embracing the ‘lightning doesn’t strike the same place twice’ law of reason.

It didn’t take long for me to spot the droplets of blood that weren’t dry anymore. Fresh red dots followed me across the ground; I swore they hadn’t been there last time I looked.

‘What the hell? Who’s bleeding?’ I said, with only a mild amount of panic. It wasn’t much blood but it was enough to take note of.

‘Ahh, Daniel!’ Aleks said, pointing. Sure enough, somehow Dan had cut his hand on some glass and was now trailing around the missile strike site with a fresh wound. ‘We have a major casualty!’ Aleks said humorously, jumping into action with an intensity you’d expect to see only on the battlefield. It was a scene worthy of a hearty chuckle: the three of us, standing in a bomb site with an air-raid siren sounding while a man who’d spent two decades in the Special Forces applied a sticky plaster to Daniel’s injured pinkie finger.

‘Ow,’ Daniel offered, and we howled with laughter.

‘Thank goodness you are here with your first-aid kit, Aleks,’ I said.

‘Exactly right,’ he replied.

That evening, we got the green light.

'We've looked at the schedule you sent through — it's great, thank you, you're good to go,' Sarah Bristow said.

'Okay, great.'

'I'm sorry it took a bit longer than you wanted, but it was important we got this right and you guys were safe and prepared,' she added, and I was simultaneously embarrassed at the reminder of how worked-up I had been the day before, and grateful for the mutual lowering of arms. We hung up the phone to a chorus of 'Keep us updated, our phones are always on loud so don't worry about waking us up' from The Sarahs, who were still carrying on with the precious pantomime of pretending they slept a wink when we were in Ukraine.

Part of the very improved plan was a second armoured vehicle and driver so we could travel in convoy and have a backup. No one wanted to be stranded in a dangerous position because of a flat tyre or an engine breakage, so an extra car was never going to be a bad idea even though I seriously doubted we'd need it. Daniel, myself, Aleks and Jakub would travel in front in the Beyoncé-mobile, and Petro and Nikita would travel in the second car with a new driver, also called Nikita. He was a short hulk of a man, with more muscle than he knew what to do with; although that is not entirely fair or true, because it was eventually revealed to us that he was also a part-time deep-muscle masseuse. He knew exactly what to do with all that hulk.

'Lucky wife,' I said, and Daniel shot me a look. 'Oh, I'm just *saying . . .*'

The new Nikita was a Ukrainian man in his mid-thirties, again with a friendly face and again with very little grasp of the English language. The car he drove was a square black box and its previous life was instantly evident: a vault on wheels, it was clearly usually used to transport money between banks. 'Where do they find these vehicles?' I asked no one in particular when I saw it.

It was a long drive to Kharkiv, around six hours, and Daniel and I were looking forward to some uninterrupted sleep. We nestled into our plush seats in the back and hadn't been on the highway long before we were both sound asleep. The long stretch of straight road carried a steady flow of traffic made up of NGO vehicles, aid trucks, military convoys, soldiers, media cars which looked a lot like ours, and a smattering of local vehicles which were the sort of small rickety cars that even I wouldn't have tried to convince the dodgy mechanic down the road from my old flat in Auckland to give a warrant of fitness to.

I don't know what woke me up. I don't know if it was instinct. I don't know if it was the screech of tyres. I don't know if it was Jakub shouting 'FUCK FUCK FUCK!' . . . I don't know if I was even awake before the braking began. But all of a sudden I was flying through the air, crashing into the centre console as our car torpedoed towards the one in front and slammed into it with a life-ending bang.

It was a little red car, and our huge bumper was now embedded in the side of it. Our bonnet was crumpled up like an accordion and smoke was creeping out from underneath it forebodingly, but all I could see was the little red car in front of me and I couldn't look away. I couldn't look away from the two people who now sat lifeless in the front seats, contorted and not moving, as oil and blood leaked on to the road beside them. Aleks and Jakub were out of our car within seconds, but Daniel and I just sat in the back, staring forward in shock, hypnotised by the sound of the horn of the little red car. It was constant, and ringing out in a way that has cost me more sleep than any air-raid siren ever did.

They were dead. Two people were dead. A man and a woman, and they looked older in age. Were they married? Where were they going? Where had they come from? Who were they? Do they have children? They were dead. My thoughts were spiralling and none of them were helpful.

'I think we need to get out of the car, it's smoking,' Daniel eventually managed, and it blinked me back to semi-reality.

'Okay,' I replied, turning to the door.

While Daniel and I were operating in slow motion, we were surrounded by people far too experienced with situations like this, and they had sprung into action at triple speed. Military vehicles had blocked the road from oncoming traffic; Aleks was there, front and centre, assessing the little red car and trying to get to the couple, and a group of medics had pulled over to offer their assistance. They pulled the man out of the driver's seat and laid him on the road. He wasn't moving.

We were standing to the side watching in horror when Petro came rushing over to us. 'Are you okay?' he asked in a panic, and starting squeezing my arms as if trying to convince himself that I was alive.

'Yes, we're fine,' we replied.

Nikita the friendly masseuse arrived at our sides not long after. 'Okay?' he asked, in his broken English.

'Yes, absolutely fine,' we replied, growingly increasingly uncomfortable with the number of people checking on us as two people lay dying, if not already dead, in front of us.

'I don't have my phone,' I mumbled.

'What?' Daniel said.

'I don't have my phone. It's in the car.'

'Okay, let's go get it,' he replied with a calmness I will forever be grateful for. We walked back in the direction of the wreckage just as Aleks moved to the passenger's side of the little red car with his new medic friend and started to lift the woman out. It took us what felt like an age to find my phone; it had flown to the front of the car and was hiding out of sight, but the search gave me something to focus on amid the shock and I was grateful for that also. By the time we had retrieved my phone, the woman had been placed next to the man on the ground and while I was certain the driver was dead, I could have sworn I saw her leg twitch.

'Her leg is moving!' I said to Daniel, as Aleks dropped into a push-up position with his ear on her chest, listening for any sign of breath.

'I think major internal injuries,' Nikita the fixer added in his typical matter-of-fact tone.

My phone started to ring, and Sarah Bristow's name appeared on the screen just as the first black body bag appeared.

'Are you okay?' she asked.

'Yes, we're fine,' I assured her, already feeling like a broken record.

One of the security team had provided a basic report to the group chat, but we filled in some of the gaps for her as best we could. 'They were driving the opposite direction down the highway to us, but they were doing a U-turn and seem to have pulled out in front of our car at the last minute,' Daniel explained.

'The man is in a body bag, the woman might be alive . . .' I said. 'There's an ambulance here now but I don't think she will survive.' I can't imagine how shocking it was to hear this through the phone in the middle of the night, and the call was kept short. Mostly because there was so little to say other than more pleas from Sarah to call anytime and more assurances from us that we were okay and we would.

As we hung up, Aleks started walking towards us, peeling off blood-covered gloves. 'Okay, are you okay?' he asked.

'Yes. Are you?'

'Yes! Of course!' he said, as if it was just another day at work. 'It's not good, not good. They are not good. But we have to go now.'

'Okay . . .'

'We will go in the other car. Jakub will stay here to talk to police. Nikita will drive us to Kharkiv. We will get another car to come and collect Petro and other Nikita and they will catch up with us in Kharkiv tonight.'

I couldn't fathom how he had formed this plan among all of his other responsibilities in the last half-hour, but we nodded in agreement and piled into the vault. It was tiny, and we were squashed in tightly. That wasn't a problem but it did bring my attention to the ache in the side of my hip and I shuffled around to get comfortable, knowing we still had hours of driving ahead of us.

It wasn't often that Daniel and I sat in total silence, but I don't remember anything being said for some time. We had been bundled away at such pace that I hadn't even had a chance to say goodbye to Jakub or check *he* was okay, and we definitely had not had enough time to process what we had just witnessed. I couldn't make sense of the fact we were just back on the road, carrying on with our journey, after such a monumental event. It felt as though the little red car had been treated as a speed bump on our mission and it made me dry-retch with guilt. But what else was there to do? It wasn't safe to just stand around and talk about it, and now more than ever it felt like we had to get to the front line and tell the stories that desperately needed telling, to make this all worth it. As soon as I had that thought I scolded myself — because, of course, nothing was worth two lives.

My internal battle was still raging as we pulled into a petrol station forecourt. 'We need to stop and wait here,' Aleks explained. 'The missiles have started again up ahead, and it's not safe to go any further right now. We will wait and when we get clearance, we will continue driving.'

He was back on track with our mission as if nothing had happened. Aleks was the ultimate professional, and the past few hours had proven just how valuable he was to our team. He might not have had Dmitry's eyes, but he was very impressive and despite us heading towards our most dangerous destination yet, he managed to make us feel safer than ever.

Waiting at the petrol station was a bizarre, almost out-of-body experience. Nikita the masseuse ordered a full meal and got stuck in, and I went to the bathroom. 'Shit,' I said, spotting in the mirror a hand-sized welt appearing on my hip, bruised and swollen already.

When I returned to the forecourt Aleks had bought us each a coffee and a hotdog, which Daniel didn't look at all interested in eating. I was still jittery from the crash, but drank the coffee for something to do and filmed a selfie video about the hotdogs for a behind-the-scenes story I was compiling for *The Project*.

'What the fuck am I doing?' I asked myself out loud.

'Yeah, this is pretty fucked,' Daniel said.

'I'm talking nonsense into a camera about a hotdog while we wait for the missiles to stop so we can continue to the front line having just killed two people.'

It felt even worse than it sounded.

'We have to tell the best stories of our life here, Daniel.'

'I know,' he replied, and I could tell he'd already thought the same thing.

Halfway through the final stretch of driving to Kharkiv

that evening, Aleks turned around: 'I have just heard from Jakub. The man who was driving did not have a licence, because of poor eyesight. It wasn't Jakub's fault.' I was relieved for Jakub, who was a good man and would no doubt be feeling dreadful, but I also couldn't help but think the only reason someone like that would get behind a wheel would be to escape the nightmare of war, and that's exactly where the little red car had been coming from.

When we pulled into Kharkiv that evening it was getting dark, but it was darker than normal. A blackout was being enforced across the city and there were no lights on at all. It was both an attempt to conserve electricity, as the attacks on energy infrastructure continued, and to avoid any unwanted attention from drones.

I had booked for us to stay at a high-end hotel in central Kharkiv that Aleks had requested for various reasons. Some of his colleagues had stayed there, he was happy with its internal bomb shelter and the materials it was made out of, and it was also well-regarded among media as a good base. But as we pulled up to the hotel I had an awful sinking feeling. The towering building was completely boarded up, with no one in sight; and the way this day had gone I was convinced that I had also now booked us into a hotel that had shut up shop months ago.

Aleks jumped out of the car to go looking for answers and, like the hero he was, returned within minutes having found them. As we drove around the side of the hotel to a ramp that led underground to the basement, I was relieved for something to have finally gone right. A fancy doorman was waiting for us at the elevator and ushered us quickly into the hotel, where the lights were on but dimmed. We made it to the lobby and the check-in desk, and handed over our passports as I struggled to take in our surroundings. You could tell the hotel was expensive: it was dripping in chandeliers and luxurious gold trimmings and velvet chaise longue chairs. It was designed like a doughnut, with all the rooms around the outside, so when you stood in the lobby you could look all the way up to the ceiling and see every floor of the hotel in between. But every floor was near-empty and the chandeliers weren't glowing as brightly as they were designed to.

We were handed our room keys, shown the way to the bomb shelter, and told to keep our blinds drawn. It was quiet; anyone you did cross paths with was whispering in soft tones and mentally categorising us: 'Media.'

We did the same back. 'Aid workers.'

Months later, the hotel was bombed in what was reported as a 'revenge' attack by Putin. Twenty-eight people were injured. There were rumours that Ukrainian soldiers had been staying there prior to the attack — always something that would prompt us to move out pretty quickly — but reading the news made me think of all the incredibly kind staff we had met there, who greeted us with such warmth and professionalism amid such difficult times.

The evening work call went a bit differently that night. There were more-important people joining than usual: the boss's big boss had logged on, along with a representative from HR, wanting to check we were okay.

'Yes, we're fine,' I heard myself saying yet again. We were reminded of the requirement to engage in therapy sessions at the end of every trip to Ukraine, and we nodded that we knew and we would. Then came an instruction from a member of the CNN team that was jarring in tone, but necessary and, honestly, welcome: 'Right, you need to forget about it now.'

We knew exactly what he meant. It was not the time to wallow, or even to process what had happened. There was no way we would ever forget it and obviously we would need to address it eventually, but right now we couldn't afford any distractions. We needed to be fully focused on the job in order to keep each other safe and get the stories we came for.

An hour later we stood in the hotel lobby, going live into *The Nation*. Both of us were wearing the hotel-provided slippers that we had been thrilled to discover upon check-in. My hip was swelling up larger by the minute and Daniel had finally revealed that his neck had seen better days; the little added comfort and the cheap laugh of those hotel slippers was a much-needed reprieve. After the cross we each retreated to our own room, knowing that tomorrow would probably be an even bigger day than today. I showered quickly so as not to be caught out naked when an air-raid siren sounded and then started the agonising process of drying my hair. It was agonising because I would turn off the hair dryer every ten seconds or so, having convinced myself it was drowning out the sound of sound of a siren.

When I finally completed my hair routine, I found a WhatsApp message from Daniel: 'I'll wait for you on the stairwell when the siren sounds.'

'Yes, great,' I typed back.

'But just get to the middle of the hotel as quick as you can. The glass will do the most damage. Even if it's not a direct hit, if it hits two or three blocks away, the windows will still explode into your room from the shockwave. That's my TED talk.'

'Thanks for that.'

'Sleep well.'

It was my sister's birthday when I woke up, and I was delighted that Putin had honoured the occasion with no strikes near us overnight so we'd managed to sleep through without any shelter time. Petro and Nikita the fixer had now rejoined us, and after the trauma of the day before we were determined to make today a successful one. Our first stop was a central park where humanitarian aid was being given out to residents. There were 300 people lining up when we arrived, and that was the maximum allowed. The need was much greater, but there had been attacks on people waiting for aid in the past and the organisers didn't want to risk becoming a target so they kept the numbers capped. It was freezing and families were lined up in their warmest clothes, waiting patiently for their free bag of oats. I smiled at a mother standing in line who was cradling a baby to her chest. 'She was born in the shelter, when the bombs dropped,' she told us, and I was shocked as I thought to myself that her story had become a familiar one.

There was a new deadly threat facing Ukrainians — and that was the winter. With houses destroyed during eight months of brutal fighting, and Putin now aggressively targeting the power infrastructure, the cold weather was making life even harder for already vulnerable communities. But Kharkiv was tough. Within 24 hours of the war, Russian troops had reached the northern suburbs. The Ukrainian city was close to the Russian border, so it was easy and fast to get to. Also, its mayor publicly opposed Zelensky so Putin had been counting on an easy win. That wasn't the case. While more than 1000 civilians were said to have been killed in the fierce battle that followed, eventually Putin's men had been forced to exit and Kharkiv had kept its freedom. Nearly half of the 1.4 million residents had left, though, and the city felt lonely. The scale of destruction was breathtaking, with whole apartment buildings destroyed and left abandoned, and teddy bears and children's shoes strewn outside their bombed homes.

As we walked around the deserted streets we spotted a middle-aged lady emerging from an underground bunker. Her name was Lina. Nikita stepped in to start translating, and told us how she had hidden in the basement with her dog for ten days during the worst of the strikes, and now her four-legged friend was too frightened to return to the real world so she came back here to feed him every day. Lina walked us towards her apartment, where she had lived for 32 years, and when we arrived at an obliterated building she pointed towards the top and a blackened slab of concrete.

'That's it,' Nikita said. 'That was her home.'

Lina's dog was far from the only frightened animal in Kharkiv. Many pets were left behind when people fled, and they cowered under cars and buildings everywhere. We said goodbye to Lina and drove to another suburb where we knew there had been constant bombardments. There were no people in sight but cats everywhere, and Nikita turned to us: 'I have a good story for you.' He walked towards a basement hatch where the cats were gathering and knocked politely. A woman named Natalia Pasternak emerged from behind the concrete wall. She was short and dressed warmly, but looked exhausted and suspicious. They spoke for ten minutes or so before Nikita came back over.

'She says if we buy her some cat food, she will do the interview. I'm telling you, it will be worth it.'

'Okay, no worries, we can get some cat food.'

'Okay — come on quickly before she changes her mind.'

We followed Nikita towards the woman. Natalia didn't wait for introductions. She turned on her heel and led us through her underground maze where she had lived for eight months while the Russians were shelling her home. She had refused to evacuate even when aid workers came to save her, staying there to look after all of the neighbourhood pets that had been left behind. The basement walls had been covered in blankets, hanging like curtains to separate areas of the concrete cave. Natalia showed us the 'kitchen' where she cooked, which was really just a table with some pots and a kettle. It was filthy and freezing everywhere and she took us through one partition to reveal hundreds of animals, mostly cats, snuggled up for warmth next to each other. She stroked their fur and lifted some of them up to show us while I blinked away my shock. Firewood was Natalia's only option for heating and she was frantically stockpiling kindling. I prayed she would survive the winter. We thanked her profusely for showing us her home and sharing her story, and we promised to return with some food for the cats; and we did, although I felt we should really have been finding her something to eat as well.

Nikita was pleased with himself. 'That was good, yes?'

'Yeah, that was good.' But for once my feelings aligned more with those of Petros, who looked pale at what he was seeing of his own country.

As we drove out of the suburb, we passed a large brick building that had clearly been bombed incessantly. The metal structure remained standing with scorched brick crumbling off it, but there was no roof and there was rubble and debris everywhere. 'That was a high school,' Nikita said casually.

'Let's stop,' I decided. You could easily have convinced me it was a Hollywood film set. The overturned classroom desks, burnt and discarded, the lessons taught here far more chilling than what the students had signed up for. Daniel and I headed straight into what used to be the school corridor to start filming, but I could hear bickering behind me and it shocked me just as much as my surroundings. It was Petro, worried about us being inside the building without a helmet on, arguing with Aleks who didn't consider it a great risk as long as we were quick. A world where *Petro* was pushing the health and safety agenda and being the cautious one in the group was so unfamiliar that it reminded me yet again that the impacts of war went far beyond brick and mortar.

By the time we finished filming at the school, and at the nearby kindergarten where children's toys were scattered among the shattered glass and a broken globe lay on the floor in a sad symbol of the state of our world, I knew we had more than enough content for the day's story and we headed back to our palatial hotel base to start the evening routine. Daniel had been speaking to the receptionist about getting access to the roof for our live crosses. It wasn't great television to film from inside a fancy hotel lobby but we couldn't be out on the street after curfew, so the compromise would be to stand on the roof of the hotel, which would technically still be within the rules.

'He's very helpful. Keeps saying it will be okay for us to make a "movie" on the roof,' Daniel reported back with a chuckle. 'But it's bloody pitch-black out there.'

'Are we going to be okay?'

'Yeah, just hope we don't attract a drone strike,' he said, his chuckle morphing into a nervous laugh.

'We'll just keep the light off until the last minute.'

Daniel set up the camera in the darkness and we called through to Auckland to get ready for the technical checks with the studio.

'Can't see much, can you flick on a light?' they asked us a few minutes before our cross.

'No thank you,' we replied. 'We'll turn it on when you give us the 30-second call.'

Those next few minutes were long and painful. Standing on the roof in negative degrees and darkness, Daniel and I were staring at the sky, pointing out glimmers of light up above and asking 'Drone? Or star?' on repeat. Once the live started, though, it was easy to ignore the fear and just talk, even with the light shining brightly, but as soon as it was finished we packed up and got inside as quickly as possible.

The tortured town of Izyum was about 50 kilometres from the front line and had recently been liberated. It lay about two hours from Kharkiv so should have been an easy day trip for us, but nothing is easy in a war zone. The roads were abandoned except for the military tanks that still sat in the forest on either side, and there were signs everywhere warning of landmines.

We had driven for about 45 minutes when we hit our first major roadblock; the bridge we needed to cross had been exploded and we needed to find a new way. Izyum had lived under Russian occupation for months and there were reports of mass graves and torture chambers, which Nikita the fixer had arranged for us to film at. We had stocked the car with masks and Vicks VapoRub to put under our noses, to help with the smell of dead bodies, and we had been advised to buy a stash of chocolate bars because sometimes even a simple sugar rush can help alleviate the depression around you. We had plenty of water too, although I wasn't going near it. We were on strict instructions not to leave the road because of landmines, and told the safest place to stand on the road was in the tyre tracks of our own vehicle, land we had driven over already without hitting anything lethal. It meant the boys would get out of the car, stand in the tyre tracks and turn around to relieve themselves with ease, while I was left to battle with my bursting bladder, knowing any shot of privacy behind a bush or tree was out of the question. Squatting behind the car didn't excite me much.

Nikita managed to find access to Izyum and we drove on in hope. Eventually, houses with four walls started to become the odd ones out and we knew we were getting closer. If they weren't blown up completely, the buildings were scarred with holes from artillery fire. In the town square, people were gathering, slowly, meandering past destroyed buildings, sandbag barricades and craters caused by shrapnel in the ground. I wondered what they were all doing when suddenly a truck pulled up and everyone started running towards it, fighting for a free loaf of bread. One woman, grasping her bread, told us through tears that Putin's men had tried to take her brother's car but he had fought back, so he had been taken, beaten and interrogated for three days before being killed.

'I feel like I'm going to have a heart attack,' she told us. Strangely, Nikita, staring at me intensely through his aviator glasses, dismissed it entirely. 'I'm not sure you can believe her,' he said.

'Why not?' I asked.

'She has no proof.'

More than 400 bodies had been found in a mass grave in Izyum and Nikita agreed we could head there next. We had been driving for 30 minutes and something didn't feel right, so we pulled over and I asked 'How much further are we going? This feels like a long way out of the town.'

'I am trying to find the cemetery,' he replied.

'We need to go to the mass grave,' I said, 'like what we discussed in Kyiv . . . remember?'

'Yes, cemetery, where you bury dead people.'

'No, not a normal cemetery,' I said, growing increasingly

suspicious. 'The mass grave where the bodies were dumped.'

'That sounds to me like a cemetery,' he said, 'and I don't know where it is, but I know someone who might. Follow my lead.'

I got back in the car with Daniel, Aleks and the other Nikita behind the wheel.

'Something is off with him,' I said. 'He is suddenly insistent that there is no mass grave, but a couple of days ago he said he had it all planned.'

'He's giving off Russian vibes,' Daniel agreed.

Aleks nodded, and so did friendly Nikita.

'He is speaking Russian,' Aleks confirmed, and I think deep down I had known it since the beginning. The team had not been totally at ease around Nikita since he'd joined, and I'd had a feeling it was because of the language. While almost everyone in Ukraine could speak Russian and the languages had long been interchangeable, the use of it had dropped off substantially since the war started, as part of the continued resistance. Nikita speaking Russian around everyone was obviously ruffling feathers, but they had been too professional to mention it or raise the issue.

We pulled over to a warehouse and I saw Nikita jump out to speak to a local, presumably asking for directions. We were wasting time, and losing light, and with a long drive ahead we didn't have much longer to film before we'd have to head back to Kharkiv. I stepped out of the car in a huff and on a mission to find out what was going on, and accidentally pushed the alert button on my phone. This triggered a series of processes all around the world to check I was okay and not being held hostage or shot at.

'Yes, sorry, false alarm,' I said down the phone, and saw Daniel and Aleks doing the same on theirs. I was mortified at my clumsiness and felt like I was losing control of the day, so I barrelled towards Nikita, rallying my best no-nonsense voice.

'Nikita, do you know where the grave is or not?'

'Listen, Miss Lisette, there is no mass grave. The Ukrainians liberate the area, and when the Russians are all gone, the Ukrainian authorities take all the elderly people who have died naturally over the past few months, and put them together in a graveyard that they dig in the forest, and then they call all the media together and say, "Look at the evil Russians who made a mass grave." But they made it themselves!'

The conspiracy theory was disturbing and knocked me silent for half a second before I remembered we only had 30 minutes before we needed to leave and just one short interview in the camera so far. We had to move fast and there was no time to argue.

'Right, forget the grave. Let's just go to the torture chambers and then get out of here.'

'What torture chambers?' he said in response.

I couldn't believe what I was hearing, and even Aleks shook his head in frustration.

'Everybody knows the torture chambers!' he yelled in support.

The torture chambers had made international headlines and we had discussed them in depth, on multiple occasions, before even arriving in Kharkiv. Nikita had never tried to deny their existence in any of those conversations but now seemed to be suffering a total loss of memory. While evidence of torture had been found in Bucha, the northern city had only been occupied for a month while Izyum had served as a hub for the Russians for closer to seven and there were widespread reports of multiple dedicated torture sites all across the town. One of those discussed in depth was an underground jail cell at the police station which had desperate messages carved into the wall.

'Nikita, we need to go to the police station now.'

'It is not a torture chamber,' he argued.

'What do you mean?'

'Where do you put people that disobey the law? You put them in a prison cell. Do not call that a torture chamber,' he replied.

It was clear now that our work was being sabotaged, and Daniel looked at me with a sense of urgency he didn't often have. 'We need to get moving, Lisette, this is ridiculous. We have to get something on tape.'

He was right. We had been through far too much to get to this point and have Nikita the Russian compromising our coverage. I took it as permission to fire up, pointing at our troublesome fixer like my scary primary school teacher used to do to the naughty kids and raising my voice in front of everyone.

'Listen, Nikita, you need to do exactly what I say now, because you are not in charge here. We need to get back to the town square, and you need to find us one family to speak to and we will do the rest. Understood?'

'Okay, okay,' he said, backing down slightly and getting into the car.

'Good, let's go.'

By the time we made it back to the town square, Aleks had agreed to give us some extra time to work, a full 45 minutes before we'd have to leave. We had no time to muck around. While we filmed at a house where a 'liberated' family were now living in squalor, without food, water or electricity, Nikita managed to find us a mother and her little boy to speak to. Conveniently, the mother had a happy story to share of how the Russian soldiers had given her son lollies.

'Were you ever scared?' I asked her.

'Yes, every day for my life, but as long as my boy was happy,' she said.

'Good interview,' Nikita concluded.

It was a miracle that we got the story we did that day, and in the end I was actually quite pleased with what we had gathered. But I was furious at Nikita. As I sat at the dinner table scripting that night, he stopped by my table with a piece of cheesecake, which, I make clear to anyone who will listen, is my favourite sweet treat. He had likely remembered, at some point during dinner, how he was currently making a living — and how easily word could get out among the media that he was more trouble than he was worth. I took the cheesecake as a peace offering, which I am certain is how it was intended, and he left me to it with a polite smile.

Our days were getting more and more ambitious: longer, busier, and closer to the fighting. I knew Daniel and I were still being both haunted and motivated by the little red car. We wanted to get as close as possible to the front line and Nikita the fixer was happy to lead the way. We were ten kilometres from the Russian border when we saw a group of five or so Ukrainians huddled on the side of the road. Nikita jumped out of the car and started to speak to them, and they looked in our direction and nodded.

'Come on, they will show us their village,' he reported back, and we hastily started pulling on our protective gear. We were following two sisters and a brother, who looked middle-aged, along with their parents and their aunty, who were all elderly. They started walking through a forest which looked to us like exactly the sort of place we shouldn't be heading, given the signs everywhere showing a red skeleton and warnings of mines and booby traps.

'Come, come,' Nikita urged, 'they walk this way every day, they know it is fine and safe.'

Aleks nodded, and we continued forward through the bush and over a railway crossing. Sure enough, we emerged into a clearing and a village stood before us — or what was left of it. It was the aunty's first time back there since it had been liberated. She had fled to safety before Putin's men arrived; now, tears filled her eyes as she saw what had become of her hometown. The houses were battered, many without windows, walls or roofs, and there were tanks in the middle of the streets, left as horrifying new monuments of war. The sister, Rita, pointed out the house where she and her brother Vitali had been born, the primary school they attended, and the church where her family would pray; all now scarred by war, riddled by bullets or completely destroyed by missiles and artillery.

'The man who lived in this house was killed after he was caught helping people to escape,' Vitali told us, pointing to one abandoned house. The Russians had been gone for a couple of weeks by this point, and Vitali and his family were still trying to track down their old neighbours. 'We will take you to our home,' they said and continued to lead the way.

As we walked, the path became more overgrown and less clear. There were signs to the left and right of us warning of mines, and we now seemed to be stomping single-file through more of a field than a street. I could hear the mumblings behind me that we were getting into nervous territory, but I told myself that as long as we stood in the footsteps of the family leading us, we would be okay. The discontent from Petro and Aleks was getting louder and Daniel said, in a warning tone, 'Lisette, this is getting dangerous', but we had come so far that I didn't want to turn around now.

Nikita, for once, was on my side, still doing his utmost to mend our fragile working relationship. 'Their house is just up here, it will be good for your movie,' he promised, and he was right.

We stood outside it in disbelief. The roof had collapsed, the windows were shattered and the fence was riddled with shrapnel and damage from artillery. Aleks wouldn't let us leave the 'path' and so we watched from some distance as the aunty walked up to the house in shock, silently crying. Daniel had remarkably trained the camera on her from afar and was focusing intently on what he was filming. It was the perfect image to explain the tragedy occurring and I knew we had struck gold for our 'movie'.

'No one move,' Aleks said out of nowhere, pointing to the ground, and Petro turned a ghostly white.

'What is it?' I asked.

'It is a landmine,' Aleks replied, with a growl that told me I'd put us all at risk.

'Oh shit.'

Petro was starting to fret and Aleks was trying to calm him down. Daniel was still filming and I was making sure he didn't step an inch either way, now terrified that his worst nightmare was about to come true and already imagining having to explain to his mum that her eldest son had lost both his legs because I wanted a stupid shot of a house. Vitali had sensed the panic and walked over, entering the conversation with a lot of wild gesturing and Ukrainian ramblings. The languages were flying and everyone was getting very worked up.

We were all standing very close to the mine when suddenly I saw Vitali kick it. He kicked the mine we were all staring at in terror, and honestly: that thing with your life flashing before your eyes happened to me. Swear words were screamed in English, Ukrainian, Polish and Russian and I dived on top of Daniel, pushing him and the camera out of the way. I thought it was quite heroic of me, really, saving him and all that, but hero was not the four-letter word he used. Instead he turned at me and yelled, 'What the fuck, Lisette! Don't ever fucking do that again! Fuck!'

The mine had not exploded, obviously, so my heroics had come across as having suddenly jumped on Daniel without warning while screaming for no reason whatsoever, giving him the fright of his life. Fed up with the language barrier, Vitali had tried to prove that there was no risk and we were safe by kicking the mine — because he knew he had planted it there, disabled, to scare off any returning enemies. If only language hadn't been a barrier, he could have told us calmly and saved us all the heart attack.

It was not our finest moment and I was just about to apologise and vow not to push the team any further into the long grass, when Nikita piped up: 'You need to film this.' Everyone was keen to turn around and get out of the minefield, especially after the scare, but Nikita was insistent. 'There are human bones up here. They think they are the neighbours.'

As soon as I heard that I wanted the shots. Daniel did too, so we negotiated a few steps forward with Aleks, to allow us to film the bones from a distance before retreating to a more comfortable position. I knew we were pushing our luck with our team, who we respected immensely, so I promised myself we would behave from that point on.

Once we were back on the main street, Rita and Vitali led us to the local grocery store but I was almost too frightened to step inside. Vitali was a big man and he was charging around without any care for booby traps despite having just told us they had found some inside the day prior. Russian soldiers had camped out in the store for months, and Vitali pointed out their uniforms left discarded on the floor, their army rations, their medicine, their ammunition, even their cash. Then he pointed to a drawing of two tanks on the wall. 'They were drawing their tanks firing at Ukrainians!' he thundered. He was angry, and understandably so. Six generations of his family had grown up in the town, and both his great-grandfather and his grandfather had fought alongside the Russians in the past. That border brotherhood had clearly now been obliterated.

There was much to film inside the store, but it was so cluttered and messy that I could barely see the floor I was stepping on and I kept imagining one of us standing on something deadly. I was keen to get the hell out of there; once I did, I started calling for Daniel to follow suit but he was getting too many good pictures and ignored my anxious pleas.

'Well, well, well, now who isn't listening?' I thought to myself, still feeling a bit sheepish from the earlier incident.

Daniel eventually emerged and Petro and I were genuinely relieved to see he still had both his legs as we trudged further through the town. It's fair to say we were all a bit on edge after the events of the day so far, and tiredness wasn't helping the squabbling between Daniel and me. Every minute or so we would hear the rumbling of artillery, the sound of the Ukrainians and Russians firing at each other on the border's edge, just a stone's throw from where we were. I was desperate to get the sound captured on camera, but whenever it happened Daniel seemed to be filming something else and we'd miss the opportunity to record a piece to camera with the artillery firing in the background.

I was midway through another complaint about it — 'Well, are you going to . . .' — when we heard it again.

'Boom!' The sound of war burst into life around us once more.

'I'm always rolling, Lisette,' Daniel said, and the camera was facing me this time so I started immediately.

'You can hear that because we are just ten kilometres from the border, the constant but faint rumble of artillery being fired in this direction. It makes your skin crawl,' I said to the lens.

'Got it, great work,' Daniel said, and I returned the compliment.

'We've got a good story,' I said. 'I think we should quit while we're ahead.'

Everyone agreed and we said our thank yous to the family and headed back to Kharkiv.

The producers were delighted with the package when it played the next day, and we had messages from home saying it was our best yet. Then a text came through from my friend Ed, the one who had provided snacks during the Queen's death and was now providing light relief for us through a war zone. 'I'm laughing out loud at Dan saying, "I'm rolling all the time" at the start of your piece to camera,' he wrote.

'Oh my god,' I replied. 'I didn't know you could hear that. We were midway through a bit of a tiff . . .'

'I was listening with headphones at work so you probably couldn't hear on TV. But it's definitely there.'

Daniel fired up the laptop and we listened back. And, sure enough, there it was: the bickering of two emotionally fraught individuals, loud and clear even without headphones.

On the day we were due to head back to Kyiv, I was walking around the breakfast buffet searching for scrambled eggs when there was a series of thundering bangs and the hotel shook all over. The bombing sounded near, close enough to halt the activity in the room for a second as everyone weighed up the information to hand.

A man I had never met before, who was also eyeing up the egg offerings, raised an eyebrow at me. 'Be careful, those ones were close.'

Daniel and I continued piling food on to our plates and then wandered towards Aleks, who was already tucking in. 'Should we go to the shelter, or nah?'

'No, we're fine. They're targeting the powerlines,' he said, and if that meant I could eat my eggs before they went cold then that was fine by me. My phone started ringing just as I picked up my fork — The Sarahs, of course, who always seemed to be running off some weird sixth sense. They were calling to check that everything was all set for the big drive ahead, and I was midway through my usual reassurances when another bomb hit. I cut my sentence short and shot a look at Aleks, who again looked unbothered.

'Oh sorry, there are just a lot of strikes this morning . . .'

'What?' The Sarahs responded. 'Do you need to get to a shelter or something?'

'Nah, nah, we're fine, we're just having breakfast then we'll head off,' I continued, and Daniel murmured his agreement through a mouthful of sausage and hashbrown.

After breakfast, Aleks asked the hotel to organise us some takeaway lunches so we didn't need to stop for food on the way to Kyiv, and he proudly arrived at the car door with a collection of brown paper bags. 'Here are your rations,' he said, handing them out. We did end up stopping, though, for petrol and, obviously, a hotdog for good measure. We actually got rear-ended by another vehicle in the carpark, but after our previous accident this was barely worth mentioning and while the insurance conversations were being carried out, Nikita (the fixer, not the masseuse) and I got talking on the forecourt.

'What do you think of what you have seen?' he asked me.

'I think it is incredibly sad and wrong,' I replied.

'You think it's wrong?'

'Yeah. Do you not?'

'No . . .' he said slowly. 'I support the fight.' I noted the lack of absence of the word 'war'.

'You grew up in the East?' I asked.

'Yes. My parents are Russian.'

I was happy to finally have it confirmed, but I was not at all surprised.

'They still live in the East?' I asked.

'Yes, they will never leave, it is their home,' he replied.

'So, are you Russian?' I asked.

'I used to work for the Ukrainian government,' he started, 'and then after 2014 when the fighting started, I did not work for the Ukrainian government.'

He was speaking very deliberately, clearly relishing my attention. I was eager to learn as much about him as possible so kept pushing for more detail.

'So you lost your job because you supported the Russians?' I pressed.

'I am a Russian national but a Ukrainian citizen,' he said, and that made a lot of sense. Like many who live in the far east, Nikita had been born and raised Russian but his family settled on the Ukrainian side of the border long before that country gained independence. Now they found themselves living in a country that didn't match what they considered to be their identity, but they also didn't want to feel pressured to move out of a place they had always considered home.

'Who do you think started the fighting?' he asked me.

'Putin,' I responded.

'No, NATO started it.' I had heard this argument too many times to engage in it, but there was no doubt now that we had a Russian sympathiser, with government connections, as part of our team.

'I think I will leave the country soon,' he continued.

'But you can't,' I replied, referencing the laws prohibiting men of fighting age from leaving Ukraine.

'For a price you can,' he said with a coy smile.

'How much?'

'$5000 USD,' and he said it as if he knew for sure.

'Could you get back in?'

'For a price.' His smile was getting broader by the second, and I found myself laughing. Nikita was unlike anyone I had ever met, maybe a bit scary and definitely with questionable links to the Russian agenda, but charming in a concerning way.

'I have to be careful what I tell you,' he said. 'You could be a Russian spy.'

'It's pretty clear *you're* the Russian spy, Nikita,' I prodded back.

'I can't be a spy, I have accreditation,' and he gestured to the documentation we each had on a lanyard around our neck that confirmed we had security clearance from the Ukrainian armed forces to be working in the country.

'Yes, but how much did you pay . . .?' I asked, nudging him.

He only laughed in return.

I never could nail down Nikita. He was a fascinating character who I developed a strange soft spot for, but I was also very wary of him. I might have been growing paranoid, but he seemed like the sort of person who could easily be feeding information about our work back to Russia, or hacking our laptops or phones. In the days and weeks that followed, things grew increasingly strange when Nikita started sending me videos of him singing and dancing to a variety of songs, including 'I want to break free' by Queen and 'I'm sexy and I know it' by LMFAO. In case you're wondering, there was nothing sexy about Nikita. I couldn't help but feel like viewing his videos was compromising my security somehow, and eventually I stopped opening his messages altogether.

It was a long slog of a journey out of Ukraine. From Kharkiv to Lviv is a thirteen-hour drive, plus another couple to get to the Polish border, and we were relieved when we finally made it there. After goodbye hugs with the wider team, Daniel, Aleks and I hopped in the car with Oleks, who was there waiting to pick us up. As we did, he clocked Petro's Glock in its new holster and pointed at it, laughing kindly: 'Ahh, Sheriff Petro!' I was thrilled that Petro's transformation had been noticed by more than just me.

Finally in Poland, Daniel and I had a date with our regular table in the town square and copious amounts of gin, but the phone rang before we even managed to get our bags down in the hotel.

'The Sarahs are calling!' I yelled in Daniel's direction.

'What do they want?' he yelled back, and I was wondering the same thing, given we were usually left alone to drink in peace once we'd made it into the safe zone.

'Hello?' we answered on speakerphone.

'Hey, how are you guys?'

'Yeah, all good; tired, but happy to be in Poland.'

'Yeah, we bet. So home to London tomorrow?'

'Yep, we fly out in the morning.' Daniel and I were looking

at each other, like 'What's with all the small talk, they know this stuff already?'

'The reason we're calling . . .'

Here we go, I thought, what have we done wrong?

'. . . is to let you know that we've just found out you're finalists at this year's TV Awards . . .'

We were shocked enough at that, and probably didn't say much before Sarah went on: '. . . and we want you guys to be here for the ceremony. So, you're coming home next month for the party!'

These bombshells were shaking me more than the real ones we'd been dealing with in Ukraine, and I think we were both a bit lost for words. When the phone call wrapped up we were more eager than ever to get to our gin, although two hours later it was clear that perhaps we'd been a bit too eager. Daniel, who can identify every flag of the world with outstanding ease, was starting to muddle up Qatar and Bahrain — a sure sign he was well under the influence — and I was starting to do my impersonations of the gaggle of British tourists sitting next to us a little too loudly when the push alert came through.

'Liz Truss to make Downing Street statement,' the banner announced.

'Oh fuck off,' I said, still in my Geordie accent.

'Yeah, fuck off Sky News,' Daniel echoed.

'Can we just get one day?!' I started ranting, while already positioning my phone up against a bowl of fries and settling in to watch the livestream of what we knew would be the UK prime minister's resignation.

'Can we get another round?' Daniel asked the waiter.

'Just one for the road . . .' he said to me.

'They were doubles!' I reminded the waiter as he walked off.

Liz Truss did resign, after just 50 days in the job, making her the shortest-serving UK prime minister in history; and we eventually stumbled back to the hotel to get to work, knowing it was a story too big to pass on due to exhaustion or intoxication or both. I started scripting the story while Daniel sobered up with some sleep before having to begin the edit. It wasn't my best work, I'll admit, but I recorded the voice-over without a single slur and it went to air without any complaints, except for our own of course.

'Back to Downing Street we go . . .'

MIDDLE OF NOWHERE, POLAND & KYIV, UKRAINE
November 2022

We were due to fly to New Zealand in mid-November, but of course we should have known better. After almost a year of calling for the New Zealand prime minister to visit Ukraine, we finally got word that a Kiwi politician would be making the journey to Kyiv and we had been invited to cover the trip. The dates clashed, but they always do and thankfully I hadn't even told my family we were coming home so didn't have to deliver any major disappointment. By this time I had learnt my lesson and subconsciously started not to commit to anything.

It wasn't Jacinda Ardern who was making the trip, it was Defence Minister Peeni Henare and the decision still frustrates me. Earlier in the year, when Ardern was touring Europe, she turned down an invite to Kyiv, citing scheduling issues and the need to get back to Australia for a meeting with the new prime minister Anthony Albanese. Somehow Albanese, who was in Europe for the same NATO summit as Ardern, managed to fit in both. I'm not going to pretend to know anything about the inner workings of the Beehive or the political strategy, and I'm sure there was a lot more at play than I could ever imagine, but I always felt that one of the most impactful contributions to the Ukrainian war effort that New Zealand could have made would have been for Ardern to visit Kyiv. Not the New Zealand prime minister; specifically, Jacinda Ardern. Following her handling of the Christchurch mosque attack, the eruption of Whakaari White Island and the pandemic, she had the global name recognition of an A-list celebrity. She'd been on American talk shows and even the cover of *Vogue*. When Petro's friend Angelina Jolie had visited Lviv it had dominated headlines for a few days; reigniting the world's interest in the wider story, reminding people not to forget and also reminding Putin that those with influence and power were not in his corner. Ardern, with the stardom of Jolie alongside her own political credibility, would have generated similar headlines. The New Zealand Defence Force has made a significant contribution to the war effort by training Ukrainian soldiers in the UK, but I would argue that seeing Ardern in Ukraine's capital would have had a longer-lasting impact than any of our millions of dollars for ammunition and weapons.

Two days before we were due to leave London to meet the New Zealand delegation in Warsaw, a missile struck Poland; the first time a foreign missile had landed in NATO territory since the war began. The threat of an escalation was obvious; if it was deliberate, then Article 5 of the NATO treaty would be triggered: an attack on one is an attack on all; potential World

War III. I abandoned the tomato pasta I had been cooking for dinner, grabbed a coat to disguise my 'at home' clothes and ran on to the street outside, where Daniel had arrived within minutes of my call, to do a live cross into the morning news.

When I rushed back upstairs to start packing a bag for the airport, my housemate the chef remarked, 'Were you seriously just live on television outside our front door just now?'

'Yep,' I replied as I started stuffing the usual staple of double puffer jacket, boots and beanie into a bag, wondering how he wasn't used to this TV thing yet.

'Were you talking to the redhead?' he asked.

'No, Sam presents a different show.'

'Well, you had pasta sauce on your face . . .' he said, and walked out of the kitchen. It wasn't until we were in a taxi on the way to the airport that I finally wiped away the full splattering of tomato.

We flew to Kraków, then drove for hours to the remote location where the missile had landed. It was snowing and pitch-black and we were travelling through kilometre after kilometre of isolated farmland. As we arrived and set up for our live cross, we were surprised to find we were the only media there. It was a big story and I had imagined there would be a huge media presence, but it was 4 a.m. so I should have known better. Halfway through our live cross in the morning, my eyes started watering from the cold and a tear slid down my face. I remember thinking that people watching were going to think I was far too emotional about this missile strike when I had reported on far worse.

We bundled into our lonely rental car to warm up, and with hours to wait until our next live cross we set an alarm and nestled deeper into our puffer jackets for a nap. The nap turned into a longer sleep than I got on most average nights in the job. Four and a half hours later, our alarms brought us to our senses and we woke to find hundreds of camera operators and journalists busily at work around our car. While we had slept, the sun had risen and the world's media had descended on the Polish patch to do their live crosses in their much kinder time zones. I wiped away the dribble from my chin, smiling in a daze at one foreign journalist who caught my eye through the window. I often wonder how many people have photos on their phones of me and Daniel with our mouths wide open and dead to the world, snoring in the middle of the Polish farmland in our car that morning.

The timing couldn't have been better. We drove straight on to Warsaw, where we all met for a pre-trip briefing. With the minister on board, security protocols were tighter than usual and everything was planned with precision. We were soon ushered into a motorcade and raced for three hours towards the Polish border with Ukraine. It's amazing how much faster you can get to places when you have a police escort. We had never taken the overnight train to Kyiv, but I had read an article about the French president, German chancellor and Italian prime minister making the journey and I was imagining a slightly less fancy Air Force One in train form.

'Why don't I ever learn?' I scolded myself as we arrived at the train station and I must have let out a slight sigh on realising that we'd be taking the standard train.

'What, were you expecting Air Force One in train form?' Daniel asked, looking far too amused.

We were, to be fair, in the 'first class' section. There were two single bunks in each compartment of the train and some ham, a white bun and a piece of lettuce was delivered to us for dinner. We were off just as night fell. Stopping only once to cross the border and show passports, when we woke for good it was daylight and everything was blanketed in snow. Ukraine in winter is stunning. The train took us through farmland that looked like Narnia, and the closer we got to Kyiv the more it felt like we were going home.

On arrival we were taken straight to the main media hotel, and the doorman greeted me with a warmth it's hard to imagine can come from someone living in the Eastern European winter amid war.

'Welcome back,' he said with a smile.

'When were you last here?' one of the minister's team asked me with a raised eyebrow.

'A few weeks ago,' I said, and as I did I realised how strange my life had suddenly become.

What followed was a day of handshakes and landmarks, meetings with the Ukrainian defence minister and the same tour of some of the worst-hit local areas that world leaders had been taken on for months now. By midday we realised that our visit coincided with that of Rishi Sunak, the newly appointed UK prime minister. His footsteps followed ours; we know because we watched his tour unfold on the BBC. To the shock of no one reading this, Rishi Sunak's presence got a lot more international coverage than Peeni Henare's. But I believe to this day that had it been Jacinda Ardern who had visited, it would have rivalled the Downing Street VIP for headlines.

We were about to leave the hotel for the train station when we remembered the slightly sad dinner we'd been handed the night before. Grabbing a wad of Ukrainian cash out of Daniel's pocket, I ran to the hotel restaurant in search of sustenance.

There wasn't anything quick and easy, but it was Daniel's last overseas assignment as Europe Camera Operator and I couldn't go back empty-handed.

'I'll have a bottle of red, please.'

'Any one in particular?'

In a hurry I pointed to the top of the list. Ukrainian prices were so notoriously cheap that I didn't bother to look properly. The delegation was going to leave without me if I didn't hurry, and assuming it was a bargain as always I quickly counted out the notes. Rounding up, I told them, 'Keep it. I don't need the change.' The cash was worthless outside of Ukraine anyway, and I doubted we'd be back again. I had already pushed the budget with The Sarahs one too many times.

It was closing in on 1 a.m. and we were finishing up our final story together on the sleeper train when we finally had time for a toast.

'To a hell of a ride, and the perfect way to end it.'

'To a farewell tipple on the midnight train.'

Preparing to make my usual exclamations of how 'It was essentially free!', I googled the price of the bottle.

'Well, I hope you enjoyed your farewell tipple, Daniel, because that's a $280 red and I gave them $300 for it.'

Approximately four hours later, Daniel threw a pillow at me from his bunk half a metre away. 'You're going to wake the whole carriage and embarrass us in front of the minister!' he growled.

Apparently an expensive bottle doesn't pay any dividends when it comes to my snoring.

Ever since I'd arrived in London, I had known that Daniel would leave the job before me. His finish date had been pushed out and pushed out, but it was inevitable that there would be a changeover in camera operators during my time. It's deliberately arranged that way, so that one half of the team always knows what they're doing and can guide the other half through the basics in the initial weeks and months.

It's hard to properly explain the bond that is formed in a television news team. You see each other at your very best and your very worst, and splitting up when we knew how finely tuned our bureau had become didn't feel good. There were lots of big things I was going to miss; but I also have a bad habit of not charging my phone and I was increasingly concerned about whether the next camera operator would be as understanding when I pestered them with 'You don't have a power bank handy, do you, I'm on 2% . . .' right before a live cross.

Beyond his hyper-organised nature, Daniel was a master of his craft and made me a better journalist, and I didn't want to lose that either. Sarah Bristow had warned me that it would take three months to adjust; she actually used the words 'grieving' and I remember thinking that was a bit over the top. But it wasn't. I was so proud of everything we had achieved and the stories we had told, but I was worried that without him I wouldn't be brave enough to do any of it. As we headed towards the airport I told myself that it would be incredibly self-involved to cry, because it was Daniel's day and if anyone had a reason to cry it wasn't me. But as I took a final team selfie at the Gatwick Airport gate, I realised, very fittingly, that my phone was on 11%. This was going to make it hard to get home.

'You don't have a charger, do you?'

Obviously, he did. And obviously, I did end up crying.

I joked with HR that they should have advertised Daniel's

job as 'Lisette Reymer's best friend' and while they, shockingly, didn't take my advice, I was remarkably lucky to work with back-to-back legends. Alex Parsons, an incredibly talented operator and all-round phenomenal human, would soon become the better half of the bureau and a lifelong friend as well. He's also a born-and-bred Cantabrian; I felt that was a good omen off the bat and I was not disappointed.

'Dan told me to always have a charger handy. No stress.'

İSKENDERUN, TURKEY
mid-February 2023

News broke that a 7.8-magnitude earthquake had hit Turkey and Syria on the 6th of February 2023. It struck in the middle of the night while everyone was asleep in their homes, and they were buried in their beds. Thousands were killed and thousands were trapped; and at the time, I was trapped in London without a cameraman. Alex was out of town, taking his turn at being fake-kidnapped and put through the paces of hostile environments training, and I was becoming increasingly hostile as a result. The drama, logistics and cost of pulling him off the course and getting him back to London so we could go to Turkey meant that The Sarahs were hesitant in hitting the green light to go. As the death toll continued to rise, I watched as every other foreign correspondent I knew deployed to Turkey and my housemates started avoiding me at all costs.

The sun was going down in New Zealand and The Sarahs were readying for bed without a decision to deploy having been made, and I took my frustration out on the London footpaths. Having decided to distract myself with the most delicious grilled-cheese sandwich money can buy, I had just arrived at a busy lunchtime market when a phone call came through from one of our CNN guardian angels (a man too humble to want his name included in this book, although if it turned out he was actually some sort of secret agent I wouldn't be surprised). He'd already helped us carry out many of our Ukraine trips, and now asked cheerfully down the line, 'How are you?'

'Well, I'm incredibly stressed so I'm currently pacing

around the city,' I replied, knowing full well I was doing more storming than pacing.

'Why are you stressing?'

'Because I want to be in Turkey!'

'Well go to Turkey, then!' he replied, in a way that suggested I could be on a plane within an hour if I really *wanted* to be.

In typical guardian-angel fashion, the conversation then progressed to him offering to price up options for a campervan that we could sleep in and use to get around Turkey if we were to deploy.

'That would be incredible, thank you,' I said, feeling a surge of optimism thanks to both the call and the grilled cheese.

I sat on a bench in the middle of the market and made a flurry of calls: organising a Turkey-specific carnet for the camera, trying to determine the cost of pulling Alex off his course, booking a courier to deliver a satellite phone to my house, and trying to price up flights.

An hour or so later I got a call back from CNN.

'I've got you a campervan, a driver and a security officer, available for as long as you need. They'll meet you in İstanbul and you can drive from there, and you'll all be able to sleep in that campervan. It has a generator.'

'Amazing — how much does it cost?'

I genuinely can't remember the daily figure he quoted, but I know it wasn't a tiny bit over our budget; it was well beyond. As in, probably-not-even-worth-waking-up-The-Sarahs-to-pitch beyond our budget. We're talking thousands of pounds. I said as much, but thanked him for all of his help as always. Of course I woke The Sarahs anyway. It was early afternoon in London and if we were going to deploy tonight, we needed to get Alex on a train back from his course very soon, or we'd miss all the evening flights out.

Sarah Bristow answered the call almost immediately because, of course, she hadn't been asleep at all. 'I'm on the deck outside, trying to work out how we make this happen,' she said. 'Everything in me is screaming that we need to be there.' On that we agreed instantly, but obviously it wasn't that simple. I filled her in on the offer I'd had from CNN and I could hear her gulp at the cost.

'If we did this, Lisette, you wouldn't be able to go to Ukraine for the anniversary.'

The 24th of February 2023 would mark one year since the war started, and the plan had been for Alex and me to travel to Kyiv and cover it; something I was deeply passionate about. Apart from blowing the budget for the Ukraine trip on Turkey, if Alex was taken off the training course he wouldn't be able to get on another one before the anniversary, so he wouldn't be certified to travel to Ukraine. Having had experience with the Christchurch earthquakes, Alex was approved to go to Turkey without extra training — but a war zone was a different beast and there would be no exception made. Without a camera there was no point in me going, so we were suddenly faced with an ultimatum.

'It's going to be one or the other,' Sarah said. It was immediately clear to me which one.

'Then it's Turkey, definitely,' I responded. The tragedy was unfolding now, the pain and suffering was raw and developing and we needed to be there. Privately I also harboured a small belief that through some miracle between now and then I'd be able to change the outcome of Ukraine, too, so I reasoned it was better to get Turkey across the line and tackle Ukraine next week.

As we dove into the details my phone started buzzing. Another call was coming through.

'It's CNN,' I said to Sarah. 'Should I answer it?'

'Yeah,' she said, 'call me back.'

'Hello?' I said, trading calls.

'Listen. I've got you two cars, two drivers and a security officer, for five days. But that's all we can give you.'

'I only need five days!' I was trying to contain the excitement in my voice but I was never very good at playing it cool around these big network guys.

'Well then, you've got it.'

'How much, though?'

'You just sort your flights.'

I told you — guardian angel.

I was pretty much lost for words but managed a thank you and quickly called Sarah back with the update. 'If you can get the carnet and get Alex back to London in time, let's do it,' she said.

It was like she'd just fired the starting gun on some sickening long-distance sprint. The next three hours were some of the most manic of my career. As I raced across London in peak traffic to pick up the carnet, I called Alex with the news and he bailed from his course at pace to get on the last train back to the city and on to the airport. We would both be cutting it dangerously fine. In the back of an Uber I pulled up the flights on my laptop and very nearly vomited. They had almost quadrupled in price since I had originally priced them up for The Sarahs. I couldn't work out what had happened, but I saw the whole trip evaporate in front of my eyes.

I called them both. 'It's going to cost a lot to book these flights,' I said, my gut twisting in discomfort, 'and we need to make the call right now because Alex is about to get on a train.'

'Just book them,' they said, possibly because they were sick of answering my 3 a.m. phone calls but more likely because by this point they were as desperate as I was to get to Turkey. I hurriedly booked the flights as the Uber pulled up to the carnet office, raced out to grab the documentation and jumped straight back into the Toyota Prius to begin the race home again. It was a five-star effort from the driver; Tomlin would have been impressed. As he expertly weaved through rush-hour traffic, I started scripting my story for the news bulletin while frantically trying to coordinate with my housemate to collect the satellite phone off the courier driver. When I got home, I threw everything I needed in a bag before doing a U-turn and rushing back out the door to run to the station to catch a train to the airport. I was going to be late, for sure, but Alex was going to be lucky to make it at all.

When I finally made it to Gatwick, I raced to the counter to check in and was met with some big news, and some bad news.

'Ma'am, you're flying business class; please go to the premium counter.'

That was the big news. And I might be the first person in history to have a negative reaction to it. We always flew economy no matter what, and usually on the most budget airlines; so Turkish Airlines business class was very much not my standard approach to company card expenditure, and nor was it approved. With most flights fully booked, the only last-minute seats available must have been business class and I had booked them inadvertently. There will be some who claim that is a convenient story, but I was genuinely panicked as I contemplated the trouble I could get into for taking such liberties. I calmed myself down with a reminder that I'd had the increased price approved by the bosses *and* there had simply been no other option if we wanted to land in Turkey in time to go live into the next New Zealand bulletin.

The bad news was yet to follow.

I walked over to the premium counter where a woman was waiting to help, with a smile that said she was clocking off soon and the most extreme winged eyeliner I had ever encountered. I asked if we could start Alex's check-in in advance so we could race straight through security when he arrived and she was happy to oblige; we were business customers, after all. 'Oh I'm sorry, Miss Reymer,' she said casually, 'you've booked this ticket under the wrong name,' tapping her long acrylic nails repeatedly on the desk.

'What?'

'You've got a ticket here for Alex Stephen Parsons, but his passport reads Alexander Stephen Parsons. They don't match.'

I felt a jolt of panic and leant over the counter in front of me, straining to see her proof but already knowing she was right. In my hurry I hadn't booked the ticket properly, and given that this was my first time travelling with Alex I hadn't given a second thought to using his full first name.

'Oh, I'm so sorry, that's a wee mistake, it should be Alexander,' I said, trying to match her level of casual but failing miserably.

'I'm sorry, ma'am, you'll need to buy a new ticket. It is too many letters to change.'

Through the thick layers of fake eyelashes she was wearing I was surprised she could see the letters at all, but regardless I was now really in a state. Not only had I taken it upon myself to buy two business class flights, but this lady was now telling me my only option was to buy a third! There was no world where that would be possible; or, rather, there was no world where it would be possible and I kept my job. Instead, I did what any self-respecting youngest child would do: I started fake-crying. The feeling was genuine but I think I was running on too much adrenaline to conjure up real tears, so I explained through crocodile ones what a rollercoaster I had been on that day and how important it was for us to get to Turkey and tell these stories.

The lady wasn't buying it, but her nail tapping stopped so I took that as a small win. 'Just put it on the company card,' she said, clearly missing the crucial point that I should never have booked a business flight in the first place and my company card was not a bottomless pit like others she must deal with at this VIP counter.

As my hysteria increased, we started to draw the attention of nearby customers and one of her check-in colleagues eventually came over to assist. He looked at me with pity and gave a slight wave of his hand, which seemed to signal 'Put it through', and I wondered right then and there if God had been terribly misrepresented all these years and was actually a middle-aged red-haired man who worked as a Turkish Airlines manager at Gatwick Airport. Regardless, I was a believer.

Half an hour later, my new friend Alexander arrived at the airport and with the new carnet stamped and our bags checked in, I found myself daring to believe we were actually going to make it to Turkey.

My phone rang. CNN calling.

'All sorted?' he asked.

'Yeah, just at the airport now, thanks so much.'

'No worries. We've also got you a generator for the van, so you'll have power overnight.'

'Incredible.'

'And I hear you want to go to Ukraine? What's the plan there?'

'Oh, I don't think that's going to happen anymore because

we're doing this,' I replied, unable to process anything beyond the next few hours.

'Right. Well, let's get through Turkey and then we can talk about Kyiv.'

I hung up, once again in grateful shock.

As we raced through the rest of the airport process, I kept scripting my 6 p.m. story on my phone and managed to record a voice-over to send to Auckland where the television package would be edited together while we were in the sky. Recording a voice-over in the field is an incredibly glamorous process. At an airport it typically involves standing in a bathroom cubicle with a jersey over your head and reading your script out loud, with full journalistic gusto, into a tiny microphone while the ladies in the cubicles next to you either enjoy the news update or consider getting you some psychological help.

The flight from London to Turkey is only four hours, but with the time zone change our flight would depart at 10:30 p.m. and land in İstanbul at 5:30 a.m., roughly two and a half hours before our live cross so we'd have to go straight there. We knew that flight would be our only chance to sleep for who knew how long, and as much as we wanted to make the most of our first business class experience, I'm sad to say we demolished the hors d'oeuvres in a way that made it very clear we didn't belong in business class and I was asleep before the main course was served.

We landed in İstanbul on time, but, as always the carnet delayed us and so did the translation battle to get the necessary SIM cards to power up a live cross — so the Amazing Race continued. Our security officer Keith was waiting for us at arrivals. A sniper by trade, this middle-aged Brit had retired from the military into a life of private security that involved everything from buying gold in Africa for wealthy individuals too frightened to do it themselves, to looking after us amid this natural disaster. It was the deadliest earthquake globally since Haiti in 2010, and the final figures would show that more than 56,000 people were killed and another 118,000 injured.

We got in a taxi and headed to Keith's hotel in central İstanbul, where we would be meeting our drivers after our live cross. It was five minutes before the 6 p.m. bulletin, of which we were the lead story, and we were still driving when I got a call from one of TV3's legendary producers: Angus Gillies.

'Do not miss your slot,' he instructed with the passion of a producer who doesn't want their perfectly constructed bulletin to suddenly go up in smoke. 'Stop on the side of the road if you have to. It doesn't have to look good, just get in front of a camera.'

'Yeah, I know! Don't worry, we'll be there,' I assured him, only slightly miffed at the suggestion that I wouldn't have made that judgement call myself after everything we'd been through to get to this point.

We pulled up to the hotel and ran to a side balcony, trying not to slip over as the snow continued to fall around us. I think we got the link up with seconds only to spare, but we made it. And, Alex had set up a beautiful shot.

Turkey is a big place, and we had a huge day ahead of us if we were going to get anywhere near the epicentre. Our first stop, Adana, was a ten-hour drive away. Of course this is why we have drivers, to share the burden of the drive time, but this time our drivers were missing in action. Keith was in touch with them and they had said they were five minutes away, but it was an hour and a half before they finally showed up and by then I was in a pretty foul mood. One of them, Mohammed, couldn't speak any English, while the other could speak more than he wanted to admit when I started grilling him for an explanation of what had taken them so long. Probably in his late fifties, this man looked like some sort of mad Turkish scientist, with long unkempt grey hair and unbelievably bad time management. He would spend the next week promising he was 'five minutes away' when he definitely wasn't. It resulted in us dismissing his real name altogether (which, honestly, I can't remember) in favour of the new moniker 'Five Minutes'.

We drove in convoy to Adana, us and Keith in one car with Mohammed, and Five Minutes driving the other, and arrived late evening, parking up at a petrol station to 'sleep' for the night before doing a live cross the next morning. We couldn't see much damage in the darkness, and it was still snowing as we bunkered down. My friend Melissa Stokes, a former *1News* Europe Correspondent, had gifted me a head torch when I moved from TVNZ to Newshub years earlier, along with a note that told me I would need the torch when I was on an extreme assignment overseas one day. I was grateful for it at the time and even more grateful for it on this night, as it provided the only light we had.

Five Minutes offered to make a quick dash down the road for some food, and returned almost two hours later with completely inedible kebabs, which, I'm convinced, were stuffed with rotten meat. Keith slept in the front of our van, and Alex and I, on our first deployment as a duo, camped out in the back side by side. Mohammed and Five Minutes shared the second vehicle. As soon as we got settled, we were reminded of why we were in a car and not a hotel building. The car shook all night from aftershocks, and as the snow packed in around us I layered up with several jumpers to stop my shivering from adding to the shaking sensation.

Daylight brought clarity of the level of devastation we had driven into; and the closer to the epicentre we got, the worse it became. Street after street of apartment buildings were completely flattened, and machinery and people everywhere were working overtime, searching through the rubble for both survivors and dead bodies. Temporary campgrounds had been set up everywhere and anywhere, with the newly homeless now camped out in tents in the freezing winter, too scared to risk going home as the aftershocks continued. I was embarrassed to have a car to sleep in; it suddenly felt like an obnoxious show of riches. There was no electricity, so everyone was cooking on fires, and hygiene was rapidly deteriorating to the point of becoming an acute health risk. The public bathrooms were overrun and feral, completely unusable and driving everyone, including me, to the streets to do our business.

I couldn't get my head around the scale of destruction. We would drive for hours and see no let-up in the severity of the damage to buildings. It was like someone had taken a bulldozer to this entire portion of the country. Family and friends waited in groups around fires in front of different piles of rubble, desperate for news of their loved ones trapped underneath. Most feared the worst, pointing out duvets they recognised slammed between two pieces of concrete where their niece or nephew would have been sleeping, but in the early days many were praying for a miracle. There had been numerous extraordinary scenes following the quake of survivors being pulled out of the tightest of places, having survived in the toughest of conditions without food or water, trapped for days in the icy cold. A newborn was among those found in the early days, her umbilical cord still connected to her mother, who had tragically died when the quake hit.

The emergency services and rescue crews had been slow to arrive, held back by ruined roads, icy weather and a general lack of resources and heavy equipment, and there were simply not enough of them, so locals everywhere were trawling through the mountains of debris themselves, using buckets to dig for their loved ones. It was busy and chaotic and loud; concrete and rubble being shifted and shovelled around as people wailed for their missing family members. There was so much grief, so much overwhelming depression . . . but then suddenly there would be a shout to silence it all. It would start with just one person screaming out, standing on top of what used to be an apartment block and within seconds word would spread down a 500-metre stretch of road. Heavy machinery would be switched off, thousands of workers would stop what they were doing and the busy Turkish traffic would come to a halt. Rescuers had heard a survivor. Once there was silence, the call would go out again for a response. Everyone would hold their breath, including us, until the return cry came, often accompanied by news of how many people were trapped down below.

The confirmation of life triggered new momentum; a highly orchestrated, high-stakes effort to get the survivors out from wherever they were in the rubble and carried in the arms of strangers to health professionals. The country was so crippled by sadness, but the rescues provided hope. It was addictive, and unbelievably motivating. I have never felt elation like the moment I saw a man in his fifties, Oscar, being pulled out of his concrete prison alive. He and his wife and their two children had managed to survive together for 84 hours, but rescuers couldn't get to them all fast enough. Only Oscar survived; left to live a life without the people he loved most. The elation evaporated just as quickly as it had burst on to the scene. It didn't belong in a place so broken, anyway.

The back seat of our van was our office as well as our bedroom, and as we clambered in and out in our grubby boots all day, the vehicle was becoming filthier and less and less appealing to sleep in. We were surviving on a steady diet of Pringles, lollies and a very aggressive Turkish energy drink, and as we got ready to begin our night-time editing process we would shuffle the food crumbs around and treat ourselves to a baby wipe to clean our faces and hands. By the third morning Alex, the kindest man you'll ever meet, admitted my snoring was affecting what little sleep was up for grabs and I vowed to let him fall asleep first the next night. I doubt I was successful.

Turkey didn't have enough room in its graveyards for all of the bodies, so mass graves were being hastily dug on the outskirts of Kahramanmaraş, where the quake hit hardest. The freshly turned dirt, stretching for miles across large fields, was a sobering sight. Diggers were everywhere, creating long trenches, and a truck would arrive at the end of every one with a trailer of bodies piled on the back, wrapped in blankets or plastic bags. The bodies would be unceremoniously laid in the ground and covered in dirt, while someone walked around placing a simple wooden cross at each head.

There were thousands of bodies, yet only a handful of mourning families. One grieving group of four started unwrapping their loved one in front of us, readying themselves to lay their baby to rest, and Alex quickly turned the camera to face away as we all just stood there in shock. The moment had caught us off-guard. It was rare to see a proper goodbye, to witness any sort of ceremony. There was one prevailing reason for this: the quake had hit while whole families were asleep in their homes and most had been wiped out completely, with no one left alive to bury them or pay their respects. Those who did survive, like Oscar, often wished they hadn't. The pain of having lost everyone who meant anything to them too much to bear.

We had been filming in the cemetery for over an hour when I saw them coming. Two uniformed police officers were staring at us from about 300 metres away, and they started to walk with intent in our direction. It wasn't a welcoming walk. 'Give me the card,' I said to Alex, meaning the small piece of black plastic that sits inside the camera and holds all of our precious footage.

'What?' he mumbled in what was barely a reply. Cameramen have a tendency to 'get in the zone'. Magic happens there, in 'the zone', so it's not always in a journalist's best interests to break it. But this was not one of those moments.

'Don't ask questions, just quickly give me the card,' I replied, trying to appear calm as the officers got ever closer.

Looking very confused, Alex ejected the card and I quickly stuffed it down my bra. The uniformed men arrived at our side seconds later.

'Forbidden!' they started shouting at us, pointing at the camera. It was clear they were telling us we couldn't film there, but I turned to Five Minutes for translation assistance because it was also pretty clear that I wasn't going to be able to mime an expressive 'We're sorry!' and get us out of the situation.

I don't know what Five Minutes said, but it wasn't helpful and two minutes later we were being marched off and detained by the Turkish police. As we walked, Alex started filming whatever he could on a backup card so we would have footage to show them if they insisted on looking at it. We wouldn't want to be caught out with a suspiciously blank camera.

We were taken to an area where a large group of police officers were gathered around, trying to keep warm with hot coffee. We were told to sit in the middle of their circle and wait for the gendarmerie to arrive.

'Well, this all seems positive,' Alex managed.

The gendarmerie is a separate force to the police, and under the state of emergency now in place, they had ultimate authority in the earthquake zone. We were told by the officers that new rules had been introduced to prohibit filming inside cemeteries and we now needed to be handed over to the gendarmerie because we had committed a crime. But the change in legislation hadn't been published anywhere and we had evidence of other media outlets filming there in the days prior without issue. There was a sense that the government was trying to restrict information around the extent of the tragedy, and there was also a desire among many of the grieving Turkish to hide their loss from those families still searching for their loved ones and holding out hope of a late rescue.

Alex showed the officers the footage on his camera and deleted it in front of them, bargaining for our freedom, but they wouldn't budge. The gendarmerie were on their way. One of the officers looked younger than me, and kept smiling at me from across the group. I thought for an idiotic moment that maybe he would be our ticket out of there, so I started to engage with him. His English was worse than ropey, and the most I got out of him was a terrible instant coffee and some sad puppy-dog eyes. He quite clearly had no power at all. Eventually he pointed to my phone and asked for a selfie, which I took against my better judgement and only noticed hours later that he had been covering his police badge with one hand in the photo, as if he was temporarily off the clock.

We waited hours, and were joined by two Italian and French news teams who had suffered the same fate and were now also being held hostage. We were all offered kebabs, which we ate begrudgingly because we were so hungry, but disappointingly for our captors this didn't have the desired effect of shutting us up and we continued arguing between mouthfuls. By the time the gendarmerie showed up, the other two crews were even more fired up than we were and Five Minutes was getting in a heated debate with the men in uniform that obviously I couldn't understand a word of.

The officers retreated to their own business once the gendarmerie arrived, acknowledging their place in the pecking order, and no one had eyes on Alex and me, who were standing five metres away from the huddle of chaos that had erupted between the gendarmerie, the Italians, the French and Five Minutes. 'We could just leave and no one could notice,' Alex said, I think mostly as a joke.

'Should we actually try?' I said, realising that we genuinely might be able to get away with it. The Italians were now turning on Five Minutes. I don't think he was helping their case and the journalist was sick of him getting in the way; which I could, of course, relate to. I turned to Mohammed: 'Get Five Minutes, let's go.'

He instantly chuckled at the nickname, revealing to us all that he understood more English than he let on. 'Well that's good to know,' I thought to myself. Mohammed walked over and tugged at Five Minutes' arm, who reluctantly turned towards us.

'Let's go!' I mouthed and pointed towards the park where

our car sat. As the Italians kept fighting with the gendarmerie over how unreasonable it was for them to have been detained for so long without fair cause, and the French protested that they *had* to be let go, Alex, Mohammed, Five Minutes and I hurried off to our car and drove out of the cemetery. My friend, the young officer, caught my eye as I looked back, but he just held up a peace sign. He couldn't care less.

As we pulled out of the graveyard, I pulled the card from my bra. We'd got away with it, I thought, though I didn't feel like that two hours later when we were all dealing with vicious food poisoning thanks to that fucking kebab.

The public response to a natural disaster is so different to war. With conflict there is so much anger at the aggressor and it fuels people's engagement in the story. But with an earthquake or tsunami or a wildfire, there is a lot of initial sadness and sympathy but the story doesn't maintain its momentum in the same way. Leaving Turkey, knowing that without the cameras there the world would forget that much sooner, was brutally hard.

On my street back in London, like so many others there, households will leave their rubbish in black bags on the curb for pickup. For weeks, whenever I saw those rubbish bags I saw dead bodies in them. I couldn't stop thinking of the families we had walked away from. Unlike Ukraine, after a month the earthquake was barely in the news and no one was talking about it anymore. It made me even more determined to return.

KYIV, UKRAINE
late February 2023

For some slightly deluded reason I had still hoped we'd get to Ukraine for the one-year anniversary. Logically, I knew it couldn't happen. We'd diverted that budget to cover Turkey, Alex hadn't completed his hostile environments training course and I knew the deal we'd made, but as the one-year milestone drew closer I was not in a happy place. I felt like I had abandoned the story, and there is nothing that feels more unnatural than trying to cover something hundreds of kilometres away from where the real story is actually happening.

We were setting up for a live cross in London on the 22nd of February when The Sarahs started messaging.

'Are there any trains to Kyiv?'

'How much are the trains?'

'When would they get you there by?'

Given that we were 48 hours out from the anniversary and how complicated and long the journey into Kyiv is, I thought the entire exercise was likely a waste of time. But I searched for trains anyway, intrigued by where the reignited interest was coming from.

'All sold out,' I replied, cursing the fact that when I'd last looked they *hadn't* been sold out and if we'd made the decision earlier we could have been on an overnight train by now. The messages stopped coming and I figured the conversation was over, but a few hours later my late-night moping was interrupted by a phone call.

'CNN has a message for you — they said to tell you "Lisette *shall* go to the ball",' Sarah said.

'You're kidding?'

'No, we've sorted a plan. You'll need to get all your things together and go to the airport first thing. One of their camera operators will meet you in Poland and go into Kyiv with you. They'll help you film what you need while you're there, and then you can exit with their crews a couple of days after the anniversary. All good?'

It was better than all good. It was a near-miracle. I was gutted that Alex couldn't come, but all things considered this was a great outcome when it came to our coverage. The clock was ticking towards 11 p.m. as I started hauling my suitcases out of storage and making enough of a commotion that Eavan emerged from her room and poked her head into mine.

'Ukraine?' she asked, clocking the body armour.

'Yeah . . .'

'Right, well, see you when we see you, I guess. Be safe.'

I was in Lviv within 12 hours, filing my first report before heading to the capital on the morning of the anniversary itself. President Putin is famously a fan of marking significant days in the calendar with a big statement, and there were concerns he would unleash a barrage of missiles to mark one year. I didn't have security with me on this trip, and while a Ukrainian driver had been arranged to take me to Kyiv, driving that many hours 'alone' through a country at war, on a day when widespread attacks were predicted, was a new and slightly uneasy experience. It felt like I was missing a limb without Daniel or Alex there, but I knew I would be feeling completely paralysed if I was trying to cover things from London.

As we pulled up to the usual hotel, I was looking forward to catching up with my friends on the door when I noticed the foyer was much busier than usual, and there were a lot of intimidating Ukrainian characters standing at the door.

I pushed my way through, flashing my accreditation, and managed to get to my room, where I promptly turned on CNN. The Ukrainian president, Volodymyr Zelensky, was giving a press conference and it was being streamed live. 'Ahh, of course.' He must have been using the conference centre downstairs, which explained the massive security.

Zelensky looked much older than he did a year ago, physical evidence of the unimaginable burden he'd been carrying on his shoulders; but things were looking up for Ukraine. Three hundred and sixty-five days earlier, Zelensky had stood in central Kyiv as the Russians approached, and he had vowed not to leave the capital despite the threats to his own life and his family's. Now, in 2023, he had again spent the 24th of February standing in the centre of the capital, knowing it had resisted capture. He vowed that the war would end this year. But the sandbags around the statues in Sophia Square were starting to disintegrate, in a sad sign of how long the war had been raging, and there was a huge banner draped around it, which read in blood-red spray paint: 'World Help Us Please'. I couldn't imagine how hard it was to be living under such continued torture and fear while simultaneously becoming 'old news', and I was relieved that I had made it to Ukraine to try to remind New Zealanders of the ongoing suffering.

It was a short trip, and with the lack of security and camera limitations I couldn't travel far, but the CNN operators were incredibly generous, squeezing my shoots and live crosses into their already very busy schedules. On the second evening I was set up for a live cross on one of the hotel balconies, making conversation with the producer and camera operator who had made time for me that night. 'I work with Clarissa, usually,' the camera operator said, referencing one of CNN's award-winning war correspondents, Clarissa Ward.

'Wow. And so you work with Clarissa too?' I asked the producer.

'No,' he said, just as casually, 'I'm with Amanpour.' CNN's chief international anchor. I probably would have been better off learning this information *after* my cross, as the pressure to deliver the best report of my life now felt greater than ever, but both of them were nice enough not to comment on the sweaty upper lip I developed as a result of my growing nerves.

There was a lot to learn from our big brother network and the people who worked there, with a gulf in experience between us when it came to working in war zones, but I was delighted when we drove out of Ukraine together later that week to discover that, just like Daniel and me, they considered regular stops for Ukrainian hotdogs to be key to survival.

PARIS, FRANCE
March 2023

By 2023 we were getting pretty familiar with Kevin Spacey. The two-time Oscar winner was regularly in and out of court as part of his UK sexual assault trial, allegations he was ultimately acquitted of. There was always a hive of paparazzi and security outside the courthouses when he arrived and left, and we would throw ourselves into the mosh, shoving a microphone under his face and asking him for comment whenever he walked past. On this particular morning, he arrived at court with slightly less fanfare than usual and we got a relatively clean shot of him arriving as I talked in the foreground.

'Job done,' Alex said, 'that was easy,' and we turned our focus back to our bigger task for the day: getting to Paris.

The lights of the French capital just seem to shine a bit brighter than anywhere else in the world and the streets have a certain sophisticated sparkle to them, but for such a beautiful place it sure can turn foul quickly. It was the piles of rubbish that first caught our attention from London. Piles and piles of garbage that were no longer being collected because the rubbish collectors were on strike, furious at a proposal to raise the retirement age from 62 to 64. Yes, you read that correctly: 62 to 64. There were towers of it, 10,000 tonnes of trash, including restaurant scraps, piled up on the side of some of the world's most glamorous streets. Some stacks were metres high, and the city's rodents were showing up to feast and make homes out of what they couldn't snack on. By the time we arrived, the stench was taking over and I was using words like 'filthy' and 'repulsive' to describe one of my favourite cities.

We weren't in Paris just for the rubbish. In typical fashion, the French were taking to the streets in violent protest, too, rioting every night and leaving a trail of destruction behind them. Once darkness fell, Alex and I set out to track down and follow the troublemakers across the city. They were lighting fires everywhere they went, using the rubbish as fuel, but also targeting luxury stores and bus stops. The firefighters were struggling to keep up. So were we. The looters were moving so quickly across the city that you'd turn a corner and find a fresh fire and no trace of anyone responsible. It was hard work and a very long evening.

'Is this quite a hectic response to being asked to work past 62?' I asked Alex.

'Ahh yeah, just a bit.'

We sent two stories back to New Zealand that night. In one I was standing in front of Kevin Spacey outside a London court; in the other I was standing in front of a raging bonfire in central Paris.

'Wow! That shot with Spacey was brilliant!' the producer messaged at the end of the bulletin. Star power won that night.

An official protest was planned for the following day, and our CNN colleagues had again insisted we had someone with us to watch our backs. Max was tall and incredibly French, with wire-rimmed glasses and an almost-fedora. Unlike every other security officer I had worked with, Max had no black on at all. I felt immediately self-conscious because *I* was completely dressed in black.

'Do you have any colour you can put on?' he asked me within minutes of meeting.

'Ahh, nothing on me right now . . .'

'The troublemakers dress in black,' Max explained. 'They're called the black bloc. An anarchist group. The police will not think twice about targeting them so it's best to have some colour . . .'

'Oh, well, great,' I mumbled, feeling like a total idiot for dressing all in black and also unsure what to do about it. It was too late to do much because around me tens of thousands of people were already gathering in the square. It felt more like a festival than the looting we'd experienced the night before, so I told myself my outfit decisions wouldn't become a matter of life and death and tried to change the subject.

People of all ages were walking in protest of the legislation change, blasting music and brandishing huge banners and smoke flares, but it was all very peaceful and calm. We marched for hours that day, following the hordes of police officers who were following the hundreds of thousands who were protesting, without any whisper of chaos or violence. But as soon as the sun started going down, the tone of events changed. We were walking towards Palais Garnier, the famous Parisian opera house, where the protestors were gathering, and you could feel the tear gas in the air before you got anywhere near the heart of it.

My mum's favourite painting is of the Palais Garnier and it hangs on a wall at home. My mind drifted to her as soon as I saw the opera house, but on this night it looked nothing like the beautiful building that had watched over my childhood from the hallway. Tonight, it was boarded up and guarded from danger. Our eyes started stinging a few blocks away and you could hear the loud bangs of the police firing more gas. As comfortable as the French are protesting, the police are equally as comfortable firing at those who step out of line and the scene was becoming increasingly chaotic.

As we tried to get our bearings, one of the rioters took a bat to the Lindt chocolate store right beside us.

'They make us angry, we will make them angry back,' she said, and I wondered what role the owners of Lindt had in the government's decision to change the retirement age. Her friends started to pillage the store, and white chocolate drops were scattered across the street. People would rush past, stoop to grab a handful and rush onwards, stuffing their faces with a delicious sweet treat to get them through the rest of their evening of rioting.

'Do you want some?' our angry teen interviewee asked, offering up a handful of chocolate.

'No thank you,' I replied, but I don't have a sweet tooth so wasn't really tempted in the first place. 'Get back to me when you're gunning for the Gucci store.' She didn't laugh but I did get a chortle out of Alex.

Things were getting crazier by the minute. The rioters were constantly baiting the police, hurling rocks towards them, and the police would respond with force and without hesitation, unleashing a barrage of gas and surging forward with batons and shields regardless of whether we were in the firing line or not. The masks we were wearing were reasonably effective but not totally, and despite looking like we'd survive a nuclear attack with the amount of face-gear we had on, our eyes and throats were stinging and we were coughing and crying almost uncontrollably. More than once we ended up on our knees, gasping for breath and trying to get our eyesight back, completely immobilised. The police were not holding back, instead charging towards and hitting people with their batons, and more than a handful of protestors ended the night with blood streaming down their faces.

'Move when I tell you to!' Max yelled at me, frustrated that I would pull away from his grip whenever he tried to move us out of harm's way; in turn, I was getting increasingly frustrated at him yanking at my shoulder every time I got anywhere near the action. The violence was terrifying in how quickly it had escalated, but telling a story from the very heart of it is a seriously addictive feeling and adrenaline is a powerful thing. I yelled through the noise at one of the rioters in the crowd: 'Do you think the president is listening?' He just laughed back at me in response. I'm not sure anyone there believed they could actually bring about change, but the ringleaders were enjoying the opportunity to let loose and a lot of the teenagers seemed to be treating it as a chance to blow off some steam with their mates.

As the crowds eventually started to disperse, so did the police, and we stumbled upon a young group looking a bit lost. 'What's the plan for the rest of the night?' I asked one of the girls.

'We'll find another unplanned manifesto somewhere,' she said, in half French half English, referring to another pop-up protest she expected would emerge elsewhere in the city tonight as if it were just another club they were going to hit for a dance.

—

NEW YORK, UNITED STATES OF AMERICA
early April 2023

Our London lease was up in a couple of weeks' time and we were having a packing party. The music was playing and my incredibly chic fashion-photographer housemate Oda was taking photos on an old vintage camera as we drank gin and laughed about the absurdity this apartment had played host to for the past year. Oda had taken the chef's room when he'd moved out a few months earlier, Eavan was still there and so was the thief, who we knew by now had stolen thousands of pounds from the flat slush fund. It was a reasonably shocking revelation, but at least we finally had an explanation for how she was able to afford a personal motivator to text her messages like 'Time to get up and walk around the block' and 'You're doing amazing!' intermittently throughout the day. Honestly, Essex breeds them differently.

We were throwing around duct tape and boxing up belongings when my phone rang. A Sarah.

'Hey!' I said, feeling the flush of alcohol in my cheeks.

'Hey, how are you?'

'Yeah good, what's up?' and instantly regretted ever thinking I could afford to put my phone down for a couple of hours. I knew straight away I'd missed something.

'Trump has been indicted. Can you get to New York?'

I heard the groans from Eavan and Oda as I reached for my laptop and started typing 'skyscanner' into the search bar.

At this stage it was nearing 10 p.m. Alex was already in the USA, finally getting his hostile environments training done, and our very talented US Correspondent, who I know first and foremost as my good friend Mitch McCann, was in New Zealand for his sister Brianna's wedding.

'Have you spoken to Mitch?'

'I'm going to ring him in a sec.'

The girls watched the familiar routine play out, accompanied by the usual quipping: 'Ahh typical . . . you have been in London for a few days now.' Within half an hour I was booked on an early-morning flight and packing for a very different reason and with not a lot of time to spare. My room was abandoned in total disarray.

As the Europe Correspondent, I was well and truly out of my patch by the time I touched down at JFK Airport, but as a young journalism student it was the US Correspondent I had always dreamt of being so I was more than happy to play pretend for a week. Donald Trump was yet to arrive in New York from Florida, and we filled the day by going to visit his childhood home in Queens on the outskirts of New York City.

As a young boy, Donald had grown up in a very modest house, now derelict and an eyesore on the street. 'It's falling apart, abandoned and unsellable, just like his reputation,' one of the neighbours told us. But around the corner, less than a five-minute walk away, was the 23-bedroom house the family moved to when Trump was four years old. It was utterly American, with the flag flying, manicured lawns and four huge white pillars at its front. We stood around filming it for fifteen minutes before I finally decided 'What's the worst that can happen?' and went to knock on the door.

I was saved the walk because the door suddenly opened and out came two women and a man. They looked at me suspiciously, pulling on their glasses as if we were paparazzi and they got this all the time.

I hurriedly word-vomited something along the lines of 'Hi, I'm a journalist from New Zealand . . . but I promise I'm one of the good ones.'

They laughed cynically and responded 'Well, you would say that.'

It worked, though, because while the man got in his car, the two ladies stood around. One revealed herself to be the interior designer of the house, and best friend of the other woman, who was the owner. She and her husband had bought the house off the Trumps. In the end, one of the two did agree to speak on camera about how proud they were to be part of presidential history. But what followed off camera was much more interesting — and disturbing. She started reading from the usual menu: a monologue on how Trump hadn't committed any crimes, it was a witch hunt and the country was falling apart without him in office, but by the time she had ramped up into talk of the new world order, she was really starting to lose her crowd. We were keen to get out of there when she added:

'And of course you will be following what's happening in Ukraine . . .'

'Yes,' I responded. 'It's unbelievable.'

'I agree,' she said. 'That the media would make that all up is despicable.'

I don't think I responded at all.

'What do you mean?' Alex asked, with far more calm in his voice than I would have been able to muster.

'I have friends in Russia and there is no war going on in Ukraine,' she said. 'It's all been manufactured by the media. Just disgusting.'

We weren't going to be able to bite our tongues much

longer, so we started to politely excuse ourselves on account of a time crunch.

'Where can I watch your story?' she asked as we turned to go. 'What's your name?'

I gave her my name, and we thanked them for their time and walked off.

'She's gonna get a helluva shock when she googles you,' Alex said.

I hope she did.

Coming from Europe, America was, in so many ways, a journalist's paradise. You will not find a place in the world where people are as willing to talk on camera as they are in the United States.

There is a thankless task known as 'vox popping', so dreaded in newsrooms that over the years more than a few seasoned journalists have shamelessly tossed it to an intern. It involves walking up to random people in the street and asking their opinion on a certain topic. It's essentially an on-camera survey of the public. Typically, in my experience, Kiwis will behave like the microphone is a gun being pointed at them and scurry away. The British will keep their distance and enquire 'What's the question regarding?', then shake their heads and hurry off. The French will mime that they don't know English, and then walk off talking fluent English to whoever they are with. But Americans? Americans will come to you. I am almost convinced there is a magnet in every US citizen that attracts them to a camera. They will answer any question, even if they know next to nothing about the topic; and as a bonus, they're English-speaking, which means no hassle negotiating translations like you have to so often in Europe.

On more than one occasion I have had an American walk up to me and announce 'I'm American', as if that was going to automatically qualify them for a tell-all 60-minute interview. But I had foolishly underestimated Trump supporters. They were almost impossible to interview.

Donald Trump had become the first US president to be criminally indicted, charged with 34 felony counts of falsification of business records, and was going to be appearing in the criminal courthouse in Manhattan. His supporters were more than happy to front the camera, but would rant about fake news and the various injustices against Donald Trump for minutes on end without taking a breath. I needed them in the story for balance so of course we persisted, but I did have to tell one supporter that we weren't going to be able to fit all ten of the MAGA hats stacked on his head into the shot.

On the day Trump was due to appear in court it was like a circus had rolled into town. Not just Trump supporters but also the swarm of television networks setting up ad hoc studios on the side of the road, the immense security and police presence and of course the Trump-haters. With the number of impersonators walking around the courthouse I had to do a double-take more than once. One group dressed in orange jumpsuits like already imprisoned presidents were having a serious disagreement over who was going to hold the 'Lock Him Up' sign.

'But she always gets to hold it,' one of the sign-less men whined to another sign-less man who clearly had some power of veto.

Hammered into the grass there were mini billboards still calling for Hillary Clinton to be locked up, and for every one of those there were at least ten little popsicle sticks with Trump heads stuck on them, accompanied by the message 'Piss Here'.

Presumably it was an invite for local dogs; but then again, perhaps not exclusively.

At one point a rush of people stormed towards a car that had pulled up at the curb outside the courthouse. They were yelling and pushing like a political mosh pit and I saw a flash of blonde move from the car to the centre of the crowd. It wasn't Donald Trump, obviously, the hair wasn't bleached enough; but it was one of his most loyal supporters, Marjorie Taylor Greene. The far-right conspiracy theorist was now on a megaphone declaring her support for the former president, and as she moved through the crowd I started recording a piece to camera among the madness. I ended up with a protester's arm hooked around my neck as the crush of people pushed to get closer to her. If this is what it was like for Marj, what was the Don going to lead to? I shuddered at the thought.

In the end his arrival was actually quite muted, travelling straight into the courthouse garage in an extensive motorcade. I think I claimed to Alex that I had seen a flash of Trump's distinctive tuft, but the best view was really to be had watching on CNN. Trump was in and out of court and back to Florida to make a televised address by day's end, as we all scrambled to process the history we had witnessed and make sense of it in our coverage. At 2 a.m. we set up our camera in Times Square for our final live cross before heading home to London, and ordered McDonald's coffee and hash browns to keep us going. Two rats the size of rugby balls scurried in our direction and I immediately regretted putting our bag of deep-fried goods so low to the ground. The presenters introduced me as 'International Correspondent' and I had to stop myself beaming as they crossed to me. I later considered asking for a pay rise to match my new and improved (and clearly very temporary) title and beamed freely at the outrageousness of the thought. It was, as expected, a one-off.

When I arrived back at my London apartment later that day, I had almost forgotten the circumstances in which I had left. The entire flat was abandoned, empty of belongings and furniture and humans, except, of course, everything that was mine. I laughed to myself at the absurdity of the sight, and would have panicked but I didn't have the energy. The key was due to be handed back in three hours and I still had to pack up all my things and do my share of the cleaning. I haven't seen the thief or the chef again, but Oda and Eavan remain lifelong friends.

LONDON, UNITED KINGDOM
mid-April 2023

In my early days out of Broadcasting School, I had convinced myself I wanted to be an entertainment reporter. I was so dedicated to this idea that my first ever television news story was about Katy Perry's Super Bowl performance. I was working at TVNZ at the time and I would watch Kate Rodger, TV3's entertainment guru, with great envy and admiration, setting myself the truly unachievable goal of being 'as good as her one day'.

I was sent to cover a red carpet premiere in Auckland one evening, and both she and I were set up for a live cross side by side. I was eager to prove myself to the bosses and had prepared what I thought would be the perfect segment; but about five minutes before I went on air I heard Kate on the phone to her producer giving them a run-down of what she was going to say in hers. It was ludicrously better. I frantically scribbled down what I could remember of what she'd said on my notepad, and I completely copied it. I have already admitted this fraud to Kate and she has graciously forgiven my sins, but a public confession feels appropriate. She was then, and always will be, the Entertainment Queen, and I gave up my red carpet ambitions pretty soon after that shocking showing. But upon moving to London, and especially hot on the heels of Covid, I was able to further learn how poorly suited I would have been to my once-upon-a-time dream job, as my now Newshub colleague Kate was forced to hand off some interviews to her longtime copycat.

I don't think anything I had done in the job up until April 2023 prepared me for the email from her: 'Hey you, are you free to do this one for me? Stanley Tucci.'

It's not arguable: there is no better movie in the world than *The Devil Wears Prada*, and Tucci has been one of my favourite actors ever since its release. No one likes a name-dropper, but I have met some pretty shiny stars in this job. Not just the sporty ones, but Tinseltown and music's finest too: Cate Blanchett, Billie Eilish, Ed Sheeran, Taika Waititi, Heidi Klum . . . but for Tucci I was the most nervous. I was planning questions for weeks in advance, and working on my 'so cool, so casual' face for when I first walked into the interview room. He had a new TV series to promote and I had been booked, as is always the way, for a short five-minute slot, during which you walk into a hotel room burning with hot lights, sit down in front of the celebrity and try to ask a question they haven't already heard from half a trillion other reporters who have sat in that same chair that day.

I don't remember much of what was said in the interview. It is a cruel reality that there will be a copy of it somewhere on the internet which I'm not brave enough to seek out for verification purposes, but I do remember that halfway through Stanley started looking at me with the sort of pained expression on his face that you have when you know a kitten needs to be put down for its own good. At the end of my five minutes I was sweating profusely, but broke my own rule and asked for a selfie anyway, my hand shaking so much I almost dropped my phone and my final shred of dignity with it.

I thought that was embarrassing enough, but as I left the room and stepped into the lift, I looked in horror at myself in the mirror, discovering that the most intense heat rash had taken over my neck and climbed up half my face, which instantly explained what Stanley had been so distracted by. I rushed out of the hotel into the cool London air, and as I walked down the River Thames, heading home, I left a hysterical voice message for Kate:

'Send me back to a fucking war zone, your job is bloody torture!'

Every celebrity interview I've done since, I've worn a turtleneck.

KAHRAMANMARAŞ, TURKEY
late April 2023

What isn't widely publicised about Turkey is the dog culture. There are dogs everywhere. The government estimates that about four million strays roam the streets and rural areas, and that feels like a major undercount. They stroll through the towns and sunbathe in the middle of busy roads as if they are the priority residents; remarkably, the cars swerve around them happily enough (although the Turkish do have quite a fast and loose approach to driving generally, so a little swerve every 100 metres is actually quite unremarkable).

To be crystal clear, these dogs aren't pedigrees. There's not a poodle in sight, no handbag accessory in the mix. They are mutts. Most are missing half their hair, or half a leg, or a whole leg, honestly, and flies usually follow them quite closely. But I've always been quite impressed with the temperament of these strays. I'm a farm girl at heart, growing up with wild possums as pets, so I'm not about to be worried by a few teeth being barred in my direction. But at 2 a.m., as I stood in the middle of the small Adana Airport carpark alone, guarding our several bags and all of the camera equipment while a group of seven Turkish strays started circling me, I did feel slightly uneasy. The one with a nasty limp and a chip on its shoulder was looking at me strangely and his prowling was becoming fairly sinister. Alex had gone to get the rental car sorted and there was too much gear for me to move, so my only option was to whimper helplessly until, fortunately, the ringleader's barking drew Alex's attention. I think they were rallying for some sort of attack but I was saved just in time.

'Oh shit,' Alex said as he rushed over, making enough

noise to delay the attack long enough for us to grab the gear and hurry towards the car. It was a hell of a welcome back. We had flown directly to Adana, a central spot that would cut the drive time in half as we ventured back to the epicentre of the earthquake; this time getting as close to the Syrian border as we could. It had been almost three months since the quake had hit and it was now safe enough for us to sleep in a hotel rather than a car. I was praying the local standard of living had also improved.

The place was worse than when we left it.

The bodies had been buried and the aftershocks had subsided, but whole cities were abandoned and more than two million people were in critical need. I have never stood in a place so devoid of hope.

We had a low budget for this trip; there was no extravagant convoy of cars or team of drivers, security and translators. We felt completely safe so the lack of security was not a problem, but we were going to struggle to find English speakers where we were going and I soon found myself googling 'Turkish translators near Syria' and cold-calling at least 50 as we drove further towards our destination. I was about to give up hope when a woman replied to me on a translator-for-hire app I had just downloaded, offering her services. She was in İstanbul, which wasn't ideal as usually a translator would travel with us, but she explained that she donated any money she made through work related to the earthquake to aid organisations involved in the recovery effort, and I hadn't heard back from anyone else so we decided we would try to do it over the phone.

She saved our trip completely; and having never met her in person, I feel completely comfortable claiming that she was in fact some category of angel. She would answer the phone within a couple of seconds at all hours of the day, without warning, and translate interviews for us in real time as we travelled around; and she did this for our entire trip. She even negotiated us out of another meet-and-greet with our old friends the gendarmerie.

'Sorry to bother you again . . .' I said down the phone. 'I just need to know if we are going to jail please,' I asked while holding the speaker phone up to the officer.

'No, you're fine. He just doesn't want you filming him,' she replied, to our relief. Five Minutes could have learnt a lot . . .

Our return to Turkey coincided with the end of Ramadan. Eid is the most important date on the Islamic calendar, when a month of fasting is typically broken by a day of candy and family and celebration. We arrived at an old schoolyard on the border with Syria, where a temporary camp had been set up. A charity group was at work there, serving 10,000 portions of food every day. Family after family were living in tents. Many were Syrian refugees and had already suffered so much. No one was holding out any hope of a happier life. They didn't expect to leave the tents, ever, and they could tell the aid deliveries were slowing down.

Through some miracle of human spirit, there was some joy at the camp on the day we visited. The children were dressed up in their finest frocks, and they had been donated packets of sweets to distribute in keeping with Eid tradition. They wore smiles on their faces and ran around sharing lollies with their loved ones and offering them to us so generously that I felt guilty for showing up empty-handed. We were invited into tents that were immaculately kept, and we were offered more chai than we knew what to do with. They knew, of course, that we were there to tell their stories and that we wanted to remind the world of what they were dealing with, but I could see in the eyes of every parent I spoke to that they were too disappointed by the past to believe the future could be any brighter. Better days were not coming for anyone there; it was completely and utterly depressing.

It was their faith that kept them going, and the love they had for each other is what woke them up every morning. I offered them words of promise, that New Zealand wouldn't forget about them, and when I said it I believed it. Alex and I would return to our hotel every night and work into the early hours of the morning trying to produce a story that would have some cut-through, that would affect people at home as much as we had been affected by hearing the stories first-hand. But every morning I would wake up to find the story had been placed near the bottom of the bulletin, languishing below the latest local council drama or some story that might as well have been about a cat being stuck up a tree as far as I was concerned. I felt like I had failed everyone we had spoken to, like I hadn't done their stories justice. If we couldn't get the producers to care, I concluded, none of the viewers would.

It was late evening when we arrived back in London. I had been homeless couch-surfing in the city since my post-New York move, but that evening I was finally able to shift into my new apartment. I was going to be living with Ed, who, knowing my schedule, didn't fancy living by himself the majority of the time and had insisted on a third housemate, a British guy called Ethan who was made of protein powder and honestly wouldn't have looked out of place among our Special Forces mates. Neither of them had moved in yet, though, and I was grateful for the night to myself. As soon as I opened the door to my new home, I started crying. I stayed up far too late re-listening to our interviews on repeat, and re-watching all of our stories one after another, trying to figure out where we went wrong and how we could have told them better.

Three days later, Alex and I were in the thick of all things happy and glorious, covering the King's Coronation in London, and I was pushing the emotional whiplash down below the overpriced gimmick crown I had bought for a celebratory live cross that ran at the top of the prime-time show *The Project*.

BUCKINGHAM PALACE, LONDON
May 2023

I had never seen the gardens in front of Buckingham Palace look so beautiful. The red tulips were blooming with divine intervention and the grass was so perfectly green I had to pick a blade to check it was real. Crisp white tents were being set up around Canada Gate for the media to base themselves out of, and with spring in the air the anticipation was genuine.

In the buildup to Coronation Day, the usual camp-out had begun. Young princes in costume were everywhere and hardcore royalists were setting up tents for sleepovers, fully stocked with champagne and cardboard cutouts of the entire Windsor family. I was beginning to recognise some of the most loyal fans from previous royal events we had covered, and was waving at a group of them brushing their teeth on The Mall when I noticed some more familiar faces: the Japanese team from the hostile environments training course were also circumnavigating the crowds hunting for good interviews.

They looked at me in confusion. 'A new cameraman?'

'Oh yeah,' I said with an exaggerated sad face. 'No more Daniel, unfortunately.'

'Oh no! I'm sorry,' one of them replied.

'Since when?' asked the other.

'He did his last shoot in Ukraine last year.'

'Our sympathy' and he bowed slightly.

'Oh shit. No, no, he didn't *die*! He just moved back to New Zealand.'

'Oh!' and they laughed.

The broken English hadn't helped the situation, but as I pushed on through the crowds I couldn't help but feel as though they could have been a bit more shocked to learn Daniel had got himself killed in a war zone. They were clearly still holding our less than perfect training course performance against us.

The King's Coronation, like the Queen's funeral, had been in planning for a long time, but given the cost-of-living crisis and general growing discontent with the traditional royal grandeur, Charles had given clear instructions for the celebrations not to be outrageously over the top. Instead, he opted for a simple four-day affair, with all the King's horses and all the King's men and the gold carriage rolled out just the once for the big day itself.

Despite all of the talk of Commonwealth countries like New Zealand and Australia becoming republics, by the time Coronation Day came around I had fully contracted royal fever and standing outside Westminster Abbey felt like a fitting full-circle moment, having survived the Queen's death coverage the year prior. It poured with rain all day, yet somehow spirits were not dampened at all. People were hysterical with happiness, and it was contagious. I even contemplated buying a $150 Coronation mug, but fortunately I ended up too busy to be so ridiculous. By this point I'd seen The Mall filled with people on several occasions, but this time the feeling was purely celebratory and when the famous flypast occurred and the King and Queen stood in their crowns on the Buckingham Palace balcony, I felt a pang of something special. It was like an internal alert had gone off, to signal that we'd just witnessed something with our own eyes that others would look at in photos and videos for centuries to come. The pang was followed by a more familiar *ping*.

'Have we got an obit written for the King?' The message from the newsroom hauled me straight back down to earth.

'Oh, don't even put that out into the universe!' I said out

loud, relaying the message to Alex, horrified at the suggestion of covering yet another major royal event.

'I've got one written, but it needs updating now, obviously,' I fired back to the bosses. 'I'll sort it once this Coronation weekend is done.'

'God save the King,' Alex said.

There was a party planned at Windsor Castle the following day and we headed there straight after the Coronation, checking into the same accommodation we had used for the funeral. 'I left the earring I found from your last stay in the fruit bowl on the bench,' the lovely Airbnb host had messaged, securing herself a five-star review and a third booking if ever required.

'I'll take the bunk bed,' Alex offered as we walked up the hallway, and I happily reacquainted myself with my old friend the master suite.

We spent the next day filming Princess Catherine and Prince William meeting with the gathering crowds, before settling in to find a spot for an *AM* segment ahead of the concert. It was just a few minutes before we went on air when I felt a bird deposit its support for our coverage all over my dress.

'Guts,' Alex offered as I splashed myself with water and tried to wipe off the remnants.

I did a good enough job but I must have washed off all the good luck as well, because what followed wasn't pretty. The curse of wearing a dress without pockets meant that my phone, which was connected to my earpiece and allowed me to hear the studio, had to be tucked into my bra strap down my back. I usually get away with that as long as I don't move around too much, but just before the presenters crossed to me this time the sound started dropping out. I could hear it, but not through my earpiece. Live on air, I realised that like a fool I hadn't locked my phone and my back had somehow activated speakerphone, diverting all sound away from the earpiece to the phone speaker and making it painfully difficult to hear, especially given that the phone was stuck down my damn back.

I could see Alex had realised something was wrong, and made an educated guess that the shot was framed up in a way that the TV viewer wouldn't see my next move. The thousands of young families picnicking behind me in Windsor Great Park wouldn't be so lucky. I reached behind my back, pulled up my dress and flashed the entire crowd as I retrieved my phone, holding it at my hip so that if I tilted my head towards it slightly I would be able to hear the next question from the presenters. At best, it would have looked as if I'd had an itchy back followed by a minor stroke; at worst, the Kiwi viewers would have just had a front-row seat to me flashing the entire King's party and pulling a phone out of my behind.

'How bad?' I asked Alex as we got off air.

'Nah, I reckon you got away with it,' he replied, always unfailingly supportive. I almost believed him, but as we looked to our left two small children were in fits of giggles and their mum threw me a sympathetic smile.

'Maybe not completely,' I said to Alex.

PRAIA DA LUZ, PORTUGAL
late May 2023

I was struggling through a five-kilometre run, pounding on the treadmill at my local gym and gasping for breath while some early 2000s rap played through my AirPods when a *Sky News* alert saved me. Siri read the notification out loud, with not nearly enough gravity for the information she was delivering: 'Police investigating Madeleine McCann disappearance to search reservoir in Portugal.'

I was grateful for a reason to push the 'Emergency Stop' button on the treadmill. The most famous cold case in the world was bursting back into life, and my cardio was going to have to wait. In 2007, three-year-old Madeleine McCann went missing, vanishing from her bedroom while on holiday in Portugal with her parents. We all know the story because it has been a lightning rod for media coverage since day one. The interest in the headline has barely waned in the two decades that have passed, with the world as obsessed as ever with solving the mystery of the little blonde girl with the distinctive eye.

We flew to Portugal that day and didn't book a return trip, prepared to stay as long as it took. The search for Madeleine had never stopped, but nothing of this scale had taken place in almost a decade and officials confirmed it was linked to a tip-off. The search was taking place around a reservoir which the prime suspect, Christian Brückner, was known to have called his 'little paradise'. The convicted rapist had previously been identified as being in the same area as Madeleine when she disappeared. When I popped up on TV in Portugal, more than one person sent me a message along the lines of 'Yeah, the way your time in Europe is going you might as well solve the McCann mystery as well'.

The world's media had descended on the search site and it was hard to tell who outnumbered who: the camera operators or the police officers. Portuguese, German and British authorities were all involved in the operation and there seemed to be genuine hope around the re-ignited search. On day two we filmed at the hotel where Madeleine was last seen, and standing in a picture I had seen on television so many times over the years was incredibly strange. The beach was full of families enjoying the spring weather and it felt like I could only see three-year-olds, soaking up their holidays as every child should.

As we headed back to the search site, Alex and I decompressed the best way we knew how: singing Lizzo at the top of our lungs and pushing the car's sound system to the limit. Some of the international journalists I admire most had travelled to Portugal to cover the story and Alex and I had been star-spotting in between our work. I know for a fact they spotted us in return, and as much as I wish I could say it was our journalism and professionalism that caught their attention, the truth is that we drove into the carpark of the search site completely unaware of how not soundproof our rental car was. We had quite the audience by the time we were declaring loudly and severely out of tune that we were 'bad bitches' as per the lyrics of our favourite song 'About Damn Time'.

You live and you learn.

'Material' was collected during the three days of searching, and we were told it would be sent for testing in Germany. On the final morning we were setting up for a live cross when I got a text message from Air New Zealand saying my flight to Auckland via Shanghai was booked. I thought it was a scam and ignored it. But as soon as I got off air I had a call from Sarah de Croy.

'Guess what?'

'What?'

'We're flying you home for the Media Awards. You leave from London tomorrow!'

We landed in the UK at 8 p.m. and I went straight to Selfridges department store, suitcase in tow, to buy a dress to wear. I was back at the airport at 9 a.m., bound for Aotearoa where I stayed for 72 hours, knowing better than to tempt fate, or the news gods, with a visit any longer. Maybe I should have, though, because the mystery of Madeleine McCann remains unsolved to this day.

MOSCOW, RUSSIA (KIND OF)
June 2023

My cousin Paul was marrying his wonderful fiancée Natasha in the south of France and it was going to be a wedding of epic proportions. Family and friends had flown from all over the world to be there, and fortunately I had managed to get the weekend off work.

The morning of the wedding, though, 'off work' started to feel less likely. The leader of the Wagner Group, notorious mercenary Yevgeny Prigozhin, had launched a rebellion, seemingly ready to overthrow President Putin and his regime. Prigozhin, a wealthy businessman and convicted criminal, had been known for years as 'Putin's chef'. He had founded the mercenary outfit the Wagner Group, reportedly recruiting tens of thousands of prisoners who were willing to kill for their freedom, and they had gained a fearsome reputation for brutality on the battlefield. Having managed some significant victories in the fight against Ukraine, Prigozhin had grown increasingly critical of Russia's military leadership and was now threatening an insurrection.

From a ludicrous French villa I sat glued to the news, eating fresh cheese and baguettes and sending messages to Alex, trying to work out if I needed to leave paradise. The Russian president had accused his former ally of treason and an armoured convoy led by Prigozhin was heading towards the capital. It felt like Putin had lost control of a very fast-moving situation, and while there are very few occasions where you would trade France for Russia, Ukraine or Poland, given the situation I was starting to get anxious.

'Just about to go to the ceremony. It starts in 1.5 hours so will be unavailable from then for an hour I would say,' I updated Alex.

'Enjoy it! Will be so great,' he replied.

I switched off my phone and it felt like I was suddenly operating in an alternative universe. In a beautiful cathedral, the best opera singers I've ever heard sang 'Amazing Grace' while Paul and Natasha tied the knot, and all the while my imagination was running wild, picturing the Wagner forces storming the Kremlin and undertaking a bloody battle.

Two and a half hours later, as the church bells sang out, I turned on my phone, read the updates and let out a sigh of relief. I flicked Alex a text: 'Putin still alive I see.'

'So far.'

I was standing in the garden of the villa with a glass of lemon water in hand when Sarah de Croy called. I moved away from the canapes, knowing that talk of Russian mercenaries wasn't exactly the right wedding vibe, and kicked my heels off to sit on the lawn and spend the next half-hour building a plan of attack.

'We can't get you into Russia, obviously, but you could go to Poland and then head to Kyiv depending on what happens,' Sarah said. 'Yeah, I agree. I'll look at a flight out first thing in the morning or tonight, but it's getting on timewise now.'

In Ukraine the mood was already turning jubilant. The uprising signalled a potential end to Russia's invasion and a fresh hope was blooming like they hadn't felt in over a year.

'You look at flights, and I'll talk to the CNN guys,' Sarah said, and as she did I heard my name being yelled across the garden.

'I gotta go, I'm late for a photo,' I said to Sarah. 'I'll talk to you soon' and I raced over to the family who were waiting far too patiently for me to join.

Prigozhin's men were within two hours of the capital, Alex and I were in the thick of negotiating flights and transport and I had resigned myself to a night of sparkling lemon water when, shockingly, by mid-evening it was all over. The Belarusian president, Alexander Lukashenko, had announced that he had brokered a deal and the rebellion was off.

'Enjoy the pinot,' Sarah messaged me, and I poured a glass and toasted to love in full force while the world labelled Yevgeny Prigozhin a dead man walking.

Exactly two months after his mutiny, I was on air reporting that he had been killed in a plane crash.

PARIS, FRANCE
September 2023

The French capital had descended into absolute anarchy since our first dabble in Parisian protests a few months earlier. Cars were overturned and on fire; and the lights of emergency services shone through the smoke-filled streets. The anger wasn't an issue of retirement age this time; it was a result of a seventeen-year-old boy, Nahel Merzouk, being shot point-blank by police officers during a traffic stop in the suburbs of Paris days earlier.

Even though 40,000 police officers had been deployed across the country, they were again being overwhelmed by rioters. I don't think I expected it to be any more aggressive than what we'd already experienced, but we grabbed the riot protection gear, I wore the brightest red jacket I could find in my wardrobe and we prepared to head out. We had a briefing first, with the CNN team who were also operating in Paris, which I expected to be quite straightforward; but the updates they had were slightly more intense than we had anticipated.

'Teams we've had in the area are now being specifically targeted by the rioters, so have your wits about you. Have your vehicle nearby at all times and park in a way that makes it easy to escape.'

When the phone call ended, Alex turned to me. 'What do you reckon?'

'I reckon we leave in ten?'

We had a car this time, which eliminated the huge safety risk of having to wait for the notoriously unreliable French Ubers, and we drove straight out to the suburb of Nanterre where the young man had been shot. It could have been an entirely different city: there was no Parisian magic in sight. It was around 10 p.m. and gangs of people dressed head to toe in black were skulking the streets, ready to pounce. There were entire rows of cars that were either burnt out and abandoned or currently on fire. It looked like the entire suburb had been torched. The young people there considered themselves at war with the system, fed up with the number of police killings with racist motivations and angry at the ever-growing divide between those in central Paris with their sparkling lives and those living decidedly less shiny ones on the outskirts.

The extreme violence had spread across the country, but Nanterre was the centre of the hurt and so that's where we positioned ourselves. As we drove through the streets we noticed a large group, at least a hundred, clocked in for a night shift of revenge.

'Should we get out and walk up, or should we drive?' I asked.

'I reckon we do a scoping mission in the car first, see what we're dealing with,' Alex rightly suggested.

As we got closer, attention started to turn to us. The rioters were trying to determine who we were: local residents, police or media. There was only one right answer and we had the camera hidden under a jacket behind the front seat for that reason. We drove through the death stares, trying to get to a clear spot to either park or drive away, but the group had noticed us and started getting rowdy. As we approached the intersection, one of the men in black threw a section of railing on to the road and lit it on fire.

'Well, we're not turning left then,' Alex said.

'Right it is,' I concurred.

The situation felt about as comfortable as when you try to pull on jeans after they've been in the washing machine and then eat a three-course meal; that is to say, *deeply* uncomfortable. It felt like we had driven into a hornets' nest and they were gearing up to attack. I would have rather taken on the seven potentially rabid dogs in Turkey. We turned right out of the intersection, more than ready to remove ourselves from the situation, when a young man emerged out of nowhere and threw a Molotov cocktail in our direction, forcing Alex to swerve quickly out of its trajectory so it landed just to the left of us.

'I don't think we're welcome here,' I said, an utterly pointless observation to share with a man who just dodged a Molotov cocktail.

We parked on a side street out of the way and walked back to the main square, filming what we could, but we were well outnumbered and I was relieved when the riot police finally joined the party.

As the agro continued to escalate across the country, Nahel's family started calling for peace, and famous footballers who were themselves raised in the suburbs added their pleas for peace to the pile. Instead of stopping altogether, the rioters ultimately agreed to turn their focus away from the suburbs, realising they were burning and destroying their own backyards when they should really be turning on central Paris. Which is how we found ourselves standing on the Champs-Élysées a couple of nights later, decked out in riot protection gear, as thousands of officers with their visors down stormed towards us down the famous avenue to disperse the thousands of angry protestors before they could become mobs. The luxury fashion shops that line the premium Parisian thoroughfare had boarded up their shop fronts, some even with custom-made designer metal grills. Against the backdrop of the Arc de Triomphe, police arrested anyone who gave them an ounce of reason to, and fired flash grenades where necessary, causing chaos every time they did.

Bizarrely, as it is one of the most popular tourist streets in the world, unsuspecting travellers continued to show up to shop and eat throughout the evening — only to find a scene they couldn't make sense of.

'Excuse me, what is going on?' a young teenager asked me.

He was dressed head to toe in black, and for half a second I thought he was part of the riot so I ignored him.

'Is it safe?' he asked again.

'There's a lot of unrest in the city at the moment,' I replied, not wanting to frighten him unnecessarily. 'Where are you visiting from?'

'Dubai.'

'Do you know about the protests?'

'No, I just arrived here tonight,' he said, looking terrified.

'Well, I would just try to stay away from the police officers until you've changed into an outfit that isn't all black, but you should be fine.'

He turned on the spot, likely heading straight back to his hotel; all around him the city of light and love was burning with rage.

TEL AVIV, ISRAEL
early October 2023

'Where are you guys at with movements? We're just looking at the Middle East situation.' The WhatsApp message came from Sarah de Croy.

'Currently at St Pancras worried about the same thing,' I typed back.

It was the 7th of October, and that morning news had broken of a huge surprise attack by Hamas in Israel, the worst there had been in the country's history. Militants had stormed into Israeli towns from Gaza, massacring civilians and taking 251 people hostage. At the Nova music festival, held just outside the blockaded strip, hundreds of young Israelis were murdered by Hamas fighters and many more were wounded, with horrifying reports of rape and mutilation. Around 1200 people were killed and Prime Minister Benjamin Netanyahu had given a press conference announcing that Israel was now at war.

It was pretty clear the Rugby World Cup was no longer the priority story. We had spent the early morning at London's St Pancras International station (the one that looks like it's out of Hogwarts), waiting for our train to the French capital ahead of the quarter-finals and, more importantly, trying to decide if we would get on it.

'Now boarding on platform 4.'

The Eurostar loudspeaker announced that our carriage to Paris was ready to welcome us, and Alex and I stood to grab our many bags and manoeuvre through the crowd to the escalator. But exactly 24 minutes after her first message, Sarah de Croy replied.

'Hey guys, can you head home to get body armour?' She was just in time.

The message plunged us into familiar chaos that's amplified by the knowledge we probably wouldn't be sleeping again for days. Suddenly we had a very long to-do list and almost all of it was urgent. Alex very aptly describes this feeling as 'having a lot of tabs open'. Our passports were already stamped out of the UK, and with the race now on to get to Gatwick Airport to make a flight to Tel Aviv we were frantically trying to explain to the Eurostar lady why we no longer wanted to get on her train and instead wanted to re-enter British territory.

'We've had a change of plans,' Alex said.

'You don't want to go to Paris anymore?' the woman questioned, incredibly confused and sounding borderline offended on behalf of Paris.

'No, we're going to Israel!' I huffed, as impatient as ever and unimpressed with her distinct lack of urgency.

Thirty minutes later I barged into the house to the shock of Ethan, but not so much Ed, who were both having coffee in the lounge and watching the live coverage out of Israel on *Sky News*. 'I knew this would happen,' Ed said.

'What's happening?' Ethan asked, still new to the whirlwind of the Europe Bureau and trying to get up to speed.

'We're going to war,' I announced with a little too much enthusiasm, which again I blame on adrenaline. I dumped my entire suitcase on the floor of my room, leaving my rugby-coverage wardrobe strewn everywhere as I opened my war drawer to select long pants, linen tops, jackets, boots and body armour and chuck that into the suitcase instead.

'When do you leave?' Ed asked.

'We're going to try and get on the first flight out, it's going to be really tight,' I said, grabbing at satellite phones and first-aid kits as I spoke. I was back out the door within minutes, racing across town to collect Alex, who was doing the same hasty re-pack at his house. I booked our flights from the back of a Black Cab, and I knew it would be a miracle if we made it but there was no other option if we wanted to leave tonight. There's only so long missiles can be flying unpredictably above a country before they decide planes shouldn't be too. We were set to arrive at Gatwick Airport an hour before take-off, when usually we would be there at least three hours beforehand. We'd have to check in, drop off the bags and do the carnet at super-pace and I was praying for a notification of a delay.

The cabbie, an older man from Yorkshire with a thick accent, friendly face and the news headlines playing through the radio up front, knew we were in a rush and he was putting on a phenomenal show of why they are the best taxi drivers in the world. It is one of my favourite London facts that Black Cab drivers have to sit an extensive exam to qualify for the right to drive the iconic car. The test is called The Knowledge and essentially requires them to memorise all of London's streets so they can get from A to B as efficiently as possible and outsmart Google Maps.

My phone beeped at me. 'Check in details for your Paris stay!' the Airbnb app yelled excitedly, targeting a happy holiday-maker and not someone who was struggling to close tabs as quickly as they were being opened.

'Ahh shit, I need to call Ollie,' I said. Ollie Ritchie, then Newshub's rugby reporter, had been covering the pool games in the south of France and was on his way with Newshub's longest-serving camera operator, Warren Armstrong, to Paris, where we were all supposed to move in together for the final few weeks of coverage.

'Reymer, bonjour to you!' he answered the phone jovially,

closely matching the tone of the Airbnb notification and very clearly expecting a different kind of chat to what he got.

'Ritchie, bit of a change in plans . . .'

'Oh, really?'

'Yeah, we're actually heading to Israel tonight to cover this new war.'

'Ahh. Of course you are.'

'So I'll fire you through all the information I have for the accommodation so you guys can access it this afternoon.'

'Sweet as, mate. Do you reckon you'll make it to Paris at all or just playing it by ear?'

'I think we could get to you by the quarter-finals, but it'll just depend on what old mate Benjamin does next.'

'Roger that. Stay safe you two.'

'Will do,' I said. 'Scout out the best café au lait for us.'

'Sorted?' Alex asked.

'Yeah, tick that off the list,' I said.

'Just closing the tabs one at a time,' he noted, as level-headed as always.

I was about to start searching for somewhere to stay in Tel Aviv, partly to distract myself from anxiously checking the clock every 30 seconds, when the driver interrupted.

'Excuse me, love,' he said to me, catching my eye in the mirror. 'I don't like to eavesdrop or nuffing like that, but did I just overhear that correctly?'

'Yeah, you probably did,' I replied with a laugh.

'So just so I've got it straight when I tell my missus later this evening, you lot are gonna pop off to a war zone and try to make it to Paris in time for the All Blacks quarter-final, is it? At the Rugby World Cup?'

'Hopefully,' Alex said.

'Well I reckon that could be about the craziest thing I've

ever heard in my back seat,' he said, chuckling, 'so I better get you to this airport then.' And he put his foot down. Given the range of conversations and passengers he would have met in his time driving around the city, I have worn his comment as a badge of honour ever since.

We pulled up to Gatwick with exactly 63 minutes until take-off, and piled our bags on the trolley and raced off as our cabbie yelled after us, 'Good luck! You're bloody mad!'

I was sure we could make it if we had no more hurdles, and as we tore towards our check-in counter there were enough people milling around that I was even more certain we'd be fine. That was until I saw a new message flash up on the screen: 'Flight cancelled'.

'They're not flying,' another traveller walking away from the check-in desk said to us. 'They just closed the airspace.'

It was always going to happen, but I had been desperately hoping we would sneak through before it did. Now we'd have to go the long way round and things became ten times more complicated. Sitting on the floor of Gatwick Airport, I mapped a new route through Jordan that would involve driving from Amman to Tel Aviv; but, of course, the flight to Amman left from *Heathrow* Airport and it left soon. Alex had gone to fetch sustenance (always Pringles and Red Bull), and as soon as he was back we were off again: rushing back to the airport taxi stand, explaining the situation to a new knight in shining Black Cab who joined the race towards our third departure lounge of the day.

When we arrived in Tel Aviv, the country was in shock and the grief had barely even kicked in yet. There were still so many unanswered questions. People were still missing their loved ones, no one knew yet how many hostages had been taken, who had been taken, who had been killed or the extent of the brutality of Hamas's pillage on the Israeli villages near Gaza.

David was our fixer, driver and security and I trusted him instantly with all three jobs. He had spent decades in the military but was now semi-retired into a life as a tour guide, driving visitors around Israel and giving them a history lesson as he did. He was a proud Jewish man, but he was passionate and educated about all religions. David was equally passionate and educated about the history of his country and went into the depths of it from the second we sat in his back seat, reaching into his glove box like it was Mary Poppins' handbag and pulling out maps and models and diagrams of how the land has been diced up over the years and who occupies where now, to show us while he drove.

'Here, open this one up,' he'd instruct Alex, and then trace his wrinkled fingers down a new map which showed the borders at a different time. When he ran out of props he looked out the window and pointed at anything notable: where Jesus was born and baptised, where he died on the cross, where the crusades happened, the Dome of the Rock shrine. There were so many significant religious landmarks, sacred to Judaism, Christianity and Islam, and you didn't have to drive far to get a true sense of why this strip of land has seen so much struggle for so many centuries.

We could see the Iron Dome lighting up the sky from our hotel balcony. This elaborate air defence system is almost unbelievable in how it can detect, track and intercept incoming missiles, and I felt safer in Tel Aviv than I ever felt in Ukraine. Damage could still be caused, of course, and we spent half a day filming at a site where an intercepted rocket had landed; it had destroyed a home and left one person seriously injured.

'Innocent people get hit, on both sides,' one of the neighbours said in our interview, and there was no argument from me.

Air-raid sirens were constantly sounding in Tel Aviv, but the first that affected us cried out while we were filming at a food donation and distribution point in the central city. Women and children there were working to put together care packages for Israel's military and families affected by the massacre. A grandmother had arrived with a cake that I liked the look of so I went over to investigate, wondering if it was in fact my beloved cheesecake.

'It is my grandsons' favourite,' she told me proudly.

'Oh, it looks delicious,' I responded, still half wondering if she'd be interested in sharing.

'We're sending it to them. I want them to know their Bubbe is looking after them always.' I realised with a jolt that her two grandsons must have been among the recent Israeli reservists summoned to duty.

Our conversation was interrupted by the familiar screech of a siren and the women rushed to gather their children and push them down into a bomb shelter that was far too small for all of us. 'Squeeze in and be calm,' one of the ladies started instructing everyone, and I reverted to my usual routine of getting a couple of interviews done while underground.

It wasn't until we left the distribution centre a few hours later that Alex turned to me and said, 'Well, that was pretty crazy.'

'Yeah, that poor grandmother . . .'

'And the air-raid siren!'

'Shit, yes! Your first time!' I realised. 'What did you think?'

'Pretty hectic.'

'Yeah. Now we just want to avoid one of those going off right before a live cross . . .'

Tel Aviv is incredibly close to Gaza, just a little over 70 kilometres away, so from all over the capital you can often hear the back-and-forth of rockets firing. We were sitting outside in a residential area, interviewing an Israeli man whose family were missing — presumed dead at worst, captured and alive somewhere in Gaza at best — with a soundtrack of thunder playing constantly in the background of our conversation. Rocket fire from that distance sounds like a storm brewing on the horizon, and as it grew louder I stopped the interview briefly, to acknowledge it and take a breath before continuing.

'You guys can hear that, right?' I asked.

'What? Oh, yeah,' our interviewee confirmed, too distracted by worry for his loved ones to recognise any threat to himself.

The storm was just starting to brew, of course, and I reflect on the time we spent in Israel with great sadness. There was already so much hurt and suffering and troops were gathering at the edge of Gaza ready to launch a ground invasion, but we had no idea at that point what exactly Israel had planned and how far things would escalate in the months that followed.

Mass burials were taking place in Tel Aviv; those of Jewish faith prefer funerals to take place as quickly as 24 hours after death, and when we arrived at one burial site, it was pure mayhem. There were thousands and thousands of people, and with parking limited, everyone was parking kilometres away and then battling the mounting traffic to walk down the road to the burial location. The heat was stifling, but as unbearable as it was, Israeli families were desperate to make the journey.

When we arrived, the chaos cleared into a paddock of pain. Groups stood in separate sections, each weeping over a coffin that meant more to them than the one just a few metres to the left. It's never fun filming at funerals, it feels invasive and vulturous; so we kept our distance, standing on the edge of someone else's life-defining day. Even so, the images Alex captured were some of the most powerful from that trip.

We walked back to the car in relative quiet, not daring to complain about the sweat dripping all over us or the distance we had to trek, but as we drew nearer to the vehicle an exasperated groan or two did finally escape. We had been completely blocked in by several other cars. One old and rusty car was parked in front of us with its windows down, so Alex leant in and tried to move it out of park; but it couldn't be done without the key.

David was on the phone to the local authorities, trying to get official assistance, but I missed the genetic handout of patience chromosomes. 'We need to try and push one of these out of the way,' I said, indicating to the BMW four-wheel-drives to either side of us.

'They won't budge if they're in park, especially not those fancy cars,' Alex tried to tell me.

'I reckon we've just got to muscle it.' I was growing increasingly frustrated with the situation. 'It's our only option or we could be here all day.'

He was far from convinced, but it wasn't long before I managed to get the car rocking and Alex and David quickly saw the potential. Sweating profusely in the Middle East heat, and with just a hedge separating us from a series of burials, the three of us huffed and puffed and grunted until we manhandled the car off its perch and pushed it out of our way. It was a small win amid a tough week, and I felt like the All Blacks could probably do with our forward pack in France.

As there had been in Ukraine, there was a huge drive for blood donations happening in Tel Aviv and it was staggering to see how many thousands of Israelis had turned out.

'I have two kids in the army right now, and it's hard,' one anxious father told us, swallowing back emotion as he stood in line for his turn to donate. A huge stadium had been transformed for the blood drive and there were musical acts performing inside and out to try to keep the mood light. I've been known to faint at the sight of blood or a needle, so a blood drive is a particularly perilous place for me to be, and every time I felt myself getting dizzy I would become overly interested in those musical acts, which I'm sure Alex found slightly odd.

The blood donations were just one of the many parallels between covering this conflict and that in Ukraine: the immense suffering, the heartbreaking interviews, the air-raid sirens, the trips to the bomb shelter. It felt so familiar, yet there was a fundamental difference. Every day my inbox would be flooded with messages from strangers, colleagues — even friends — who were criticising my coverage, pointing out in what ways it was one-sided and complaining it was biased against Palestinians. And yet almost every time I did an interview with an Israeli, the person would ring me after the story went to air for a long, heated and emotionally charged discussion about all of the things I had got wrong and how I had manipulated the story to suit my narrative in favour of Palestinians.

I've heard political journalists say that when they get complaints from both sides they know they're doing something right, and I tried to rationalise this as something similar, but in truth it was exhausting. I was overthinking every line and every word and spending hours trying to justify my decisions and my stories, and every day felt like I was racking up months of Broadcasting Standard Authority complaints. It is by far the most polarising story I have ever told. Even our fixer David, who is intelligent and reasonable, would struggle to fully understand the Palestinian perspective when I questioned him about it and we'd erupt in heated debate. It was a sobering insight into the divide in the region and the more I learnt, the less I knew; but we interviewed a Palestinian living within the confines of the barbed-wired West Bank who said to me the purest truth of all: 'We are all human beings, we all want our families to live in peace.'

When Israel launched its retaliation and the war escalated into a full land invasion, it became very clear we were in the wrong place. Only one foreign journalist has been allowed into Gaza without an Israeli escort since the war started, and even the escorted trips have been rare. It restricted all of our news gathering to Israel and warped the content of our stories. The local journalists inside Gaza were putting their lives at risk to get the story out, and they were producing such moving and powerful reports that it felt wrong to try to match their efforts from the safety of Israel. We knew it was time to leave. I was devastated that Alex and I never made it to Gaza and therefore never got close enough to speak to the Palestinians most affected. It felt like a failure.

We had to exit the way we had come, via Jordan, and the plan was to take an evening flight from there to London and then go straight to the train station and board our original train to Paris for the rugby. It was going to be a mission, but there was a huge silver lining.

'Our hotel in Jordan is a 40-minute Uber from the Dead

Sea . . .' I said to Alex.

'Yeah, *that's* happening,' he replied with a grin.

By early afternoon our last live cross was done and we were packed up and heading for a float in the famously salty sea.

'Where are you from?' the Uber driver asked.

'New Zealand,' we answered.

'What is a New Zealand song?'

'Umm, anything from Six60,' we replied, and to our delight we found ourselves flying down the highway to the Dead Sea with 'Don't Forget Your Roots' blasting out the window — which we then promptly had to turn down as we hit a military checkpoint.

Our Uber driver was equally delighted with us, amazed that anyone would want to swim in the Dead Sea given its excessive salt content.

'That's the whole point!' we laughed.

'There is *fresh* water to swim in!' he protested, clearly not buying into the tourist hysteria around being able to float effortlessly in his backyard landmark.

It was a surreal experience. The Dead Sea is landlocked, with Jordan on one side and the occupied West Bank of Israel on the other — so close you can convince yourself you could swim to it. A body of salty water separating peace from such conflict.

Our Uber angel took us home via a fresh water waterfall to wash off the majority of the salt, and by the time he dropped us off at the airport for our evening flight we were beginning to feel somewhat refreshed and ready to take on the Rugby World Cup. Karma served us a fast lesson for getting ahead of ourselves. Our flight to London was severely delayed, and after finally boarding the flight, at midnight, it was ultimately cancelled. We were forced to disembark, transfer to the most horrific airport hotel I've ever tried to sleep in and undertake a mad overnight panic to finish filing our story for the bulletin and find a new way to get to Paris in time for the quarter-final. The solution wasn't pretty, and adding to our ever-expanding collection of tabs was breaking news out of Israel: New Zealander Adam Agmon had just died, killed in action.

I was barely able to string a sentence together as I stood in front of the camera outside our prison of a hotel the next morning, preparing to go live into *Newshub Live at 6pm* with the latest.

'This will be fun,' I said to Alex, pre-warning that my grasp on the English language was failing and my upcoming on-air performance might leave a bit to be desired. I muddled my way through, but there was no time to dwell on it. I hadn't been off air for fifteen seconds before Alex and I were sprinting towards the airport, where we spent the next thirty minutes chugging Red Bull and pleading with our fellow travellers.

'Sorry, do you mind, we're going to miss our flight.'

'So sorry, can we go in front . . .'

'Thank you, sorry — our gate is about to close!'

When we touched down in Tunisia, Africa, I could hardly make sense of it. It was instantly clear we were in Africa, and I knew that's where I had booked tickets to, but in the madness of the past 24 hours and the headspin of the past week I hadn't properly processed where we were headed. I had just been booking the best option, and Tunisia had been that: we would be able to fly on to Paris after a few hours' layover.

It was going to be a long few hours. The airport was run-down, stinking-hot and dirty. The security scanner didn't work, so an officer just sort of looked us over and waved us through.

'Hello, do you have bags?' one of the airport staff asked me as I walked in.

'Yes, to go on to Paris though,' I said.

'Well, you need to pay,' she said.

'How much?' I asked, slightly confused.

'200 euro, cash,' she replied.

'I don't have any euro in cash,' I said, which was true.

'Well, you can't get your bags then' — which sounded about right given our luck to date.

'I have US dollars,' I offered, 'but only 100,' not wanting to reveal our full hand of thousands.

'Okay fine,' she said, taking the money and waving me on.

'Hang on, can I get a receipt?' I asked, already wondering how I was going to justify this work expense on the company's accounting software.

'No receipt,' she said, and walked off with our $100.

'I think I just got scammed,' I said to Alex, 'but she is in a uniform.'

'Yeah, and I still reckon we'll be lucky if our bags do actually show up in Paris,' he replied.

'I can't believe we're in bloody Africa.'

'Not exactly how we pictured it,' he said, referencing our ongoing efforts to persuade The Sarahs to approve a story in East Africa where the hunger crisis was teetering on full-blown famine.

Our flight out of Tunisia was also delayed, of course. 'Is this the universe punishing us for treating ourselves to a jaunt to the Dead Sea?' Alex asked.

'We're in the bad books for sure.'

'Surely the fact that we haven't showered since we swam in that bloody sea is enough to serve us right?'

When we touched down in Paris we were delirious with

happiness. It was late in the evening, the night before the quarter-finals and it felt like a miracle that we had made it. We had no appropriate clothing to wear the next day, but that was tomorrow's problem. Tonight, we would meet the rest of the Newshub gang and we would finally shower and sleep in clean beds, in a country that wasn't broken with war; it was almost too good a thought to bear.

We were laughing excitedly in the back seat, reminiscing on our journey, when the female taxi driver interrupted. 'S'il vous plaît, s'il vous plaît,' she said, wincing and touching her ears. 'Shhh.'

It had the desired effect because we both fell silent in shock. 'She has no idea what we've been through,' Alex said.

'Ahh, god bless the French,' I concurred.

PARIS, FRANCE
October to November 2023

The All Blacks were playing Ireland and the feeling was that we'd be lucky to beat them, so we lugged our bags up the stairs of the Airbnb assuming we'd be going back the other way and home to London within 24 hours. By this stage, Newshub had also sent over Andrew Gourdie from New Zealand to present the coverage and with him digital reporter Alex Powell, so with Ollie and cameraman Wuz we were a team of six in our French abode.

I was looking forward to being surrounded by Kiwi accents, but we arrived to discover that Ollie had developed a strange local flourish and was on a mission to convince as many people as possible that he was fluent in French (to be fair, he was pretty convincing). The lounge was set up in traditional fashion for a group of sports journalists: some laptops were playing football, the TV was playing rugby, their phones were focused on the next bet they were each weighing up for their respective syndicates, and I was hearing an awful lot of 'Full credit to the boys'. We couldn't have been further from Gaza, and while it was an aggressive pivot to go from talking war to talking rugby I was quietly relieved that for a day at least I had an excuse to talk about something that wasn't a matter of life or death.

We had covered the All Blacks' very first loss against France in the opening match a month earlier and I had maxxed out on fifteen drunk French fans jumping on my back in celebration while I tried to film a piece to camera, but I was readying for an even better reaction from the Irish. We had also covered the Irish win over the All Blacks in Dublin in 2021 and I had decided then that they had the best fans in the world; they're just good craic, which means they make good TV, and we knew if they won this game it would be all on. Of course, history will show the result didn't go their way. The fanzone was heaving with distraught Irish lads, and with ecstatic Kiwis who were running around, just like I was, telling anyone who would listen 'I believed in them all along!' When I sent a picture of the fallout to Eavan in the wee hours, having finally finished our monster edit effort, she replied: 'No, I'm so sad. I cried. I actually cried,' which was a long way from her reaction when the Queen died.

Ollie reliably informed me that he was confident we would make the finals now, and with two and a half weeks ahead in Paris and only a collection of dirty linen shirts and body armour to my name, I decided the universe was back on my side. 'Well then, I *have* to go on a shopping spree!'

Of course the war between Hamas and Israel wasn't going away and Alex and I were trying to do both stories at the same time. My scripts were merging into a strange interchangeable mix of headlines with very different meanings: 'The All Blacks are preparing for battle'; 'Hamas suffers a big loss overnight'. The semi-final against Argentina came and went without any upset. Gourdie had labelled Ollie's story in the bulletin *ABS_WIN* hours before the game had even started.

'Subject to change, that one, I suppose?' Ollie asked, but there was no real concern that it would.

By the time the final came around, we were firm friends with Philippe, the coffee man downstairs, who made a perfect cheese omelette. But he must have put something strange in the mix that morning because by the time we arrived at Stade de France that evening I was crippled with food poisoning, darting in and out of increasingly filthy portaloos on the concourse in between interviewing the arriving crowds; and all in the pouring rain. That should have been enough of an omen that it was not going to be our night. The South Africans were beside themselves with joy when the final whistle blew, but the New Zealand fans were strangely subdued about the whole ordeal, with most still riding high on the win over Ireland in the quarter-final.

'If only that London cabbie could see us now,' I thought to myself as we headed home to settle in for one last Parisian all-nighter of editing. 'From war zone to fanzone all within a month.'

THE HAGUE, NETHERLANDS
January 2024

When the new year rolled over, the tone was set for a happier 2024 with an early trip to Copenhagen to join the Danes in celebrating their new king. Looking back, we were probably more excited about it than the Danes, who were typically understated in their partying but kept assuring us they were delighted by the occasion while waving their flags politely. King Frederik's mother, Queen Margrethe, had abdicated after 52 years, and as his wife is an Australian we had managed to convince the bosses it was worth a trip.

Our high hopes for a celebratory year were short-lived, however. We were promptly pulled back to reality when we were diverted to The Hague first, on a 6 a.m. flight to cover the accusations of genocide that the International Court of Justice was considering over the war in Gaza. I am the proud holder of a Dutch passport, with both sets of my grandparents having immigrated to New Zealand in the 1950s, and so am always pleased to visit the Netherlands, but this was a little less tulip- and kroket-focused and a little more centred on war and suffering, which made the vibes infinitely less jovial. The war had escalated into a horrendous attack on innocent families and the global outcry was becoming deafening.

It was the type of freezing weather where your nose runs constantly and your eyes weep incessantly in a way that makes it difficult to appear professional, and both the mood and the skies were gloomy. Still, thousands were out to march and protest, from both sides of the conflict. Police had separated the protest groups, with supporters of Israel and supporters of Palestine held on different corners of the road in front of the court. We spent two days darting between both sides, trying to tell the story fairly, but I had learnt by then that this was an impossible task and the flood of scathing messages that arrived in my inbox was fully expected. There was, however, one message urging me to give OJ Simpson his gloves back; a sad reflection of a recent New Year purchase I'd made. I'll admit that when I reviewed the footage I agreed the bulky brown leather gloves really shouldn't have made it on to TV.

KYIV, UKRAINE
February 2024

As the calendar clicked closer to February, I became borderline-obsessed with getting back to Ukraine to cover the anniversary of the war. Two years had now passed, and with Gaza dominating the headlines, there were fewer people talking about Ukraine despite roughly one-fifth of its territory still being under Russian occupation.

The budgets were tighter than ever, and even from the other side of the world we could feel that Newshub was under pressure, but Sarah de Croy told me if I could get a pitch together to cover the trip for $2000 or less then we could probably get it across the line. It was an almost impossible task. Almost. We had flight credit sitting ready from when we had been stranded in Jordan; this would cover us to Poland, and if we did the trip without any on-the-ground support that would keep the biggest expense out of the equation completely. The plan was to go to Kyiv, which would be flooded with extra military for the anniversary anyway so we would feel safe enough without security; and to avoid the cost of a car and driver we would take the overnight train in and out of Poland, which was almost free. Under my mattress, I also had the wad of Ukrainian cash left over from our previous trips. It was completely worthless out of the country, but would pay for all our expenses when we were there.

'We can do it for under $2000,' I updated Sarah. 'Just a short trip, a few nights on the ground, but strong stories with lots of Kiwi angles.'

Sarah Bristow had left Newshub by this point, and Richard Sutherland had stepped in as interim Director of News. Richard had been at Newshub when I first started in the newsroom and while he had moved to Radio New Zealand not long after I arrived (surely unrelated), it didn't take long working under his leadership to become a big fan. In conversations with him since I'd been in Europe, he'd always expressed plenty of interest in our coverage of Ukraine and seemed supportive of it, so when he returned as the new Sarah I assumed we'd have no major problem convincing him to sign off on our trips.

Having ticked the box of keeping it under $2000 I thought it was a done deal, but Sarah called me back to say Richard still had some hesitations, implying that these were safety-related. By this point, having performed what I felt was a miracle to line up all the flights and trains and accommodation under budget, I couldn't make sense of the lack of support for the coverage.

'We're going to Kyiv! It's as safe as crossing the road! And it's *our* lives at risk anyway!' I raged to Ed at home on a freezing London night, in between my phone calls with Sarah and mad messages to Alex. My ranting was getting worse by the minute, and Ed promptly started mixing up his overnight oats for breakfast the following morning; a sign that he was heading off to bed and more generally, a sign that he was sick of my aforementioned ranting.

Eventually, after I'd grown increasingly antsy on the phone to Sarah, she told me: 'Book it, all approved.'

I didn't waste a second. All of the tabs were open and ready on my laptop and I went through methodically booking the various trains and flights before anything could sell out and ruin the entire plan.

'Approved! We're off to Ukraine!' I messaged Alex.

'GREAT!' he replied, and his unabashed use of an exclamation point *and* capitalisation was completely warranted. After the nightmare of him missing out on the previous trip to Kyiv, we were mutually relieved to finally get to make the journey together. Not an hour had passed before Sarah rang me.

'Change of plans. Richard wants you in and out of the country faster.'

'What do you mean?'

'He wants you back in London by Tuesday.'

'What? It's all booked.'

'Yeah I know, sorry.'

'But it's not going to save any money doing it faster, because it's all been paid for already and it's non-refundable.'

'I know, but he doesn't want you in the country for so many nights.'

The conversation deteriorated into a flurry of frustration and bewilderment. It wasn't going to save any money, it was going to limit our newsgathering to barely one story, and we wouldn't be in Ukraine long enough for any live crosses into *Newshub Live at 6pm* or *AM*. What was the point in even going?

'Most unbelievable turn of events!' I messaged Alex, unloading a stream of updates and feelings to him over WhatsApp while still on the phone with Sarah.

'SDC has rung . . .'

'says Richard only wants us there for one night'

'despite having everything booked and paid for already'

'Apparently worried about safety'

'I have no idea what the hell is going on'

'but it's a mare'

'I am a mixture of dumbfounded and fucked off'

'Will let you know if I hear anything further'

He replied instantly.

'I can't believe that, this makes no sense'

'Speechless'

It was a bizarre few hours of flaring tempers and a lot of confusion that ultimately resulted in Sarah ringing to say: 'Okay, he says just do it.'

It still made no sense, but having ultimately ended up with the result we wanted we didn't ask any more questions.

At 4 a.m. on the 23rd of February we boarded the first of two trains that would take us from Kraków in Poland to the Ukrainian capital. The first train took us to the border, where we changed trains at the Przemyśl train station. It was the same station, of course, that had been overflowing with refugees when Daniel and I had arrived there two years earlier and gone straight on air. These places that had once seemed so foreign now felt strangely familiar; I never would have imagined that I would feel so at home in a tiny, remote town on the edge of Poland.

The Polish train had been luxurious, with a cabin to curl up in and call our own. The Ukrainian train was not so luxurious, and it was there we would spend the next twelve hours. I was momentarily concerned that Alex wouldn't have the full authentic experience because we wouldn't be able to stop for a hotdog at a petrol station, but fortunately there was a treat trolley on the train and fortunately it was offering hotdogs. By midday we had caved. 'Lives up to the hype,' Alex confirmed, and I was as chuffed as if I was the CEO of the Ukrainian hotdog enterprise.

In a sign of the times, the train was actually quite busy. After crossing the border, we'd stop in Ukrainian towns collecting more and more passengers who were heading towards Kyiv for the anniversary. There were more women than I'd seen in the country in a long time, and it was clear that everyone was adapting. There is only so long you can live in fear before you begin to live *with* fear.

It was late evening when we arrived, and we headed straight for the usual hotel. Alex and I went to check out the bomb shelter in preparation for the night ahead and I was shocked to find it had also been upgraded. No longer was it a barren room with chairs lined up around the edge; it was now set up like a hospital unit, with partitions creating private cubicles with beds in them so that guests would be able to come downstairs and sleep properly in the safety of the shelter when the sirens sounded. It was a five-star hotel, after all . . . but it also was further evidence of how Ukraine was finding comfort in the uncomfortable. There were still tanks in the square, decorated in the yellow and blue ribbons of proud Ukrainians, but the giant statues that had been covered in fresh sandbags for protection in year one and disintegrating sandbags in year two were now standing exposed, with one wearing only a symbolic bulletproof vest. It was yet another sign of the way this war was turning.

The aid organisation Kiwi K.A.R.E, run off New Zealand donations, had been working in Ukraine since the start of the war. They were set up in an old warehouse on the outskirts of the city, repurposing water boilers to be sent to the front line to help heat water and food and dry clothes for the soldiers. Others were sent to families in liberated areas who were living in bombed homes, trying to survive without electricity or gas. Every boiler was inscribed with a plaque, 'With Love From New Zealand', and the pride I felt was overwhelming. A man named Oleksii was leading the operation in Kyiv and had volunteered to show us around the warehouse. It was grungy and gritty and cold and the lack of safety around the use of grinders was almost comical: sparks were hitting the camera as Alex filmed. But in Ukraine, there were bigger concerns. Having impressed the crowd by admitting he had spent time learning the Ukrainian alphabet, Alex had unlocked new friends in the warehouse and they quickly started opening up about their reality.

'Don't film it, but look here . . .'

Near the warehouse, a man was stationed 24/7 with anti-drone artillery, scanning for the enemy. 'This is how we defend the sky,' Oleksii explained, referring to a soldier staring upward, ready to shoot down anything that looked threatening coming in his direction.

By this point, though, the war was mostly confined to the east; and as a result the west, definitely, but even also the centre of the country was beginning to compartmentalise the hardship. No one had forgotten, but for the first time I felt like people were trying to move on with 'normal' life. I reconnected with a Kiwi family we had interviewed in the days before the war, who had been preparing to flee their lives in Ukraine for a safer country. The daughter had returned to

Ukraine, but her family remained in the Netherlands where they had escaped to.

'I came back to be with my boyfriend,' she explained. 'I missed him too much.'

'Are you worried he'll get called up to serve?' I asked.

'Yes. I don't want him to go.'

'Does he want to go?'

'No, why would he? He would just die.'

Her candour was in stark contrast to everything I had heard from Ukrainians in the years prior, when not wanting to fight was considered cowardly, even traitorous. There had been an unconditional commitment to the fight, not just from the men but also from their wives and other loved ones. No one had ever seemed to question the call to duty, but now that seemed to have changed. It wasn't just this one isolated case, either. Many of the families we spoke to talked about the cost of conflict as too great. In the early days there had been a belief that the war would be a short, aggressive campaign to maintain their freedom, but as it had dragged on, people saw the call to the front line as a long-term and seemingly fruitless slog that would likely end in their death and very little progress on the battlefield. What was the point? This was not an overwhelming perspective, but having never encountered it previously I was shocked at how much it was featuring this time around. The resistance seemed to be splintering.

As we left our interview and made our way into town, we passed a store selling souvenirs. A stack of toilet paper sat for sale at the front door; the paper was covered in Vladimir Putin's face. The resistance may have been splintering but there was no mistaking the common enemy.

One of our last stops was a refuge centre providing support

and shelter to mothers and children who had fled the worst of the war. Toddlers were charging around the temporary accommodation playing with donated toys, oblivious to the emotional turmoil their mums were working through with therapists in the neighbouring rooms. Many of them had no idea where their husbands were, and if they were even alive. One, who bravely agreed to an interview, had boarded the train to Kyiv searching for help after her home in the east was bombed. Out of her pocket she pulled a small angel figurine. It was missing a wing but remained largely intact.

'I found it outside my house before I left,' she explained. 'I'm broken too. But it made me believe we could survive.'

My tears were already welling up when she placed it in my hand.

'Take it with you, for strength. I am safe now.'

I tried to protest and give it back, but she was adamant I should keep it and I slipped it into my puffer-jacket pocket, wondering how she could ever fathom someone needing the extra strength more than she did.

Alex and I headed east to Poland on the train, editing our story on the first half of the trip and sending it back to New Zealand before we resumed our usual routine of me sleeping and Alex enduring hours of my snoring.

'Good sleep, mate?' he asked as we pulled into our final train station.

'Yeah,' I said, 'but you probably already knew that . . .'

We arrived back in Poland at the crack of dawn, which was far too early to check into our accommodation. My bid to keep costs down meant we were flying out to London on the cheapest flight possible, which was scheduled for some brutal hour like 3 a.m. the next morning. Needless to say, we had some time to kill.

'We could try to get out to Auschwitz?' I suggested to Alex.

'Yeah, something cheery to end the trip on,' he replied.

The old concentration camp wasn't far out of central Kraków. It was a place I had always wanted to visit, so while it wasn't exactly a pick-me-up activity it felt like the best option at the time. It was, predictably, an incredibly haunting day, and when we returned to Kraków for our live cross into *AM* we were both feeling emotionally shattered. I put my hands in my pockets to keep warm and felt the little angel still there, which instantly provided some perspective. Sleep in an actual bed was still high on the agenda, and Alex and I said our goodnights and retreated into our rooms not long after getting off air.

I saw the email first. A company-wide request to join a Zoom call for an important announcement. I had barely opened it when the phone rang. Sarah.

'Hello?' I said as I picked up.

'Hey, how are you?' she asked, but in a way that suggested she didn't really have time or energy to listen to a full answer.

'Yeah, all good . . .'

'Have you seen that email that's just come through?'

'Yeah'

'So, you need to be on that call, okay?'

'Okay.'

'Where is Alex?'

'He's next door, asleep by now I would say.'

'Okay, I think it would be good for you two to be together,' she said.

'Okay, I'll wake him up.'

'Good idea, okay. You okay?'

'Yeah, we're good . . .'

'Okay, talk to you afterwards.'

There was no doubt in my mind. We were about to lose our jobs.

I called Alex and told him as much, and he came through to my room. We set up a laptop for the call as our work group chats burst into an overdrive of speculation and information-sharing. We were operating in a haze of exhaustion as we logged in to the meeting. The proposal to close Newshub down was announced, but the audio was tragically quiet and I was almost convinced I hadn't heard it correctly. Sitting in a cheap Polish motel, fresh out of a war zone and a day at a concentration camp, with the clock nearing midnight, Alex and I sat in a numb disbelief and felt further than ever from the New Zealand newsrooms.

There was something, though, that suddenly made a lot more sense.

'Well, that explains why Richard was so determined to get us back in London by Tuesday,' I said.

'Yeah, probably didn't want us to be hit with this, fresh out of Ukraine,' Alex agreed.

'I'm so fucking glad we went,' I said, knowing we wouldn't be back, given that our time with Newshub would be all over in just four short months.

'This could be our last ever deployment,' Alex concluded. It hit me like a tonne of bricks.

We were partially insulated from the full shock, but the news had registered enough to know we needed alcohol. Unfortunately, there was nothing in the minibar.

'I'll go down to reception and see what they've got,' Alex ventured.

'Make sure you tell them it's urgent,' I said, and he nodded.

He returned shaking his head; the bearer of more bad news.

'No alcohol sold after midnight in Kraków.'

'Are you actually serious?'

'New law, apparently.'

'Of course it is.'

Alex poked his head back into the minibar. 'So, should we crack a Fanta?'

'I guess so.'

You could barely imagine a bleaker scene. But it did get worse, because just two hours later we were hauling ourselves and our gear to the airport.

ETHIOPIA, AFRICA
April to May 2024

There are some moments in your life where you just stop and wonder 'How did I get here?'

I was almost getting used to this feeling by 2024, but as I crouched in the bushes outside Westminster Abbey right before a live cross and tried to negotiate emptying my bowels without getting any splashback on my silk skirt, I really was struggling to make sense of the life choices which had led to this point.

The shituation had begun a week earlier, in Ethiopia. Since mid-2022 I had been on a mission to get to Africa and cover the growing food crisis. The restrictions on the Black Sea and Ukrainian exports had a huge impact on global food security and I wanted to show the wider impacts of the war, to keep New Zealanders engaged with the story and strengthen our coverage. Unfortunately, the budgets weren't so supportive of my grand plans and it had been pushed down the pipeline for months. Eventually, the Kiwi branch of the relief agency Tearfund offered to fund the trip for us, in a bid to shine a light on one of their big aid campaigns in the region, and I was relieved to fit it in before Newshub closed.

Alex and I had made the flight from London to Addis Ababa, the capital of Ethiopia, by ourselves and met up with the Tearfund team there before travelling on a short domestic flight one hour south to Arba Minch. It was a tiny plane, emblazoned with the green, yellow and red of the Ethiopian flag, and we landed on a short runway surrounded by green rainforest before entering an airport that was little more than a glorified garage, with missing windows and tiles falling off the walls. I was getting flashbacks to our stopover in Tunisia, which as an airport was now starting to feel quite high-end in comparison, but there was no place I'd rather have been.

We were met by a group of men who were the local Tearfund partners and ran the aid programme on the ground. They were bright-eyed and generous with their welcomes as they led us to their vehicles. Not for the first time in my career, I hopped into a car without realising quite what journey we were embarking on, and it was probably for the best. There were two cars, but there were more people than seats. We all piled in regardless. In our Land Cruiser there were two in the front and three in the back, including me, and then I watched in disbelief as four grown men opened the boot and piled in. They crossed their legs and sat in a square formation with their heads touching the roof, and they'd take turns to lean over the back of our seats for a bit of extra oxygen. It gave the impression that we were off for a quick five-minute drive down the road but it was eight hours before we arrived at our final destination: a small village near Moyale, on the southern border with Kenya.

While the seating arrangements were memorable, they were soon overshadowed by the extraordinary scenes we traversed on our journey. The roads were ruled by the animals; tuk-tuks and other vehicles swerving around herds of cattle and donkeys and goats that would trot casually down the dirt ways followed by a farmer meandering behind with a stick. There were children everywhere, lining the sides of the road, and the children were carrying babies. Young girls as young as six, maybe even five, with babies on their backs or fronts, wrapped in swaddling. They would wave and chase after the truck, noticing our faces peering back at them out the window. We drove past houses, but not like any I have ever lived in;

or seen for that matter. Some were constructed of rusted corrugated iron, but most were made of mud, some painted in bright colours and beautiful designs on the outside and others left bare. I would stare out the window in disbelief, and then a herd of camels would wander in front of our car and my jaw would drop even further. Any river or stream was surrounded by hordes of thirsty people, gathering around to fill containers with the filthy brown water. My litre of fresh water brought from Addis Ababa suddenly felt heavier in my hand, like it had turned to gold on our travels.

Extreme climate conditions had caused widespread water and food shortages, and millions of people across Africa were in need of humanitarian assistance. The need was everywhere. By the time we arrived at our destination I was starting to wonder where we would be sleeping. I had, ignorantly, not given it much thought prior to the trip, but I was pleasantly surprised to find the only motel in the area was actually in quite good condition. We had a room each, which was a win in itself, and they came with working bathrooms. The water supply was touch and go and it certainly wasn't hot, but if you got lucky it would flush with enough enthusiasm to push a bit down the sewer and we were each provided with a precariously small roll of toilet paper to see us through.

Our days filming in Ethiopia were a confronting, unforgettable look at a region gripped by food insecurity. The stomachs of toddlers were bloated and their eyes were glassy and tinged with yellow. Their mothers' eyes were heavy with sadness and tiredness. We found Bonnie lying inside her hut, hardly moving and desperately thin. Her face was covered in flies and she barely had the energy to blink them away. She was suffering from acute malnutrition and tuberculosis and her chances of survival were unbearably low. Not far from her hut, a group of hungry families gathered on the dirt, waiting patiently.

'What are they waiting for?' we asked the community leader, who was giving us a tour.

'They are waiting for a food delivery,' she replied.

The pale face of a seven-year-old, who looked closer to three and was struggling to move, told us they had been waiting a while already. I kept asking when the food was due to arrive, but no one could give me a straight answer. Eventually someone admitted: 'They are waiting on God.'

There is a constant thread linking all of the most desperate places I have worked, and it is the reliance on faith to survive the hardships of the day. It is often all they have. The ongoing conflicts between the Ethiopian government forces, those in the Tigray region and militia in the Amhara region to the north had added to the pressure on the people living in the south of the country, and we were instructed to stay on the main roads and not venture off on our own. 'We have heard there is a lot of militant activity at the moment,' our team informed us, and we willingly agreed to follow their lead.

Despite the stern warnings directed at us, all around us young children seemed to be roaming freely, without any parental guidance. Young girls, in particular, had their backs laden with containers, walking kilometres on end to fetch dirty water for their families. Elderly women, too, were walking under the burden of heavy loads of collected wood that they were taking many villages away to try to sell at the market. Most families were operating on one meal a day, though calling it a meal feels inaccurate. Most are lucky to have a bowl of maize, boiled into a paste and shared among whoever smells the smoke of the fire first. I have always rated bread as my second-favourite carbohydrate (it's hard to compete with the potato), but I have never been so grateful for a bread roll as I was for dinner every night on that trip.

It was unbearably hot in Ethiopia and I made the idiotic decision early on that I would sleep with the doors open to avoid waking in a pool of sweat, but really the air was just as warm outside and it didn't help at all. Instead, I woke up every day not just sweating but also decorated with mosquito bites. It didn't take long before they covered my entire body. That isn't hyperbole, by the way; I was quite literally covered in bites, including on my face. When covered in makeup, it looked like I had re-entered puberty and was dealing with a thirteen-year-old's acne outbreak, but it was so hot that by the end of the day my makeup would have completely sweated off and my face of red spots would be on full raw display in our footage.

It didn't take long for me to start feeling unwell. I was sweating more than just the temperature could claim responsibility for, and would experience dizzying hot and cold flushes all day and all night. I was aching from head to toe and my stomach was cramping unbearably, sending me running to and from the bathroom to either vomit or, well, the other. It made the lack of water and flush particularly problematic, and the limited toilet paper, which soon became lack of toilet paper, turned my room into a category one disaster zone.

Around this time I was also trying to negotiate my future employment in the overnight hours and attempt to partake in job interviews, darting from Alex's edit suite next door to the bathroom to a Zoom call and back to the bathroom, on repeat. One particularly out-of-body scenario saw me sitting on the bathroom floor replying to an email chain from the Newshub publicity team, requesting that I take a photo in a white shirt and jeans that could be superimposed into a magazine shoot they were doing in Auckland with a bunch of the newsroom women as a farewell feature.

'I've got a white top with me but no jeans, but we'll do our best to get the photo and fire it through this week,' I replied.

'Cool! Please make sure you iron the shirt,' the reply came.

I looked around in despair. 'No iron here, sorry, but I'll do my best,' I tapped back.

'Steam it while you're in the shower,' they told me.

'There's not a heap of hot water going around either, but I promise I'll do my best,' I replied again, thinking that at this rate they'd be lucky to get a photo of me without the toilet in frame but already resigning myself to trying to use my hair straightener to at least improve the state of my collar.

The next morning, having admitted my deteriorating state to Alex, he suggested I ask Dr Himali, who had been travelling as part of our team, for some assistance.

'Alex mentioned you might have some anti-nausea medication I could steal?' I asked her casually at the breakfast table, while trying to avoid making too much eye contact with the food that was being served up in case it toppled my fragile constitution.

'Oh, are you feeling unwell?' she said, reaching for her supplies.

After a quick run-through of my symptoms she suggested equally as casually that, based off the bites I'd acquired, I might have also acquired a case of dengue fever. I clung to the diagnosis as any good drama queen would, and clung even tighter to her supply of anti-nausea medication.

That day we were meeting with farmers who were benefitting from Tearfund's programme. It's designed to empower locals by providing them with drought-resistant crops and teaching them to grow and harvest them efficiently. We had been filming in the fields for the majority of the day but I was getting shakier by the second and I knew I was about to faint. If I had to rank the top ten most mortifying scenarios to faint in, right at the top of that list would be in front of a field of people who are on the brink of famine. What would I have said? 'Sorry, my sugars are a bit low, does anyone have a sweet treat?' No, if anyone had a right to be fainting, it wasn't well-fed me.

We had one last piece to shoot before we would be able to head back to base, but my brain was working in slow motion and I had no idea where to start.

'I'm just going to go sit under this tree and work out what I'm going to say,' I said to Alex.

'Yeah sweet,' he replied, and carried on filming.

I found some shade and plonked myself down just as I started seeing black dots. As I stared at my phone screen, waiting for helpful words to appear on my currently blank script, I felt movement. I looked up and a group of about ten children had gathered behind me, huddled around to get a view of my phone; something they had likely never seen before. As I turned they all gasped and stepped back hurriedly, before my smile gave them the unnecessary permission to burst into giggles and rush back in, the littlest wrapping her arms around my neck. It was a sweet enough moment that I could have sworn my blood sugar levels surged right then and there and I felt brave enough to stand up and attempt to film a piece to camera.

'Who do you think you are, Princess Diana?' Alex offered in jest.

'Oh look, if the crown fits,' I laughed back.

Ethiopia was proving to be a magnetic place; the rainforest

draws you in and the vibrancy of the culture is infectious. Dressed in beautifully bright outfits and smiling broadly through their troubles, the families sitting together under the shade of a tree would often fill the air with song. Whenever Alex appeared in a new village with his camera, the children would either run and hide behind each other or stand still staring at him with suspicion. Slowly, with smiles exchanged, they would grow brave enough to edge slightly closer.

'I should show them the footage of themselves,' Alex said out loud, already beckoning them over.

When he pushed play on the recordings, it was as if magic existed. The kids exploded with laughter and joy, staring at the footage through the viewfinder on the camera and then pointing at each other as if to say 'You're in the camera!' Their delight was addictive and Alex was soon lost to the crowd of children who swarmed him, fighting excitedly for their turn to either be filmed or see the recordings. He made a beautiful Princess Diana.

The return to London was bittersweet, but my reluctance to leave was somewhat tempered by my eagerness to finally have a proper bathroom at my disposal. A week on, and I was still spending more than an acceptable amount of time in bed or tied to a toilet. I was feeling much better on the whole and my appetite was returning, but the minute I started to get too confident I would be reminded who was in charge. The dengue was. This particular early morning I was due on air for a live cross into the 6 p.m. bulletin where I'd be discussing the latest peace deal negotiations between Hamas and Israel. Alex had decided to set up in one of our favourite spots with Westminster Abbey in the background, and we had just finished our technical checks with the studio when disaster struck.

'We've got trouble here,' I said, and Alex immediately knew what I meant.

'What's the problem?' the guys said into my earpiece from Auckland, assuming there was a technical difficulty.

I didn't have the capacity to reply. There were no bathrooms anywhere near us and the panic overcame me.

'Shit,' Alex said, looking around for solutions.

'No, quite literally, shit,' I said. 'Do you have a plastic bag?' I was so desperate that I suddenly found myself rummaging through all of our kit, searching for a doggie bag.

'You've got about seven minutes until you're on air,' Alex updated me as I started walking off, not knowing where I was heading. We were in busy central London and there were commuters passing by constantly, but I was starting to get clammy and shaky, like you do when you just really need to go. I saw a group of tall bushes up ahead and started walking towards them, looking for CCTV cameras in the area and wondering to myself, 'Is this even fucking legal?'

I could hear the news bulletin had started, and the voice of our wonderful political editor Jenna Lynch was updating me on the latest out of the Beehive as I started lowering myself into the bushes outside the UK halls of power, trying to keep my silk skirt in a wide enough circle around my legs that I would be able to do what I needed to do and stand up and walk off without anyone asking questions. It was a fool's approach. I was getting understandably strange looks from people walking past on their way to work, and I think if it wasn't for the fact that I had full-on hair and makeup and a relatively fancy British coat on, there would have been calls to the police over my insane behaviour.

'Those fucking mosquitos!' I said to myself as the distress of my situation took over. I could hear the news edging ever closer to my on-air slot when I spotted a Novotel glowing in the distance. Could I make it? I wondered, and the question was not just an issue of timing. I began the shuffle towards salvation, not moving too fast that I would unleash the beast but as fast as I could given I had to be in front of a camera discussing the intricacies of conflict negotiations in about four minutes' time.

I didn't ask permission at reception; I just burst into the foyer and made a beeline for the bathrooms. I could hear the legendary voice of Mike McRoberts introducing the next story in my ear as I lurched into the cubicle, and it was a timely reminder to unplug my microphone. In doing so, I also had to disconnect my earpiece and so I could no longer hear the news playing out. It was just me and the dengue alone in the Novotel bathrooms for a horrific 60 seconds.

I didn't have time to apologise to the cleaner on the way out. I was running back to Alex, who was talking on the phone to a no doubt slightly concerned control room, and he threw up a questioning thumbs up from afar.

'We're in the clear,' I yelled as I raced in front of the camera. 'How long have we got?'

'Your story is on, so about a minute I reckon.'

It was probably closer to 40 seconds later that the light went red on the camera and I was live on air.

'I'll choose a spot next to a bathroom for our live tonight,' Alex promised, and it was a good thing too.

LUCERNE, SWITZERLAND
June 2024

No one could accuse us of not making the most of our final Europe Bureau days. We were behaving like children with 30 seconds to take as much candy from the jar as possible before their parents showed up.

'Do you even live here? Or should we sublet your room?' Ed would ask when I'd return home for a 24-hour window of washing clothes and re-packing. As well as Ethiopia, we had been to Scotland for the World Indoor Athletics Championships, to Brussels for a NATO conference, to Paris to mark 100 days until the Olympics, to Turkey for Anzac Day, to Slovakia to cover the attempted assassination of the prime minister, and to Italy for the eightieth anniversary of the Battle of Cassino.

The Slovakia trip set a new record for our fastest deployment. Prime Minister Robert Fico was shot in the afternoon while I was running around a London park. I rang the bosses mid-sweat-session and 40 minutes later Alex and I had our overnight bags packed and were on our way to the airport. We ended up being away for a week, going straight from Slovakia to Cassino, where we were honoured to film Sir Bom Gillies attending commemorations. Ninety-nine-year-old Sir Bom was the last surviving member of the 28th Māori Battalion and while we didn't know it at the time, it would be his last journey to the site. He died just months later.

We squeezed everything we could out of our final four months, and we finished it all in one of the most expensive and beautiful places on earth, Lucerne.

'It's a miserable life,' Alex remarked as we drove past the

famous lake. It summed up the feeling in the car perfectly.

Switzerland was hosting a global summit, inviting more than a hundred delegates to attend to discuss a plan for establishing peace in Ukraine. President Zelensky was going to be there, as was then US Vice President Kamala Harris, and our police minister Mark Mitchell would also be attending. Security was cranked up to Fort Knox levels and the who's who of the world's media and politics were milling around in the mountains, many flying in and out on helicopters; although, to be clear, that did not include us. As much as we had been tempted to go out in a blaze of glory on the work credit card, we were confined to using the supplied media shuttle like the soon-to-be-redundant plebs we were.

As we stood in a conference centre listening to President Zelensky give his final address to journalists, I thought to myself: 'Well, this really is the perfect finale.'

It was only a short summit, held over two days, and we had arranged to meet with Mark Mitchell at its conclusion for a quick interview before he flew back to New Zealand. I wasn't sure there was much to talk to him about, having already touched base with him the day prior, but it wasn't going to do any harm so we bailed from the press conference early and tracked him down in a separate area of the venue that seemed relatively abandoned. Alex was getting set up for the interview and I was making small talk with the minister when I felt his focus drift to something happening behind me. It was clear he was not listening to whatever nonsense I had on offer, likely something about the stunning scenery, but I didn't have time to be offended.

'Excuse me, I'm just going to say goodbye to the President,' he interrupted me, and I felt the whoosh of movement to my side. As Mark Mitchell stepped forward to shake the hand of the incoming VIP, I turned to see President Zelensky arriving right beside me. He was surrounded by Ukrainian military officers, who had assessed the unfolding situation and moved aside to allow him to step right in front of our camera shot and speak directly into our microphone.

'Thank you to the people of New Zealand, we are thankful,' he said, staring at Alex and me. I was staring right back. He looked quite old, and tired, but as determined as ever, and I tried to imagine how much his life had changed in the past few years: a man who started as an actor playing the role of president on TV, now a full-time wartime leader with no end in sight. My own life felt strangely connected to his, as if, in a very distant way, we'd been on this wild journey together. I wondered whether he or I had asked the question 'How the hell did I get here?' more. I was certainly asking it right now.

Zelensky had been leaving the press conference and was being escorted to his chopper when we had intercepted him. It was the most uncanny case of right place, right time, and as he left, even the summit officials stood in disbelief at what had just happened.

'You are very lucky,' one said to me, and a squeal of agreement escaped my mouth.

We had talked at the start of the day of plans to get a nice dinner and toast to the glory days that evening, but some things never change and the sun had set in more ways than one by the time we hopped in the car. We still had plenty to do to put the story together, as well as a long drive ahead, but there was no desire from either of us for this day to end. It had been extraordinary and exhausting, like so many of the past three years had been, and that night we ended up standing in a quintessential bureau scene: in the carpark of a McDonald's, scoffing burgers in the dark, before heading back to work.

'This is living, isn't it?' I said to Alex as he took his final bite, dusted the salt off his hands and headed for the driver's seat.

'Wouldn't change a thing.'

If my days as Europe Correspondent had to end, there was no better trip to sign off on.

LONDON, UNITED KINGDOM
July 2024

Amid a flurry of UK election madness, during which Rishi Sunak was tasked with the unenviable challenge of convincing the public that the Tories could be trusted despite churning through four prime ministers in three short years, I began the arduous and extremely nostalgic process of getting ready to leave London for good. I emptied my bedside drawers first; filled with tangled souvenirs of my time in Europe, a mess of lanyards from events and experiences I'd never had on my correspondent bingo card. A pamphlet I had kept from a protest at the Vatican City was being strangled by accreditation for a NATO bomb-defusal training in Iceland, and as I rifled through my mementos I counted 32 countries we had worked in. With multiple trips to several of them, I wasn't going to attempt to count the flights.

I could also barely count the ways in which each of those flights, and what happened in between them, had changed me. I arrived in London a stickler for routine and planning everything. These days, I struggle to commit to anything more than an hour ahead of time. I am still too scared to jump off a diving board (that's a heights thing) but I am braver in every other way. Any intimidating scenario becomes instantly less so when the answer to 'What's the worst that can happen?' doesn't involve missiles or death. My stress levels are harder to raise, so too is my adrenaline, although I crave the rush most days. I still complain, of course, but perspective is much closer to hand; and I probably won't ever eat Pringles again, having had an excess on the road for the past few years. But maybe above all, I am prouder than ever to be a New Zealander, and I feel luckier than ever to be a Kiwi.

I hear a lot of 'I don't watch the news, it's too depressing'.

I've always found people telling me 'I don't watch the news' particularly strange — given that we rarely give any other profession an indication of how often we use their services upon introduction. For example, it's hard to imagine:

'I'm a mechanic.'

'Oh, I have a mate who does all the work I need done on my car.'

'I'm a doctor.'

'Oh, I never get sick.'

'I'm a primary school teacher.'

'Oh well, I finished school years ago.'

But aside from that, I do get it. And truly, the sentiment doesn't offend me. But to be able to pick and choose what 'depressing' news we have capacity to care about and engage with also proves how incredibly lucky we are to call Aotearoa home. We get to choose, because it's not happening directly to us and it's happening so far away from us that it doesn't have a profound impact on our day-to-day.

We are lucky. Witnessing the very worst and then being able to fly 24 hours away from it has made my good fortune to have a passport that reads 'Place of birth: Te Awamutu, New Zealand' feel tangible. I will treasure that lesson for a lifetime.

BARCELONA, SPAIN
August 2024

I said goodbye to London and left with just a single suitcase in tow, having packed my life up into the other two plus six heavily gaffer-taped boxes which had been sent to New Zealand ahead of me. After all, I only needed a handful of summer clothes where I was heading. The America's Cup was getting under way in Barcelona, and in an incredibly soft landing into my new job with *Three News*, I was set to spend two weeks there covering the start of it, before moving home. Stuff had taken over producing the 6 p.m. news from Newshub, and I had signed on as Senior Correspondent.

I had envisioned a quiet end to the year, rolling into Auckland in August with a stomach full of patatas bravas and plenty of free time to write this book. Remarkably, somehow I still had faith in best-laid plans. The day before my flight was due to take off, however, I sent the traditional 'There's been a change in itinerary' message to my family, after waking to the news that my time in Spain was going to be extended. The one jersey I had brought with me to Barcelona was well worn by the time I did actually make it to the airport in mid-November.

Almost every word of this book ended up being written in Europe, but I write these final ones from New Zealand. My boxes are unpacked and yesterday I lent one of my suitcases to a friend, off on its first adventure without me. It deserves to experience life with a true holiday-maker. I still haven't put my passport away, and I have no plans to. It's sitting on my bedside table, full of memories but with one blank page left.

I won't try to predict the next stamp. But yes, the King's obit is written.

ACKNOWLEDGEMENTS

To my wonderful family: Mum and Dad, Bjorn and Lucy, Anna and Mikkel, Christina and Mark, Kate and Marco and *all* the munchkins — you are without question the best thing about being home.

To Daniel Pannett and Alex Parsons — this truly is your story as much as mine and I am so grateful you let me tell it, having been fundamental in writing it into existence in the first place.

Likewise, this book would not exist without publisher Michelle Hurley, who was the first to believe in it, editor Teresa McIntyre, who tirelessly cared for each word, or project-manager extraordinaire Tracey Wogan, who offered the perfect guiding hand. Thank you all.

Kate Harley — you are the greatest friend and pseudo-therapist, and have been there for every step from the very beginning. You know me so well you could have written this book yourself.

Mitch McCann, Ed O'Driscoll, Emma Cropper and Alice Wilkins — you four Kiwis make up the most supportive group chat in the world.

Frankie Le Roy and Alyce Gulvin — I don't know where you found the patience to listen to endless draft excerpts of this book, while trying to enjoy the holidays I forced you to come on, but I am so lucky you did.

Claire Watson — I am convinced everyone needs you in their life, you are the best of the best.

Sarah de Croy and Sarah Bristow — I still can't believe what we managed to achieve together, from opposite sides of the world.

Melanie Jones — I simply wouldn't be here without you.

And Ingrid Hipkiss — your pearls of wisdom will keep me on the right path always.

To every person who made up the best newsroom I've ever known — Newshub — thank you. And to anyone who tuned in along the way, I am so honoured that you chose to experience this journey with us.

Greg Boyed — you were a genius storyteller, and you taught me almost everything I know about how to write a script. I wish more people had the privilege of learning from you.

And finally, to all the brave and generous people I met and spoke to over the course of these years, you are the brightest stars of this tale.

Lisette

ABOUT THE AUTHOR

Lisette Reymer is an award-winning journalist now based in Auckland, New Zealand as Senior Correspondent for Three News. She was born and raised on a dairy farm in Cambridge, the youngest of five children, who together, among many other childhood antics, ran a DIY radio station out of a tiny cupboard in their home. It was called 'Big Momma's House' and the siblings would take turns telling 'Yo Momma' jokes (a favourite of the early 2000s) and speaking to their very limited audience, which was really just their dad listening from a tractor in the paddock.

Lisette fell in love with broadcasting and storytelling at a young age, and during high school she upgraded from Big Momma's House to a more legitimate radio show, on Hamilton Community Radio. Upon finishing high school, she followed her older brother's footsteps and attended the New Zealand Broadcasting School in Christchurch. She graduated with a Bachelor of Broadcasting Communications majoring in Journalism and secured an internship at TVNZ working on *Breakfast* in 2014.

After four years of producing and reporting across TVNZ shows, Lisette made the jump across the road to join the 6 p.m. reporting team at Newshub. Lisette's first experience at the centre of major breaking news came in 2019, when she was among the first journalists to arrive in Whakatāne just minutes after Whakaari White Island erupted, killing 22 people. The tragedy was of global significance, and Lisette crossed live into shows around the world for more than twelve hours straight.

In 2021, at 26 years old, Lisette became Newshub's Europe Correspondent and moved to London, where she would go on to cover some of the biggest stories of the decade. Her journalism has earned her multiple awards, including Best Coverage of a Major News Event for her work in Ukraine at both the New Zealand Television Awards and the Voyager Media Awards, and most recently she was named 2024's Reporter of the Year. Lisette is deeply passionate about global affairs and bringing Kiwis closer to the stories that matter most. And crucially, she no longer tells 'Yo Momma' jokes on air.